Shugo Chara!

9

PEACH-PIT

Translated by
Satsuki Yamashita

Adapted by
Nunzio DeFilippis and Christina Weir

Lettered by
North Market Street Graphics

KC
KODANSHA COMICS

A Kodansha Comics Trade Paperback Original.

Shugo Chara! volume 9 copyright © 2009 PEACH-PIT
English translation copyright © 2010, 2013 PEACH-PIT

Published in the United States by Kodansha Comics, an imprint of Kodansha USA Publishing, LLC., New York.

Publication rights for this English edition arranged through Kodansha Ltd., Tokyo.

First published in Japan in 2009 by Kodansha Ltd., Tokyo.

ISBN 978-1-61262-348-1

Original cover design by Akiko Omo.

Printed in the United States of America.

www.kodanshacomics.com

9 8 7 6 5 4 3

Translator: Satsuki Yamashita
Adapter: Nunzio DeFilippis and Christina Weir.
Lettering: North Market Street Graphics

Contents

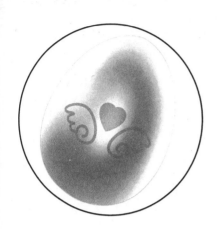

Honorifics Explained

Throughout the Kodansha Comics books, you will find Japanese honorifics left intact in the translations. For those not familiar with how the Japanese use honorifics and, more important, how they differ from American honorifics, we present this brief overview.

Politeness has always been a critical facet of Japanese culture. Ever since the feudal era, when Japan was a highly stratified society, use of honorifics—which can be defined as polite speech that indicates relationship or status—has played an essential role in the Japanese language. When addressing someone in Japanese, an honorific usually takes the form of a suffix attached to one's name (example: "Asuna-san"), is used as a title at the end of one's name, or appears in place of the name itself (example: "Negi-sensei," or simply "Sensei!").

Honorifics can be expressions of respect or endearment. In the context of manga and anime, honorifics give insight into the nature of the relationship between characters. Many English translations leave out these important honorifics and therefore distort the feel of the original Japanese. Because Japanese honorifics contain nuances that English honorifics lack, it is our policy at Kodansha Comics not to translate them. Here, instead, is a guide to some of the honorifics you may encounter in Kodansha Comics books.

-san: This is the most common honorific and is equivalent to Mr., Miss, Ms., Mrs. It is the all-purpose honorific and can be used in any situation where politeness is required.

-sama: This is one level higher than "-san" and is used to confer great respect.

-dono: This comes from the word "tono," which means "lord." It is an even higher level than "-sama" and confers utmost respect.

-kun: This suffix is used at the end of boys' names to express familiarity or endearment. It is also sometimes used by men among friends, or when addressing someone younger or of a lower station.

-chan:	This is used to express endearment, mostly toward girls. It is also used for little boys, pets, and even among lovers. It gives a sense of childish cuteness.
Bozu:	This is an informal way to refer to a boy, similar to the English terms "kid" and "squirt."
Sempai/ Senpai:	This title suggests that the addressee is one's senior in a group or organization. It is most often used in a school setting, where underclassmen refer to their upperclassmen as "sempai." It can also be used in the workplace, such as when a newer employee addresses an employee who has seniority in the company.
Kohai:	This is the opposite of "sempai" and is used toward underclassmen in school or newcomers in the workplace. It connotes that the addressee is of a lower station.
Sensei:	Literally meaning "one who has come before," this title is used for teachers, doctors, or masters of any profession or art.
-[blank]:	This is usually forgotten in these lists, but it is perhaps the most significant difference between Japanese and English. The lack of honorific means that the speaker has permission to address the person in a very intimate way. Usually, only family, spouses, or very close friends have this kind of permission. Known as *yobisute*, it can be gratifying when someone who has earned the intimacy starts to call one by one's name without an honorific. But when that intimacy hasn't been earned, it can be very insulting.

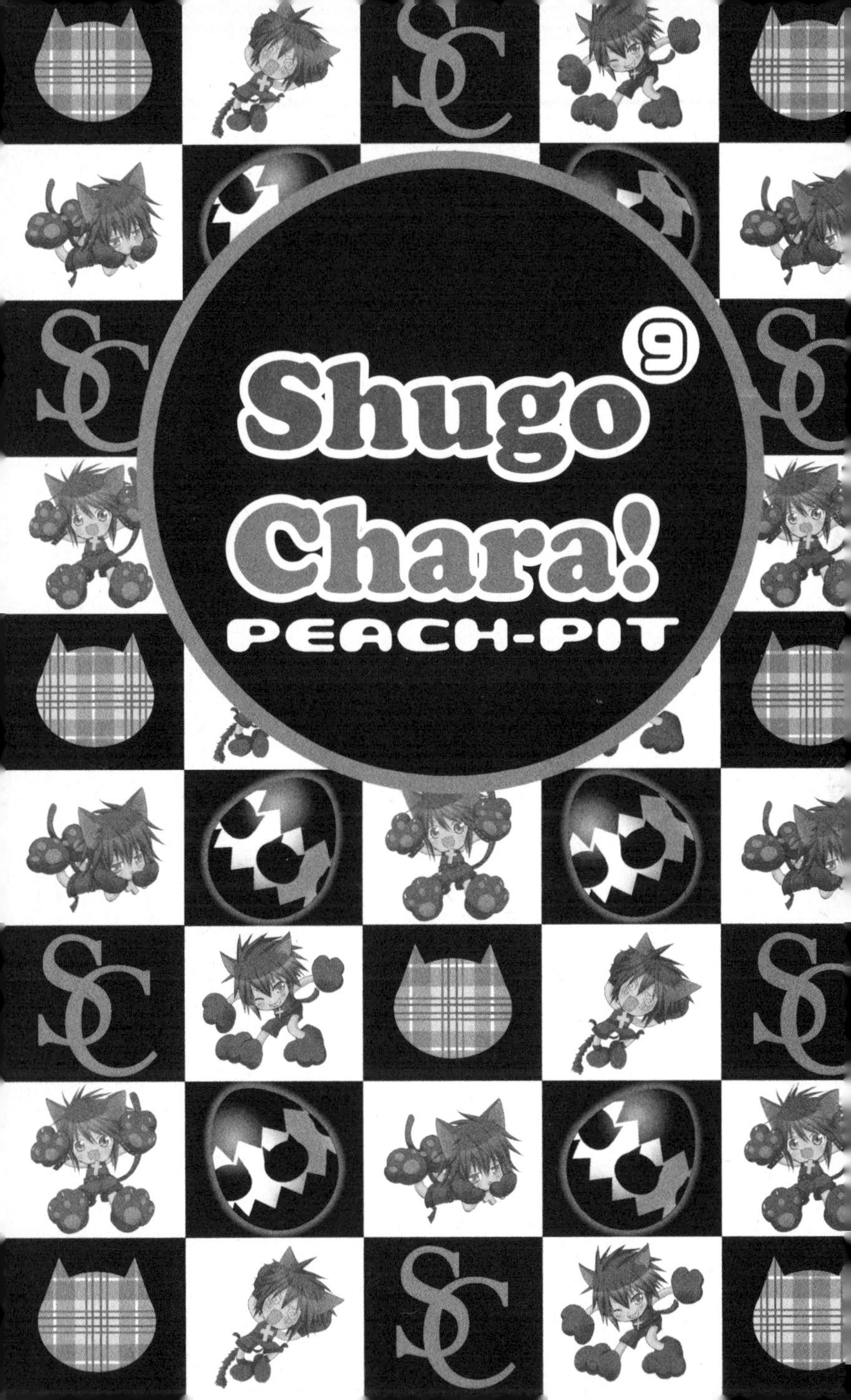
Shugo Chara!
9
PEACH-PIT

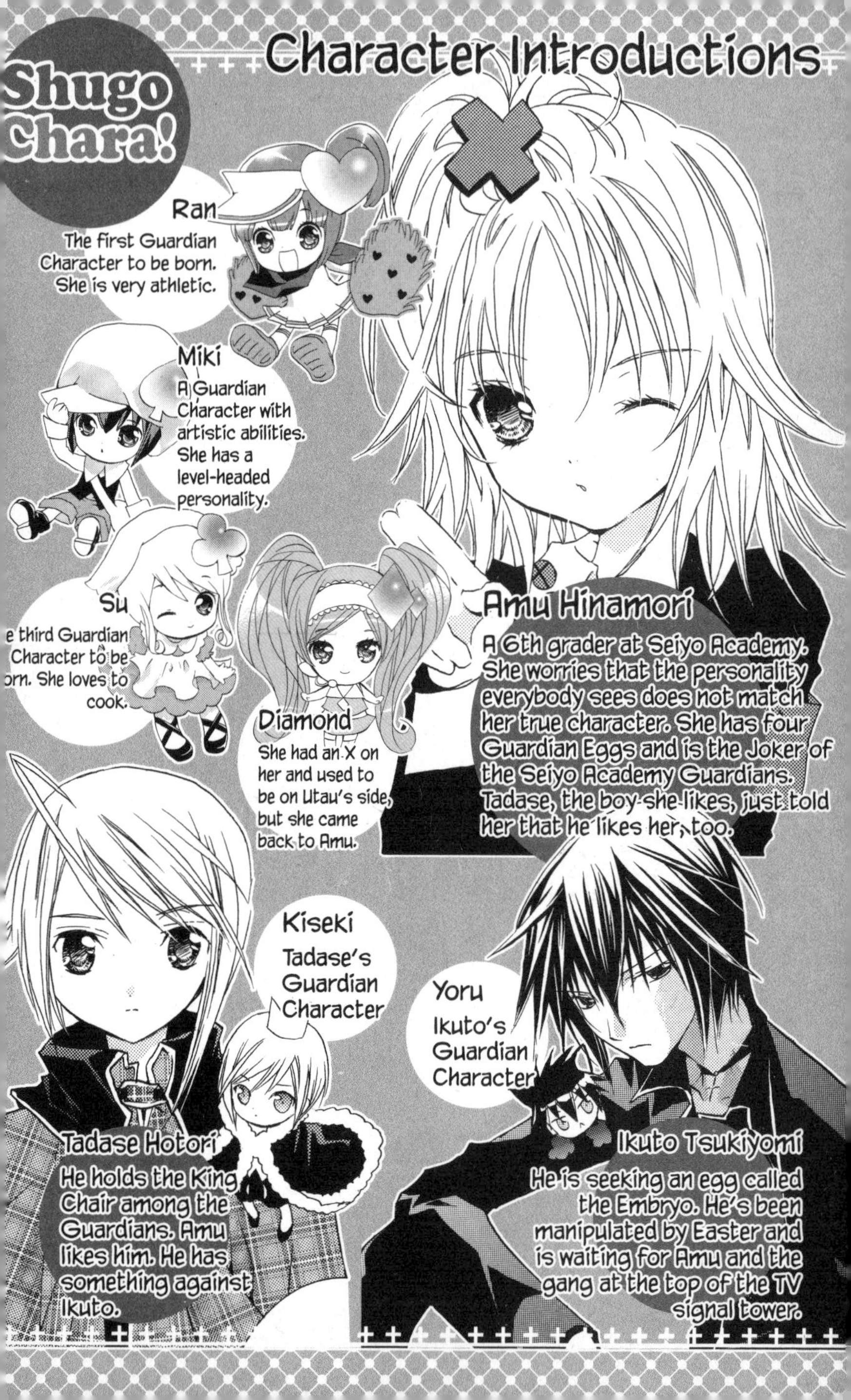
Character Introductions
Shugo Chara!
Ran
The first Guardian Character to be born. She is very athletic.
Miki
A Guardian Character with artistic abilities. She has a level-headed personality.
Su
e third Guardian Character to be orn. She loves to cook.
Diamond
She had an X on her and used to be on Utau's side, but she came back to Amu.
Amu Hinamori
A 6th grader at Seiyo Academy. She worries that the personality everybody sees does not match her true character. She has four Guardian Eggs and is the Joker of the Seiyo Academy Guardians. Tadase, the boy she likes, just told her that he likes her, too.
Kiseki
Tadase's Guardian Character
Yoru
Ikuto's Guardian Character
Tadase Hotori
He holds the King Chair among the Guardians. Amu likes him. He has something against Ikuto.
Ikuto Tsukiyomi
He is seeking an egg called the Embryo. He's been manipulated by Easter and is waiting for Amu and the gang at the top of the TV signal tower.

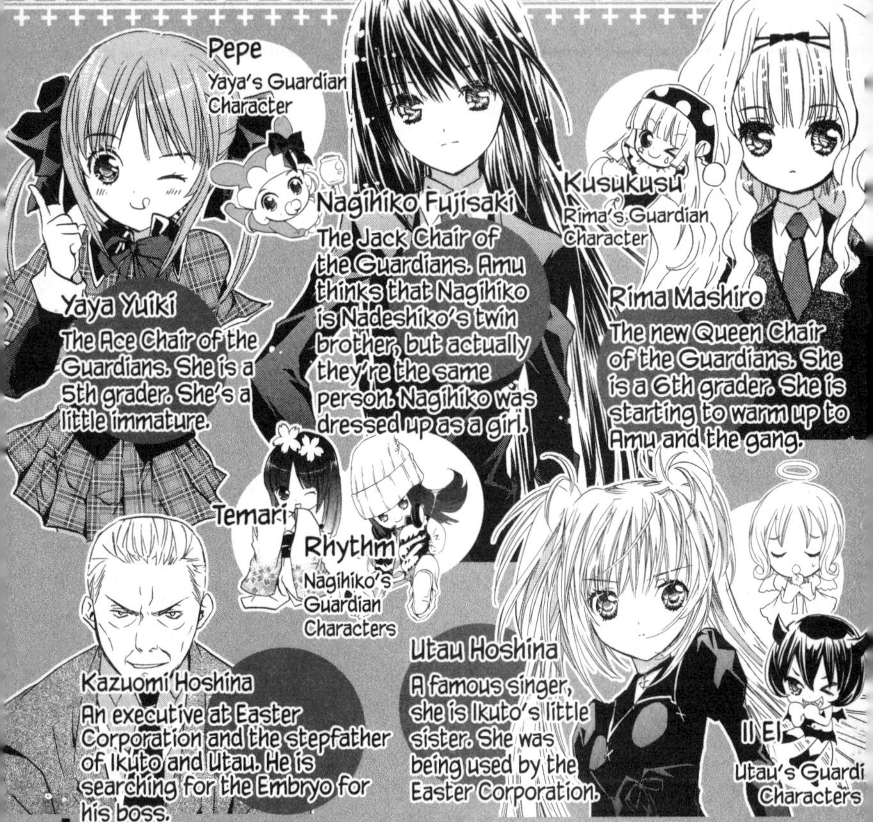

Kusukusu
Rima's Guardian Character
Rima Mashiro
The new Queen Chair of the Guardians. She is a 6th grader. She is starting to warm up to Amu and the gang.
Nagihiko Fujisaki
The Jack Chair of the Guardians. Amu thinks that Nagihiko is Nadeshiko's twin brother, but actually they're the same person. Nagihiko was dressed up as a girl.
Pepe
Yaya's Guardian Character
Yaya Yuiki
The Ace Chair of the Guardians. She is a 5th grader. She's a little immature.
Il El
Utau's Guardi Characters
Utau Hoshina
A famous singer, she is Ikuto's little sister. She was being used by the Easter Corporation.
Temari
Rhythm
Nagihiko's Guardian Characters
Kazuomi Hoshina
An executive at Easter Corporation and the stepfather of Ikuto and Utau. He is searching for the Embryo for his boss.

The Story So Far

● Amu comes across as cool. But that isn't who she really is. Deep inside, she is shy and a little cynical. One day, she wished she could be more true to herself, and the next day she found three eggs in her bed! Ran, Miki, and Su each hatched from their eggs. They are Amu's "Guardian Characters." Amu was recruited to become one of the Guardians at Seiyo Academy, and ever since, she's become good friends with other kids who have Guardian Characters.

● As the Joker of the Guardians, Amu's job is to find Heart's Eggs with X's on them and save them. But it seems that the Easter Corporation is looking for an egg known as the Embryo, and collecting countless X Eggs. The Easter Corporation's next target is Ikuto. They altered his violin and are using it to control Ikuto and make him collect X Eggs! The Guardians need to save Ikuto from Easter! Amu and the Guardians have arrived at the TV signal tower where Ikuto is. But countless traps set by Easter were awaiting them!!

● On the first floor, many X Eggs attacked Amu and the gang. With the help of Rima and Nagihiko, they were able to move forward. What awaits on the second floor!?

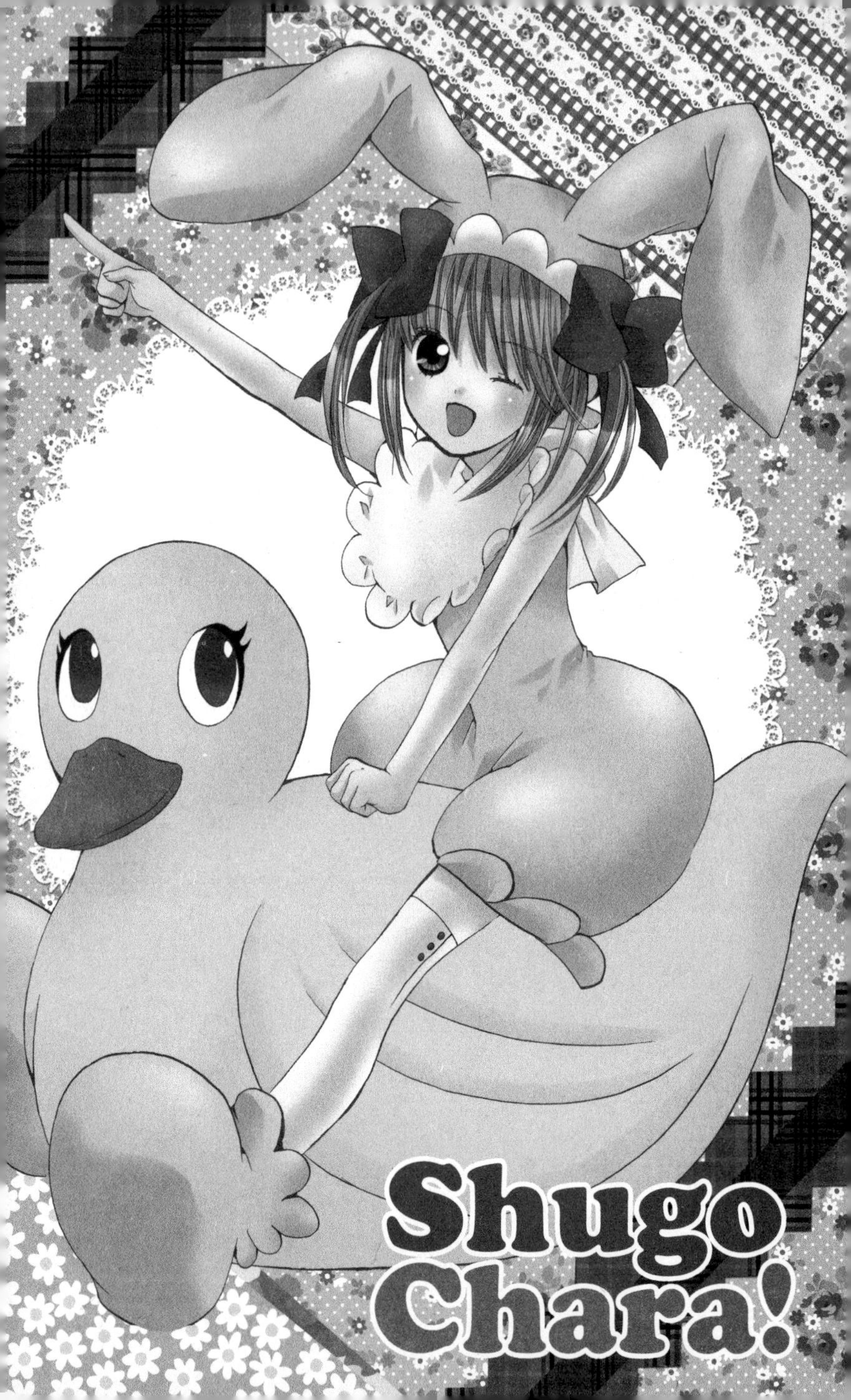
Shugo
Chara!

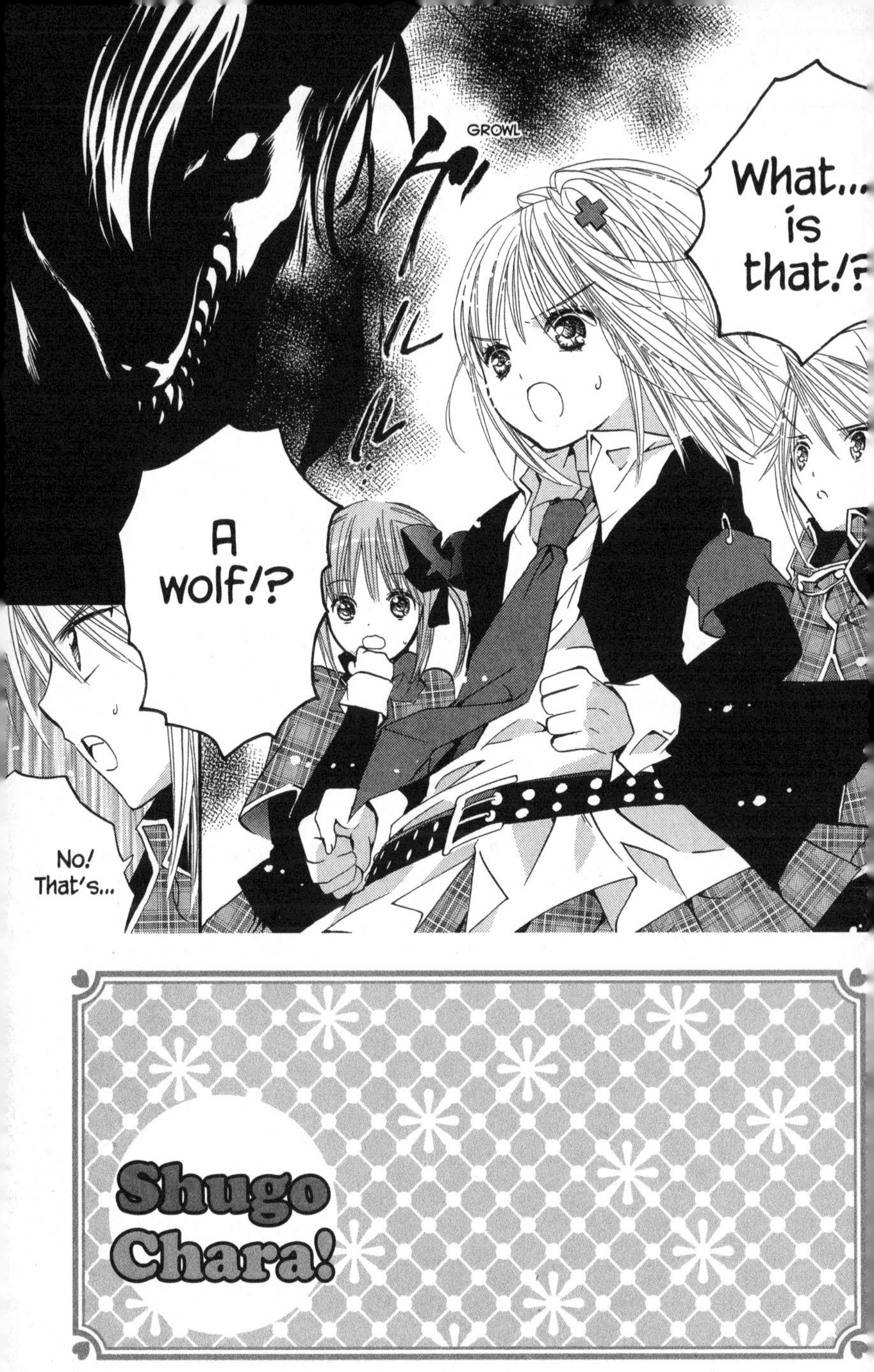
What... is that!?
GROWL
A wolf!?
No! That's...

Shugo Chara!

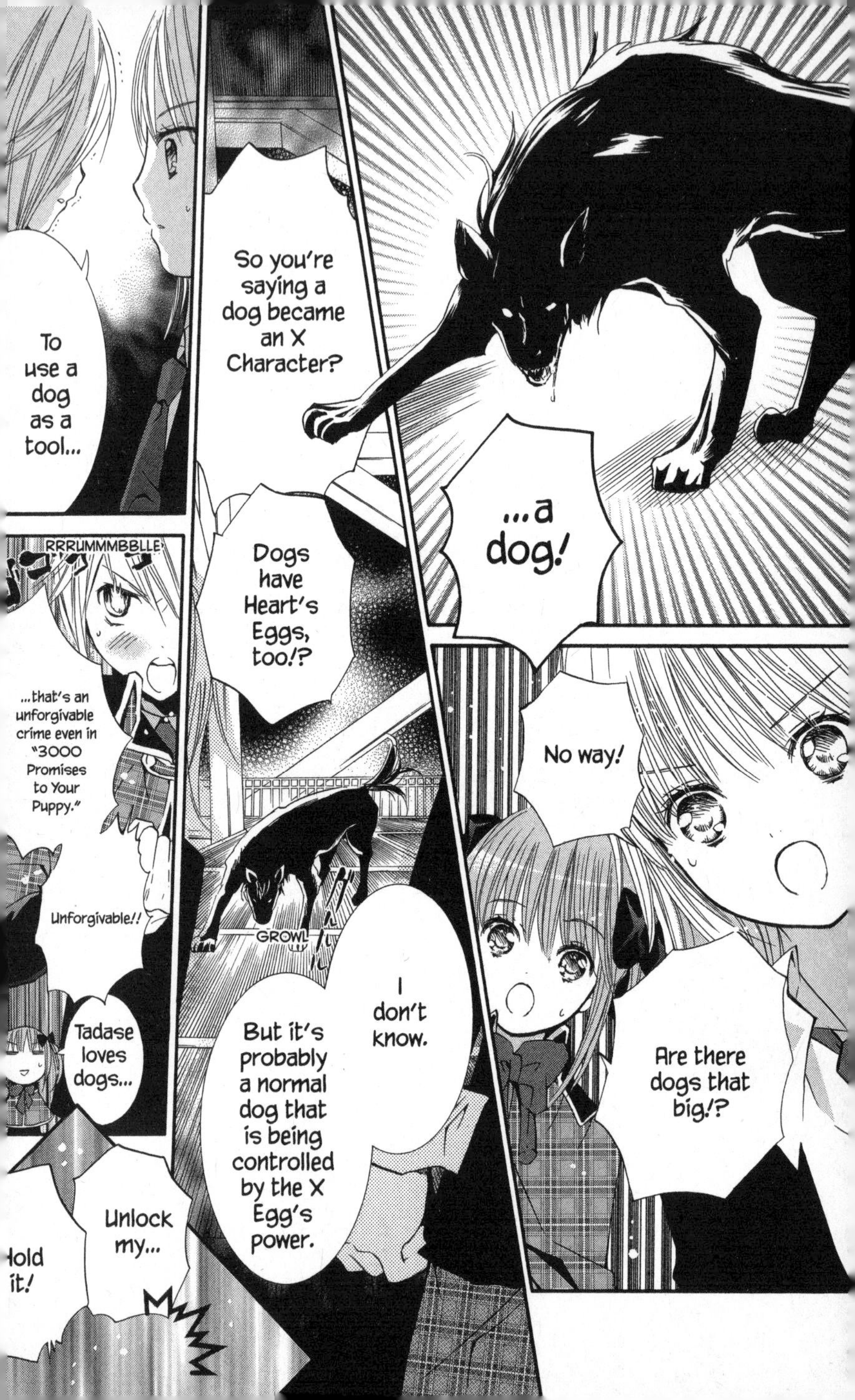
...a dog!
No way!
Are there dogs that big!?
So you're saying a dog became an X Character?
Dogs have Heart's Eggs, too!?
GROWL
I don't know.
But it's probably a normal dog that is being controlled by the X Egg's power.
To use a dog as a tool...
RRRUMMMBBLLE
...that's an unforgivable crime even in "3000 Promises to Your Puppy."
Unforgivable!!
Tadase loves dogs...
Unlock my...
Hold it!

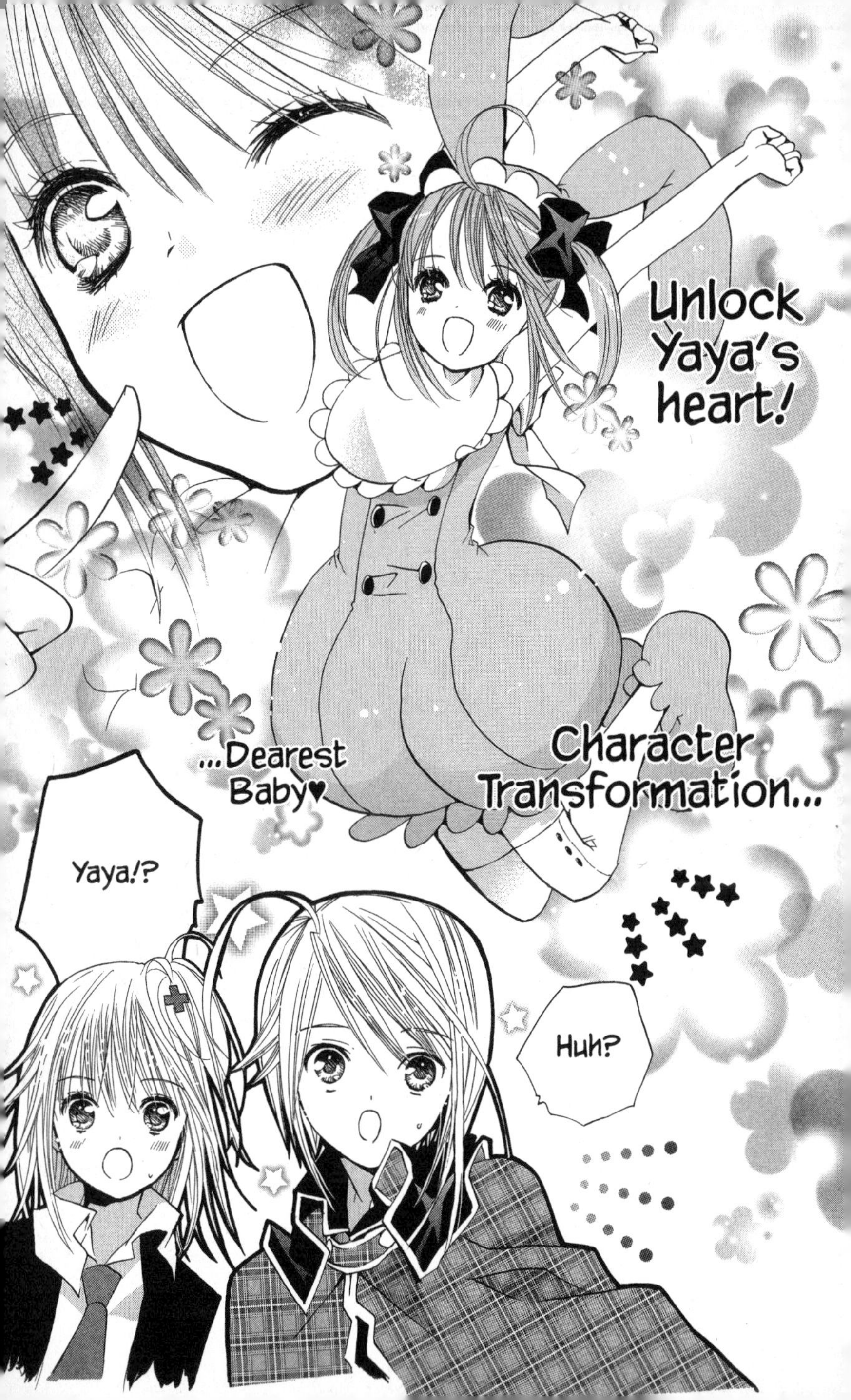
Unlock Yaya's heart!
Character Transformation...
...Dearest Baby♥
Yaya!?
Huh?

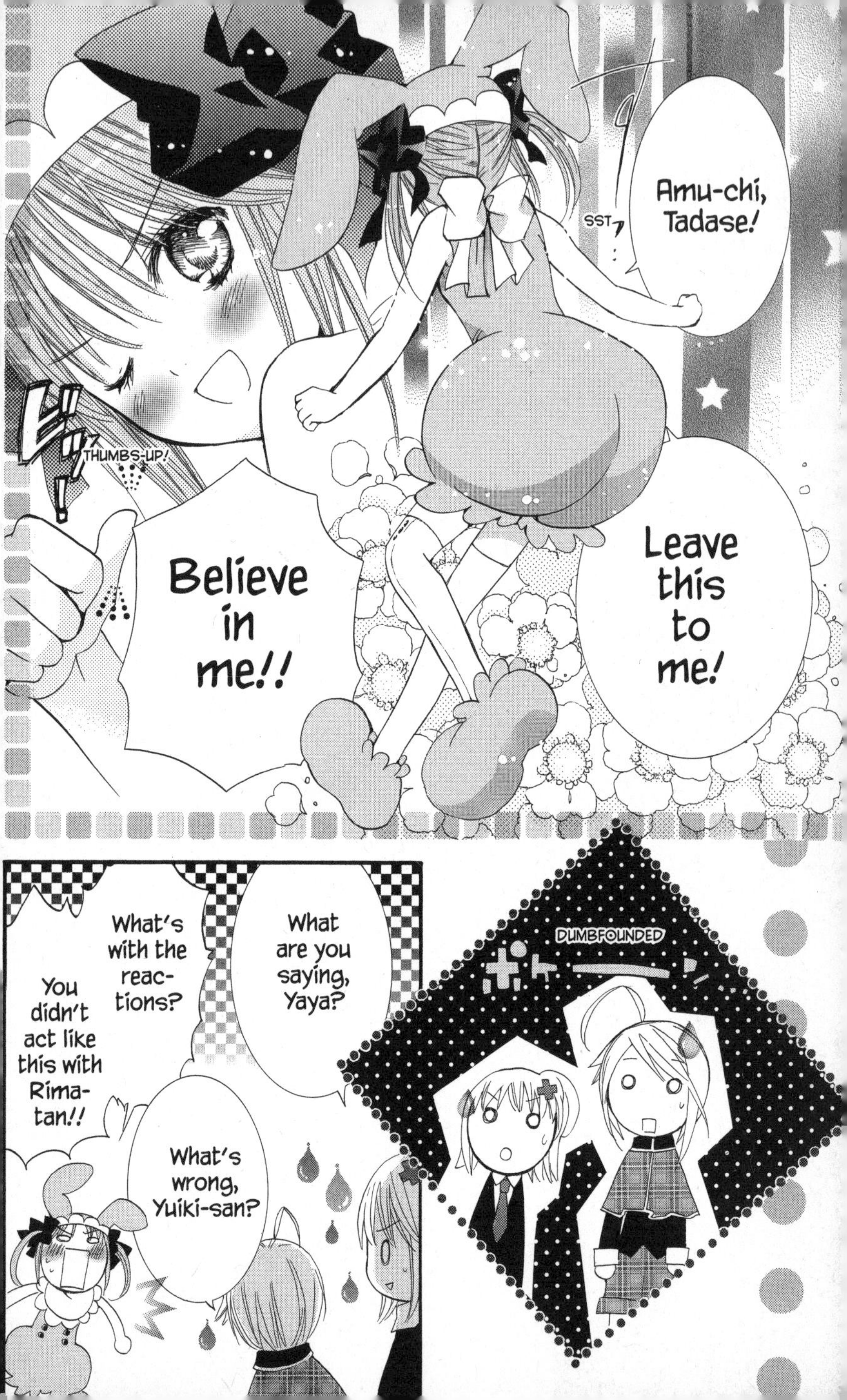
SST
Amu-chi, Tadase!
Leave this to me!
THUMBS-UP!
Believe in me!!
DUMBFOUNDED
What are you saying, Yaya?
What's with the reactions?
You didn't act like this with Rima-tan!!
What's wrong, Yuiki-san?

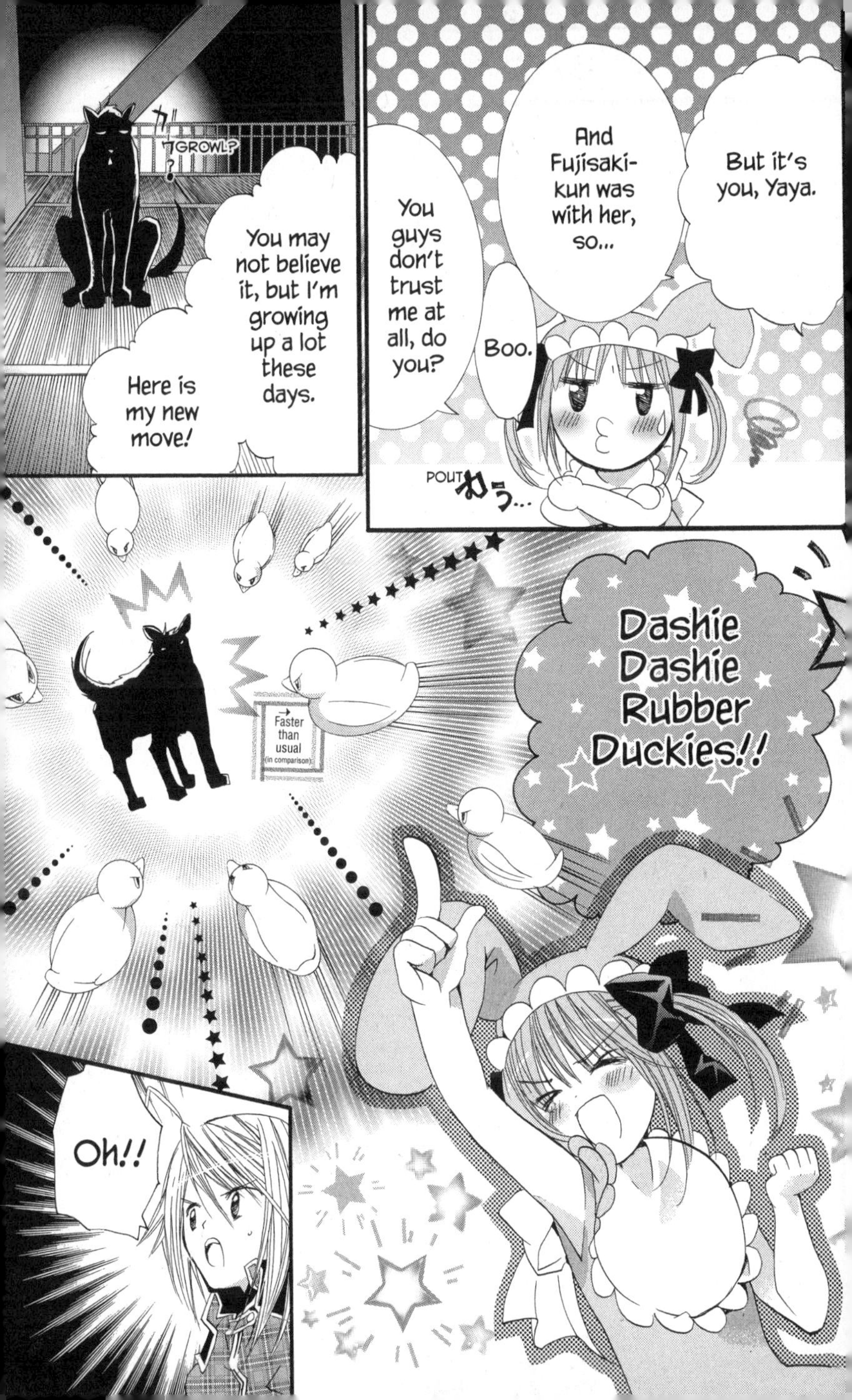
But it's you, Yaya.
And Fujisaki-kun was with her, so...
You guys don't trust me at all, do you?
Boo.
POUT むぅ...
You may not believe it, but I'm growing up a lot these days.
GROWL?
Here is my new move!
Dashie Dashie Rubber Duckies!!
→ Faster than usual (in comparison)
Oh!!

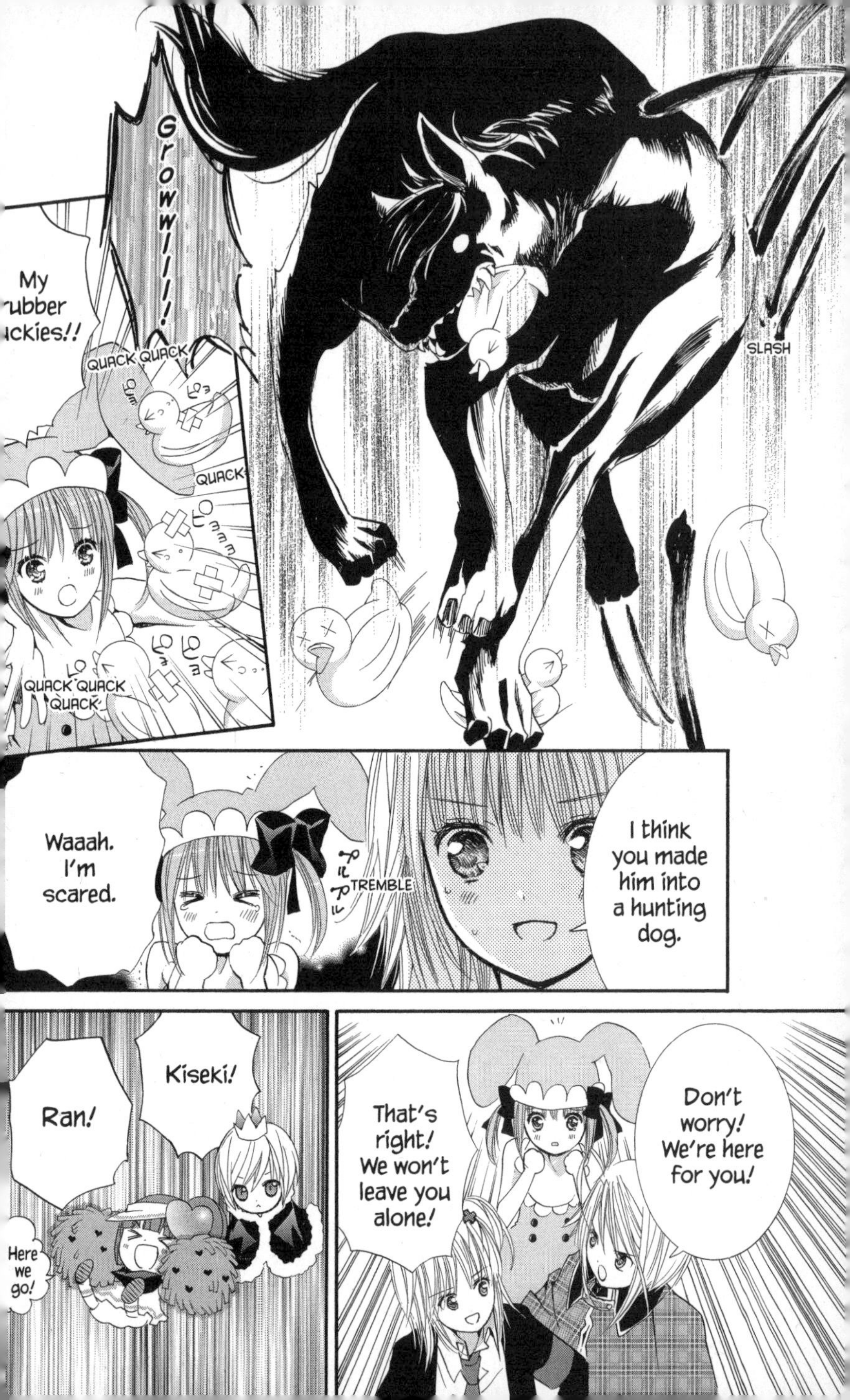

Growwlll!
SLASH
My rubber uckies!!
QUACK QUACK
QUACK
QUACK QUACK QUACK
I think you made him into a hunting dog.
TREMBLE
Waaah. I'm scared.
Don't worry! We're here for you!
That's right! We won't leave you alone!
Kiseki!
Ran!
Here we go!

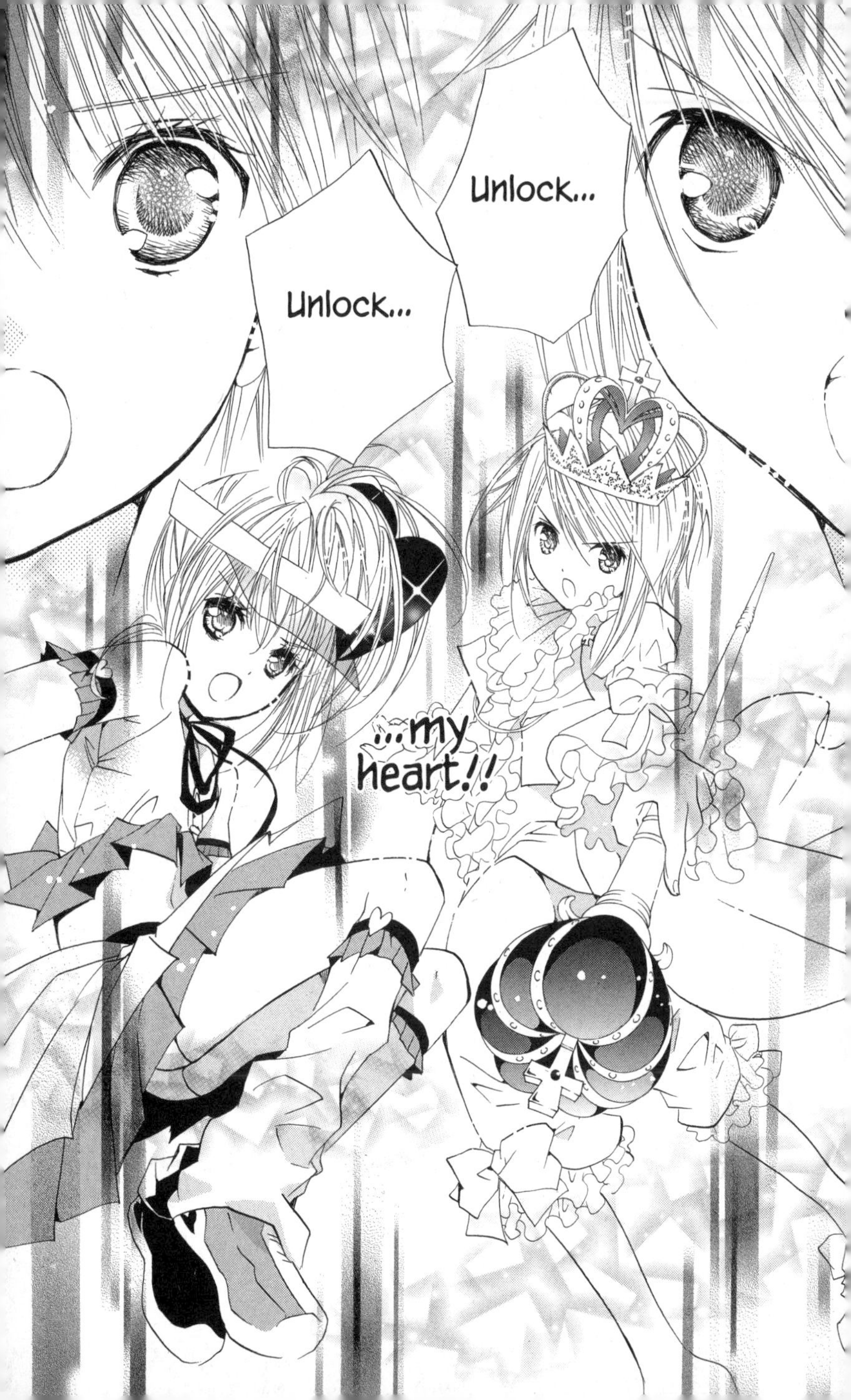
Unlock...
Unlock...
...my heart!!

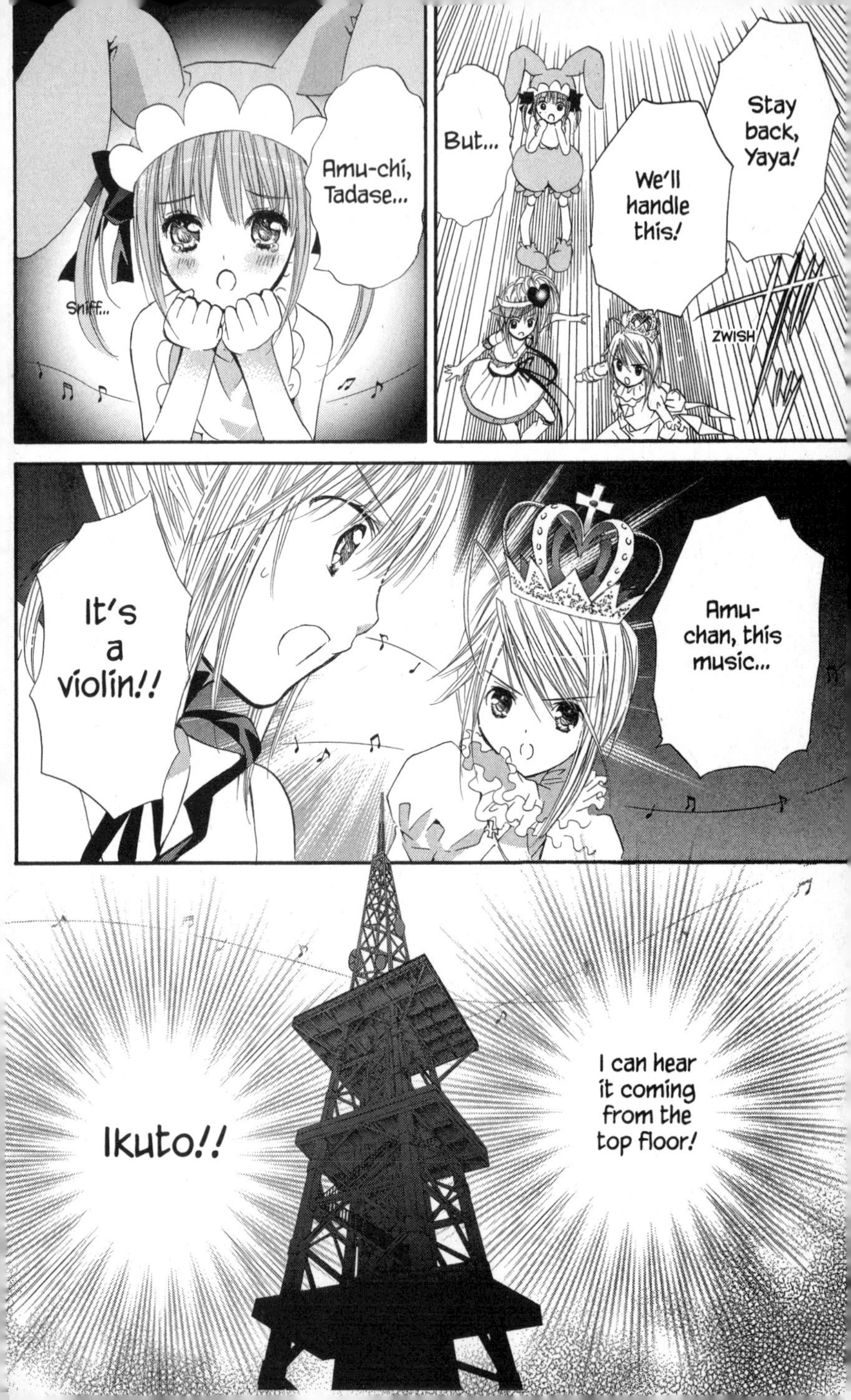
Stay back, Yaya!
We'll handle this!
ZWISH
But...
Amu-chi, Tadase...
Sniff...
Amu-chan, this music...
It's a violin!!
I can hear it coming from the top floor!
Ikuto!!

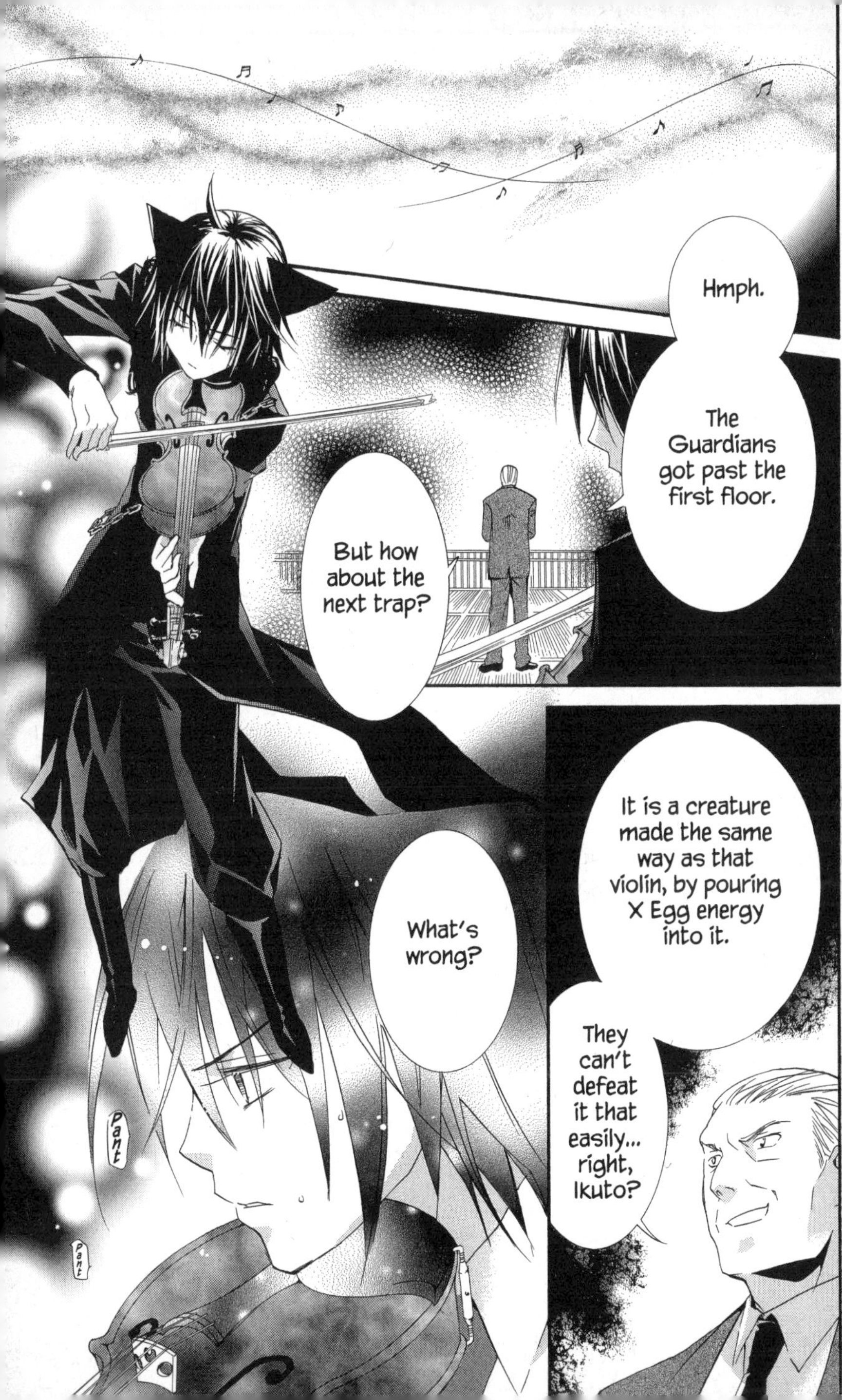
Hmph.
The Guardians got past the first floor.
But how about the next trap?
It is a creature made the same way as that violin, by pouring X Egg energy into it.
They can't defeat it that easily... right, Ikuto?
What's wrong?
Pant
Pant

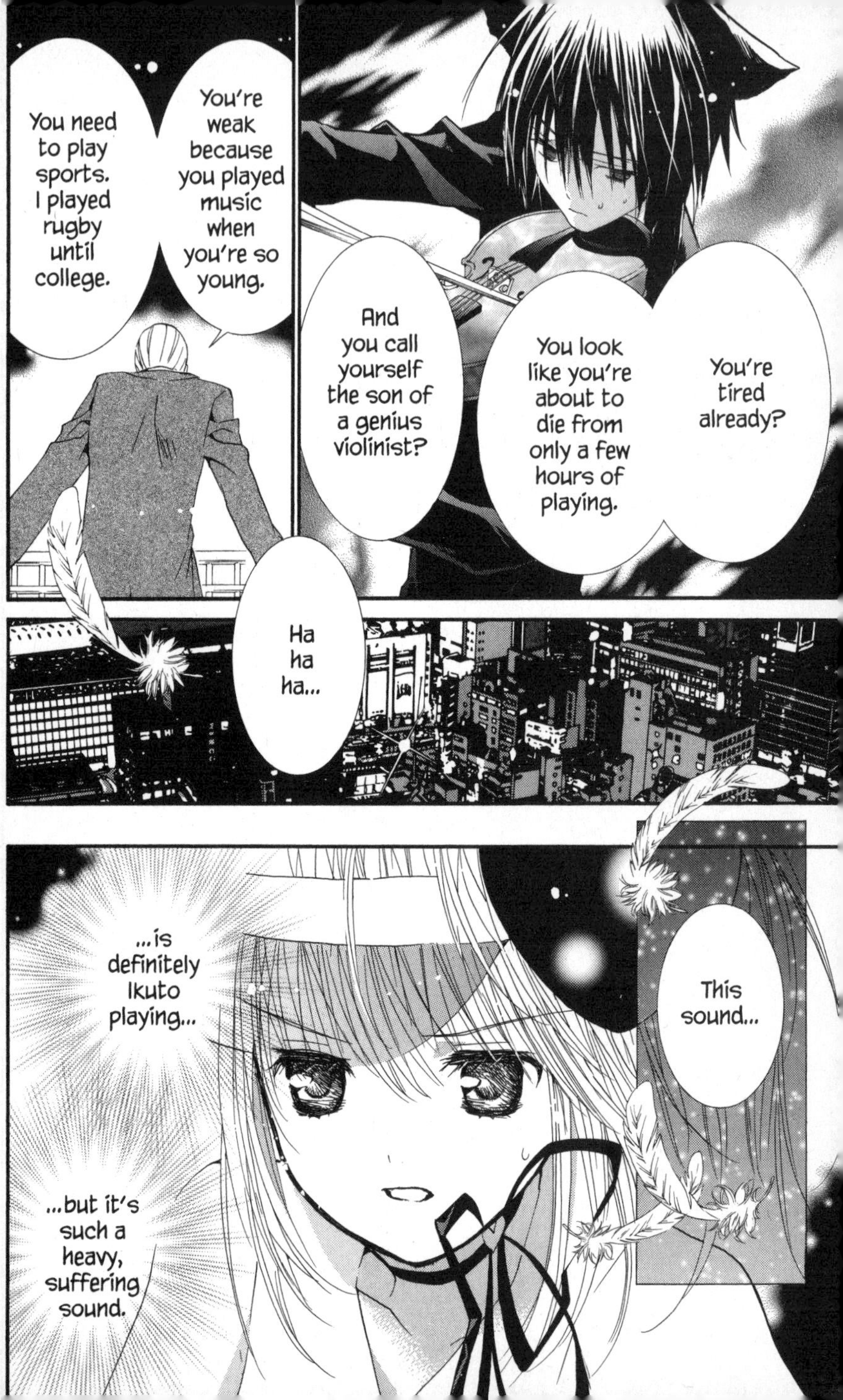
You're tired already?
You look like you're about to die from only a few hours of playing.
And you call yourself the son of a genius violinist?
You're weak because you played music when you're so young.
You need to play sports. I played rugby until college.
Ha ha ha...
This sound...
...is definitely Ikuto playing...
...but it's such a heavy, suffering sound.

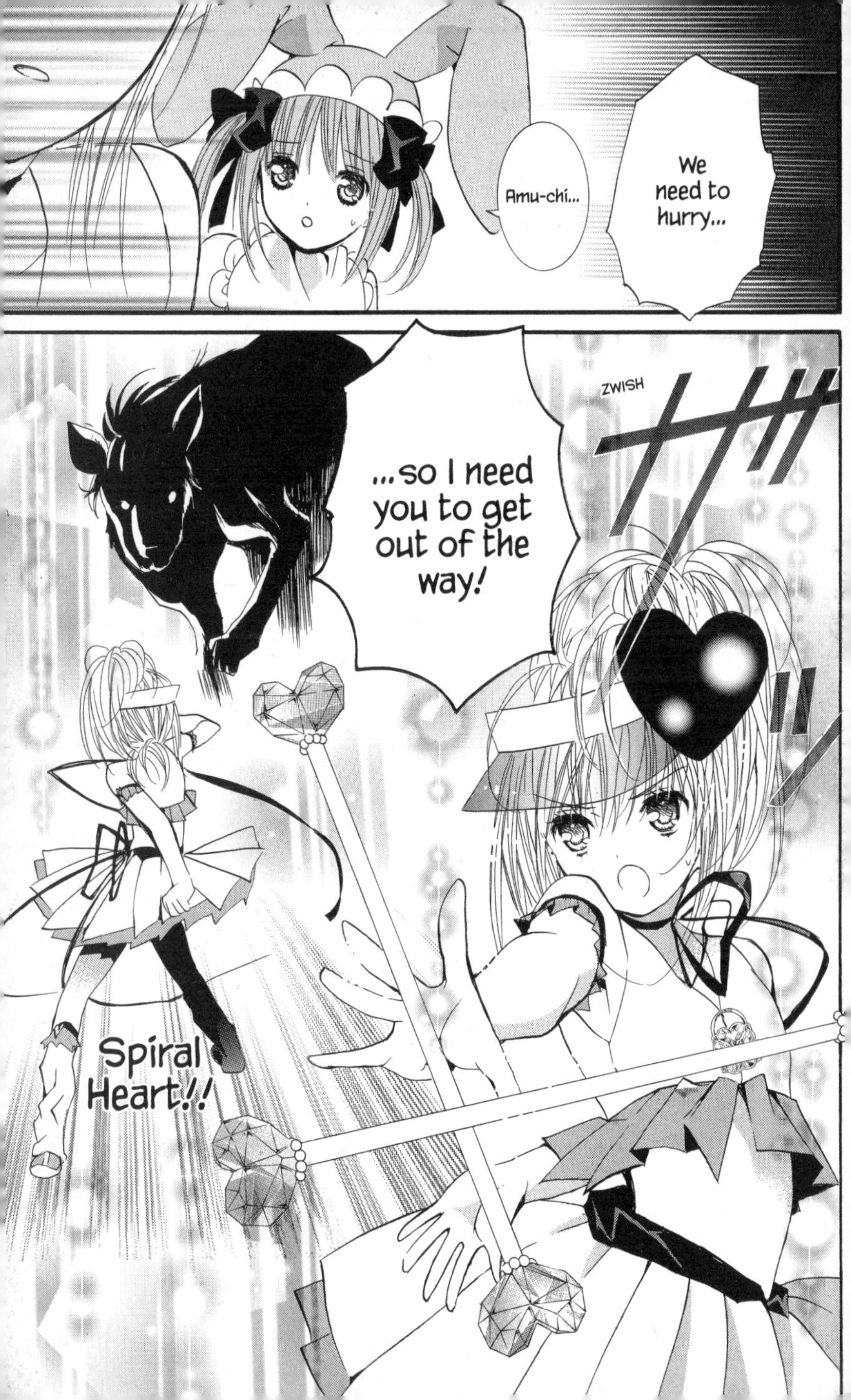
We need to hurry...
Amu-chi...
...so I need you to get out of the way!
ZWISH
Spiral Heart!!

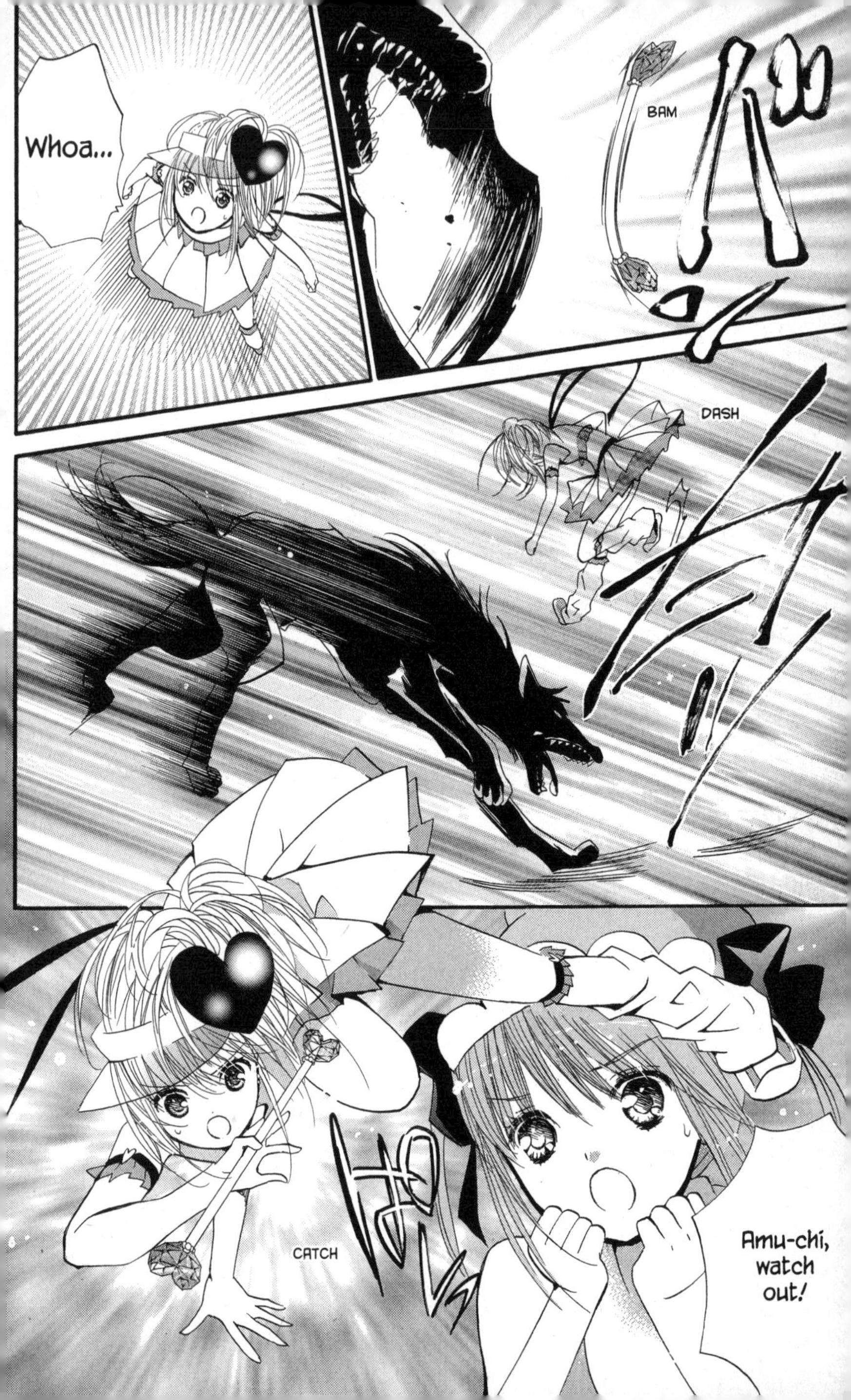
BAM
Whoa...
DASH
Amu-chi, watch out!
CATCH

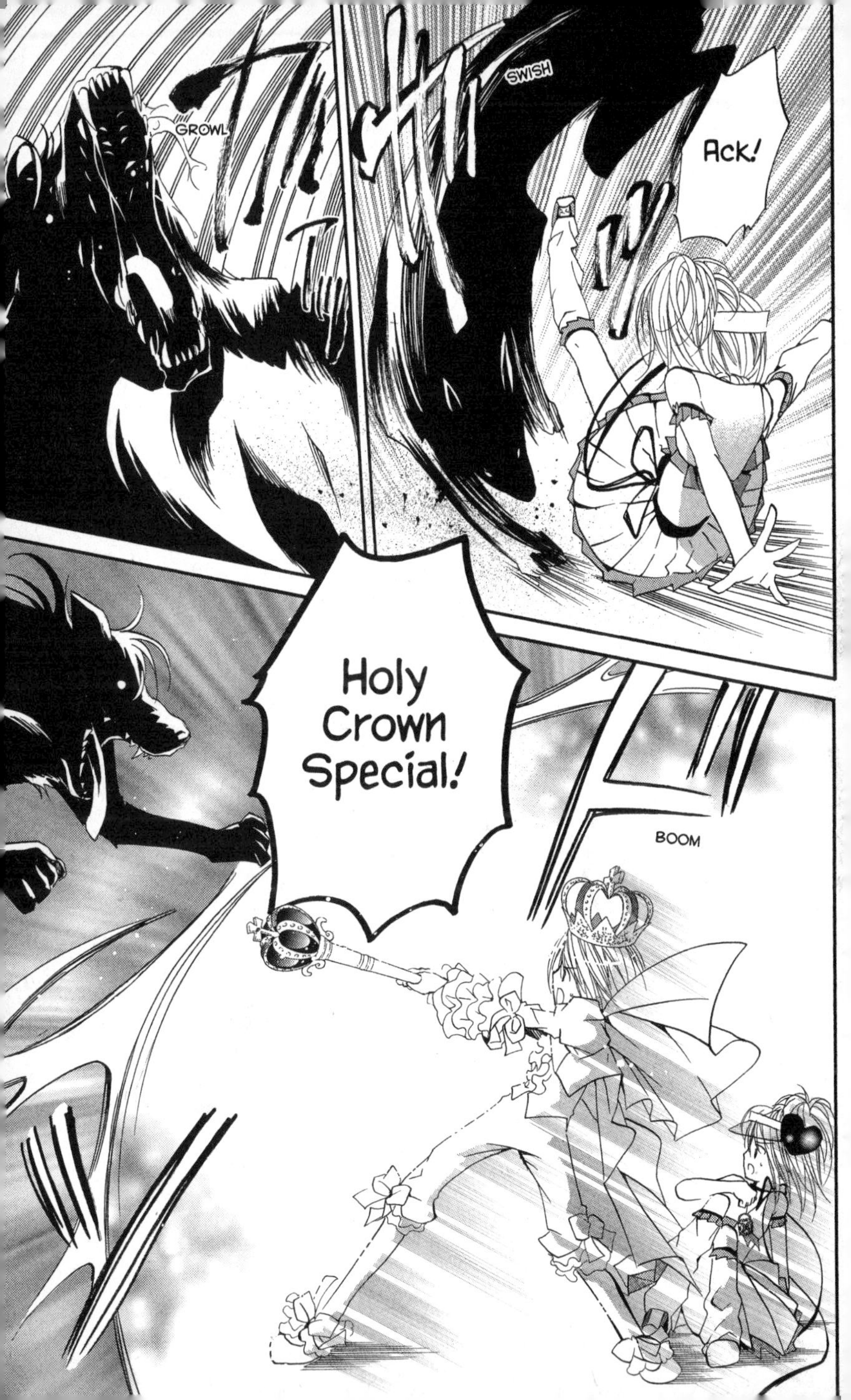
SWISH
Ack!
GROWL
Holy Crown Special!
BOOM

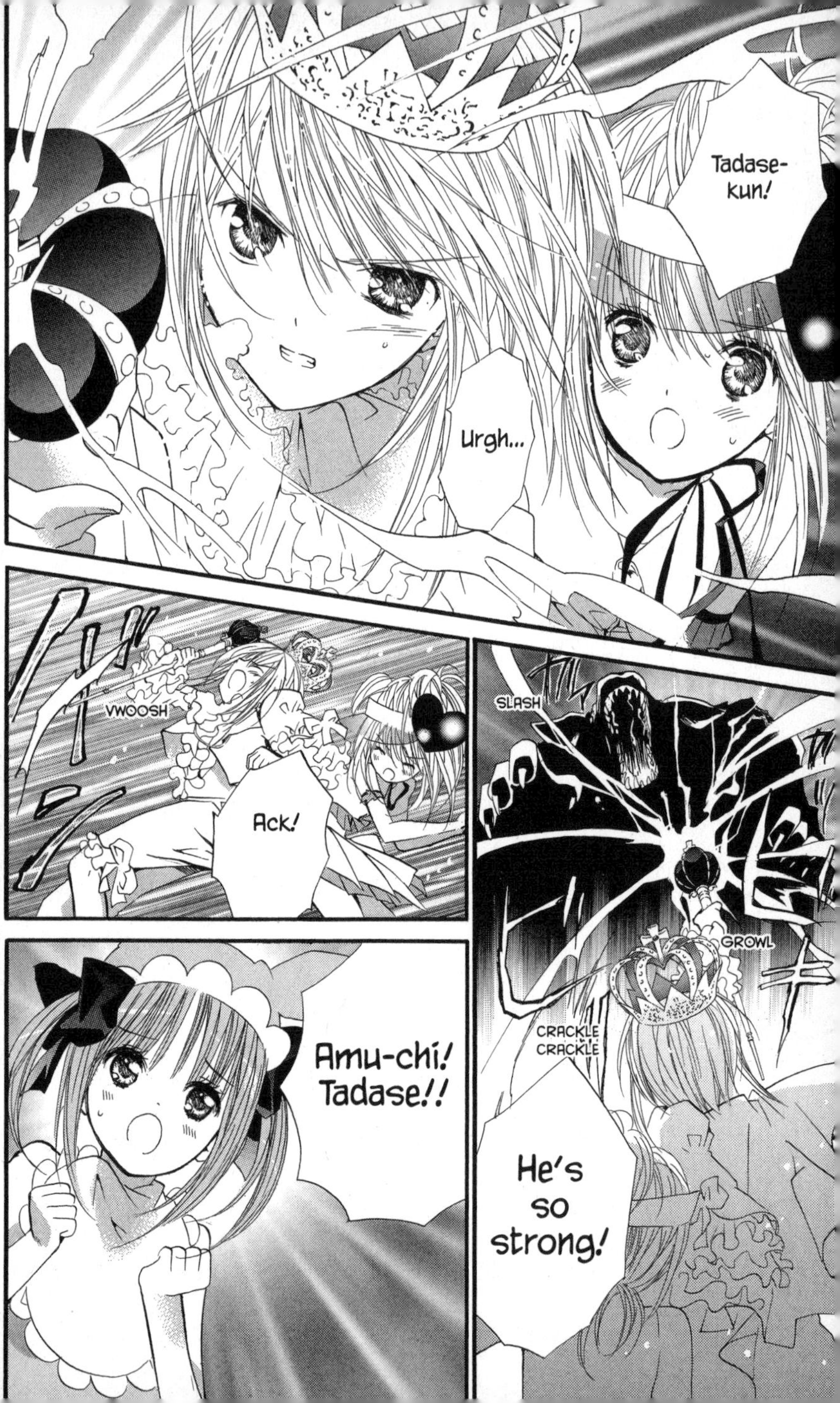
Tadase-kun!
Urgh...
SLASH
GROWL
CRACKLE CRACKLE
He's so strong!
VWOOSH
Ack!
Amu-chi! Tadase!!

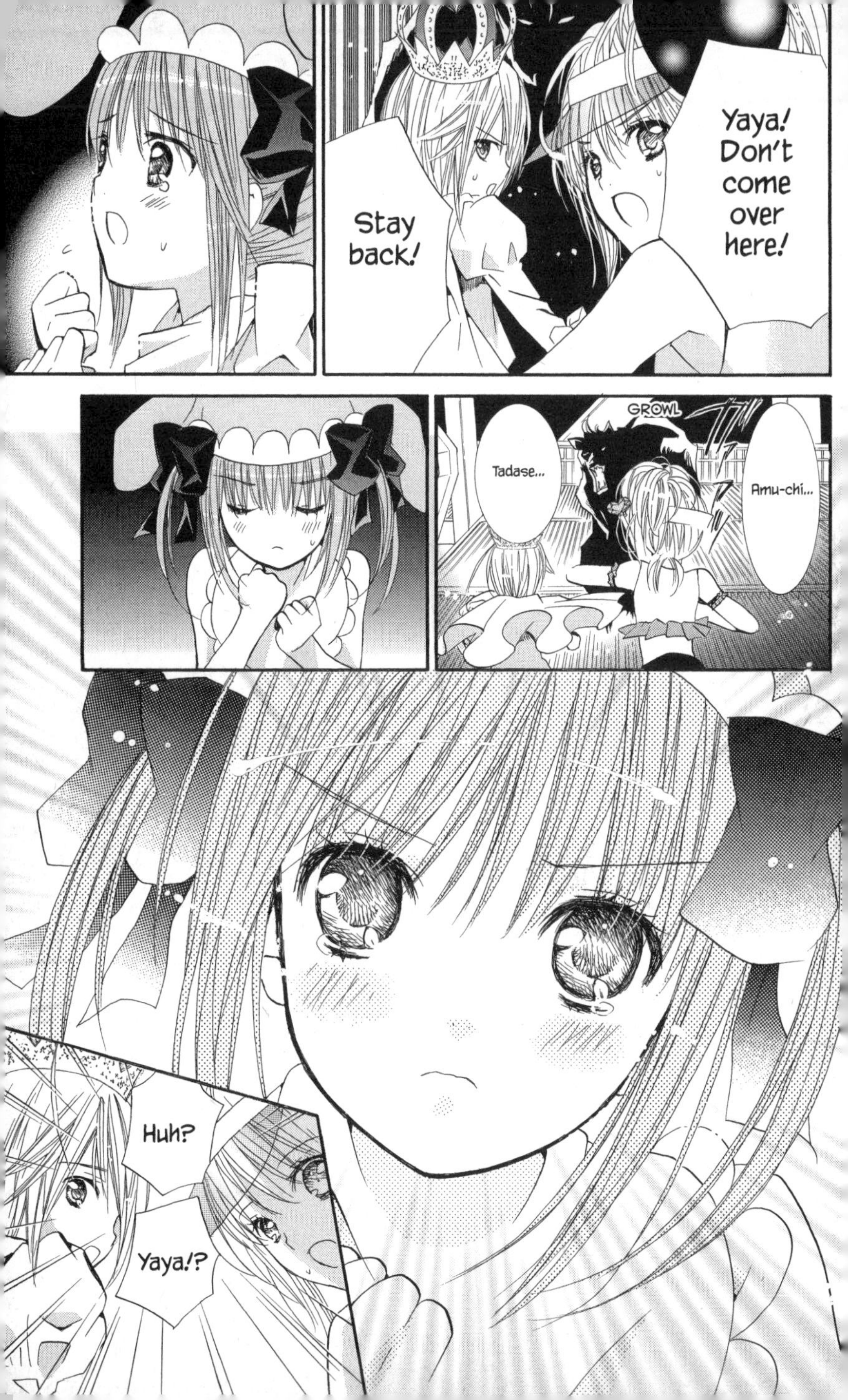
Yaya! Don't come over here!
Stay back!
Amu-chi...
GROWL
Tadase...
Huh?
Yaya!?

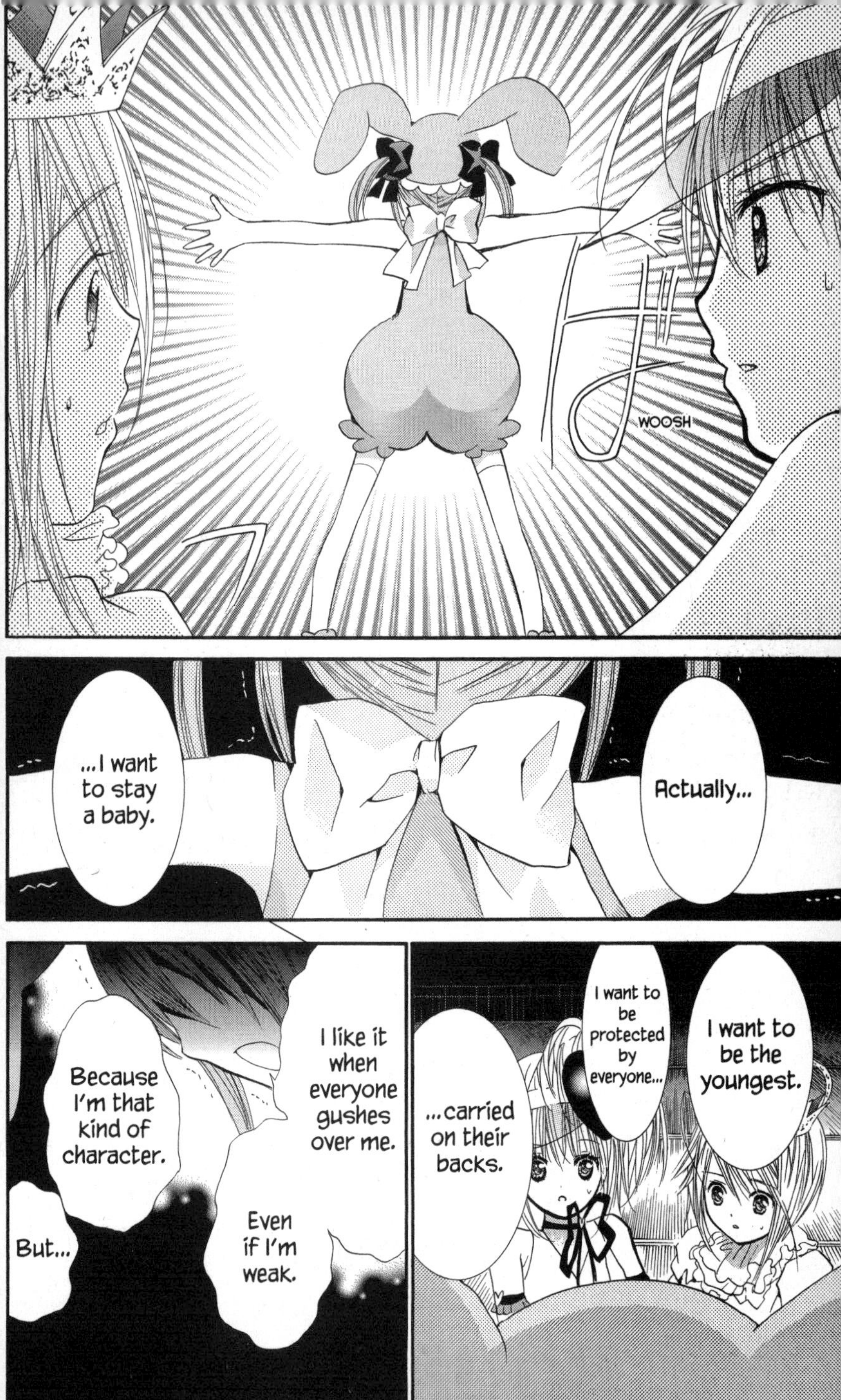
WOOSH
Actually...
...I want to stay a baby.
I want to be the youngest.
I want to be protected by everyone...
...carried on their backs.
I like it when everyone gushes over me.
Because I'm that kind of character.
Even if I'm weak.
But...

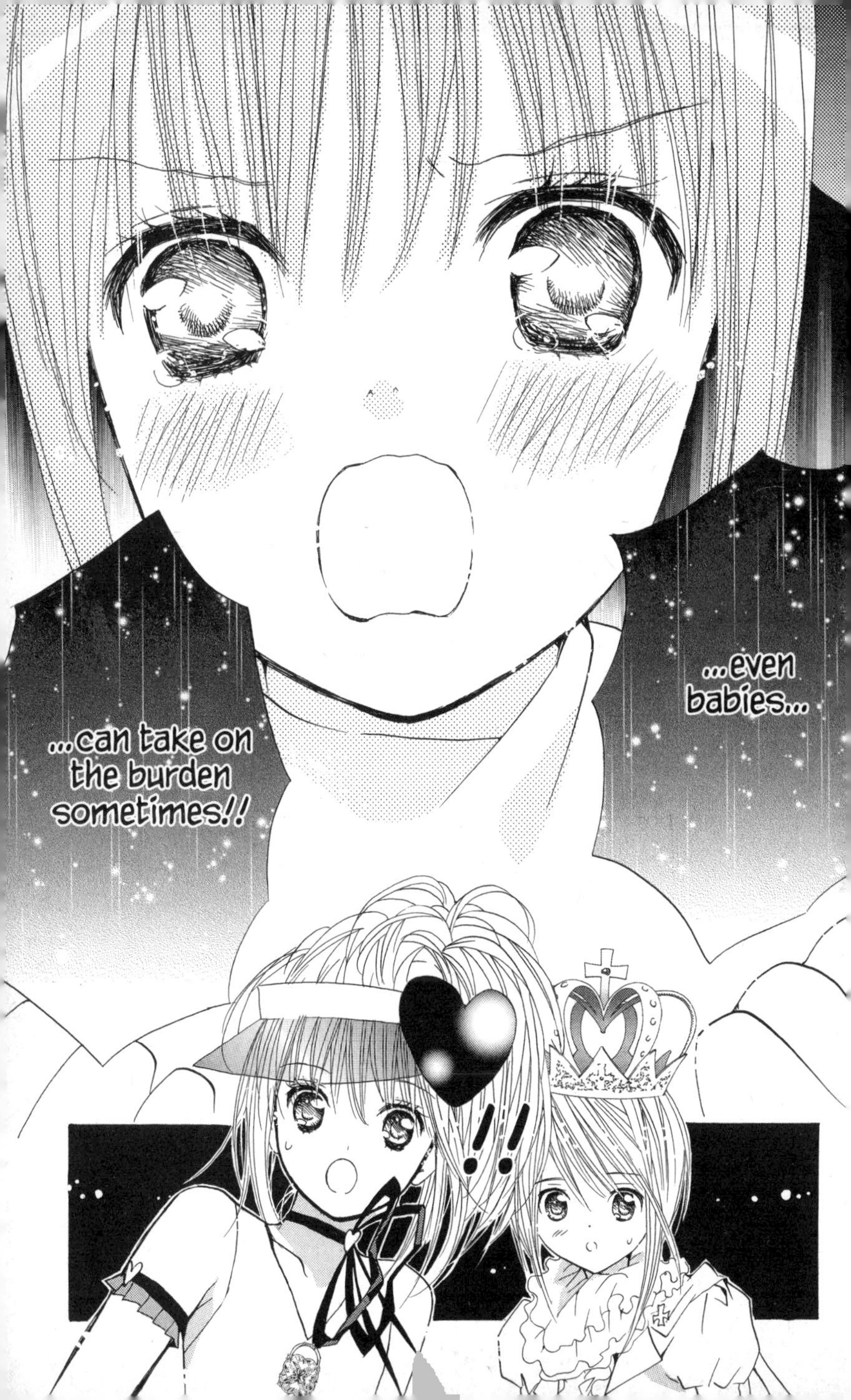
...even babies...
...can take on the burden sometimes!!
!!

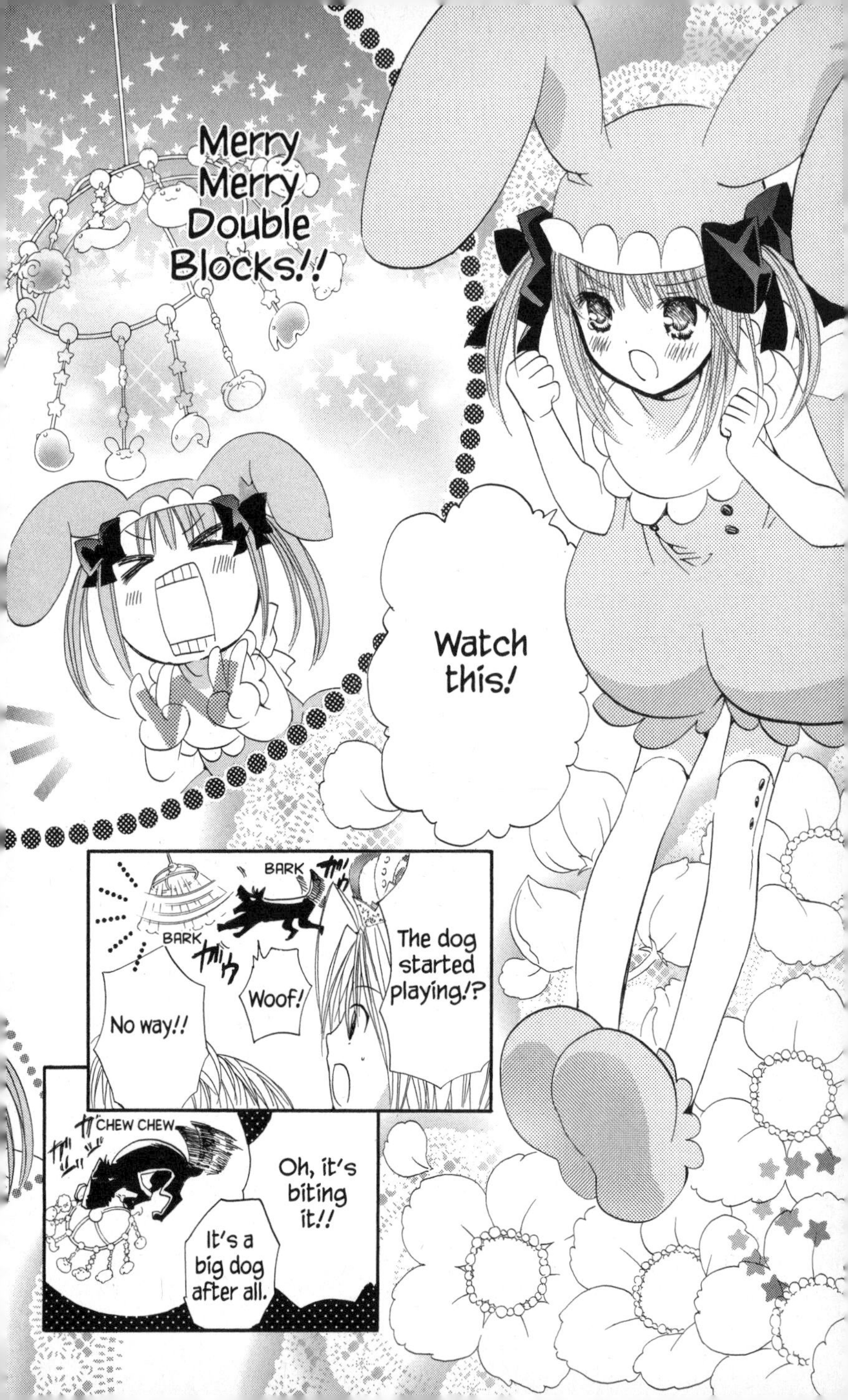
Watch this!
Merry Merry Double Blocks!!
BARK
BARK
The dog started playing!?
Woof!
No way!!
CHEW CHEW
Oh, it's biting it!!
It's a big dog after all.

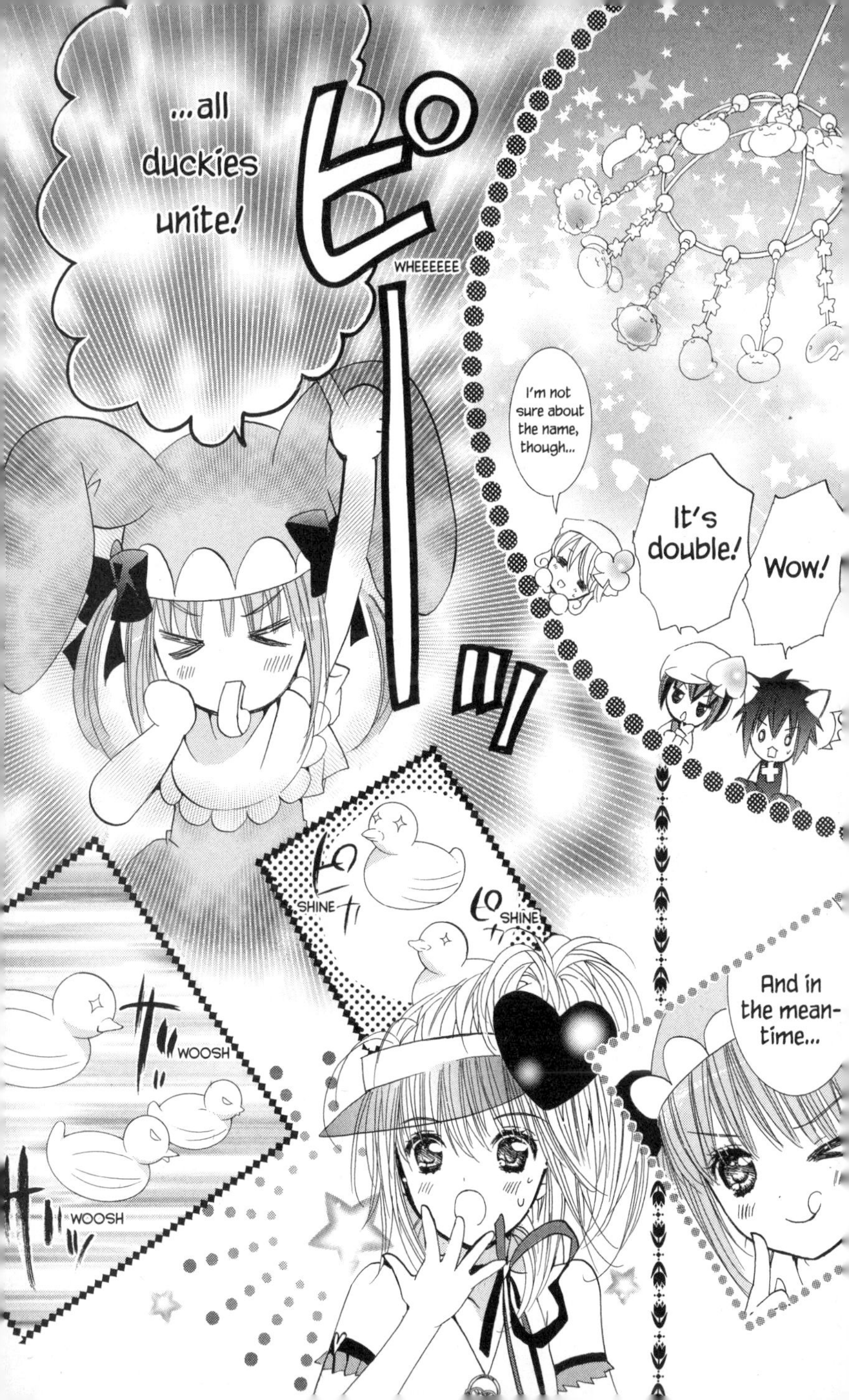
Wow!
It's double!
I'm not sure about the name, though...
...all duckies unite!
WHEEEEEE
And in the mean-time...
SHINE
SHINE
WOOSH
WOOSH

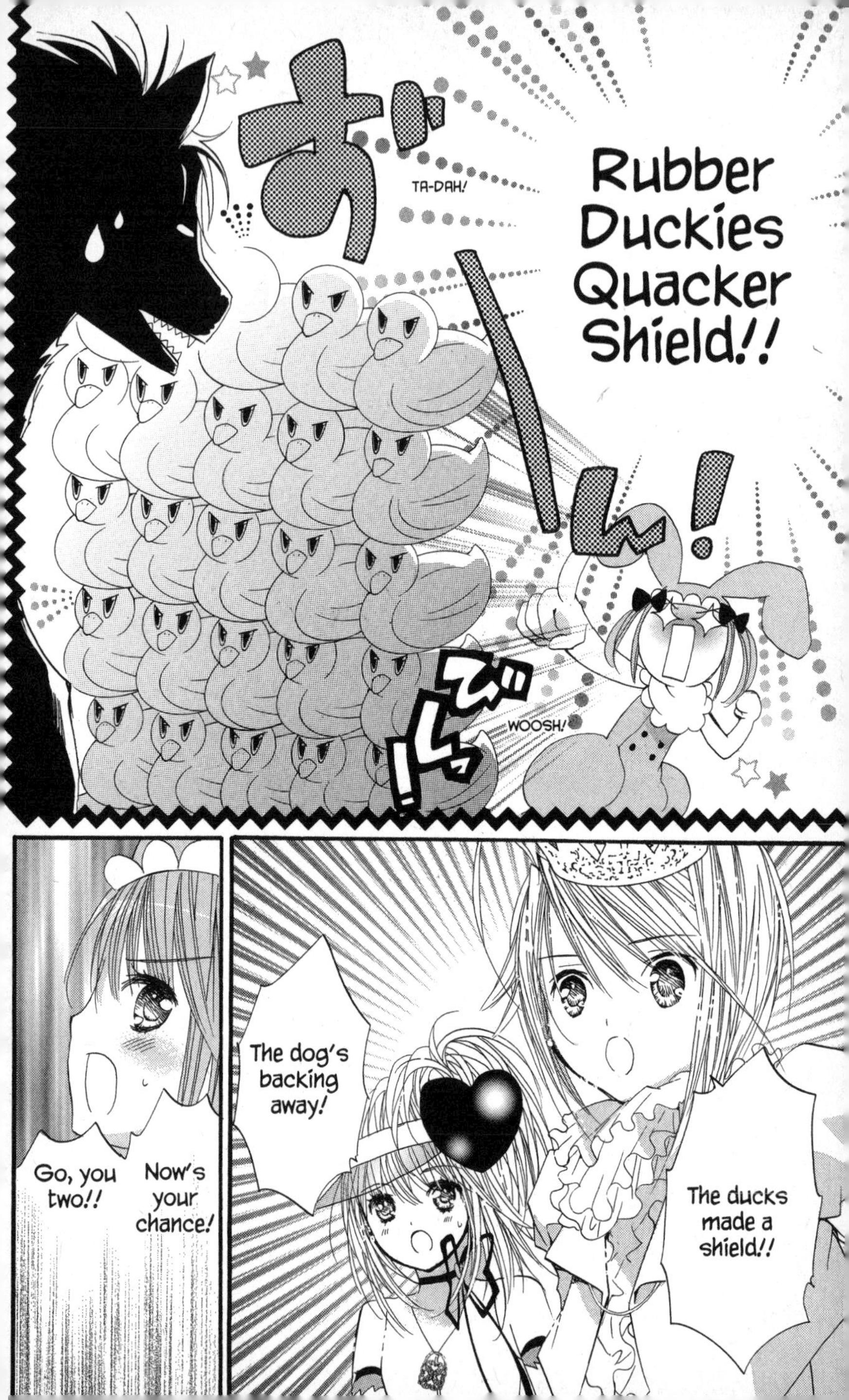
Rubber Duckies Quacker Shield!!
TA-DAH!
WOOSH!
The ducks made a shield!!
The dog's backing away!
Now's your chance!
Go, you two!!

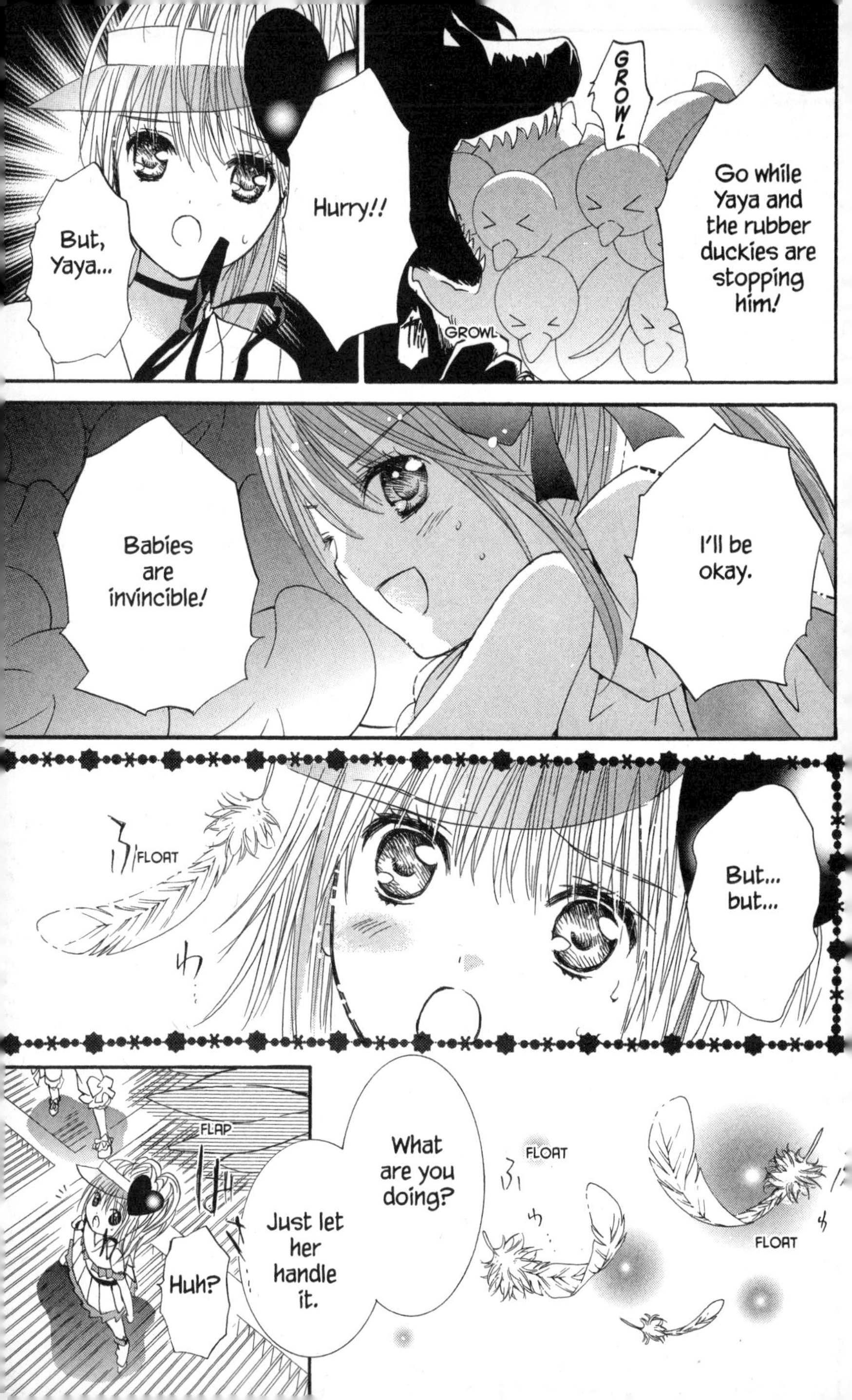
GROWL
Go while Yaya and the rubber duckies are stopping him!
GROWL
Hurry!!
But, Yaya...
I'll be okay.
Babies are invincible!
But... but...
FLOAT
FLOAT
FLOAT
FLOAT
What are you doing?
Just let her handle it.
Huh?
FLAP

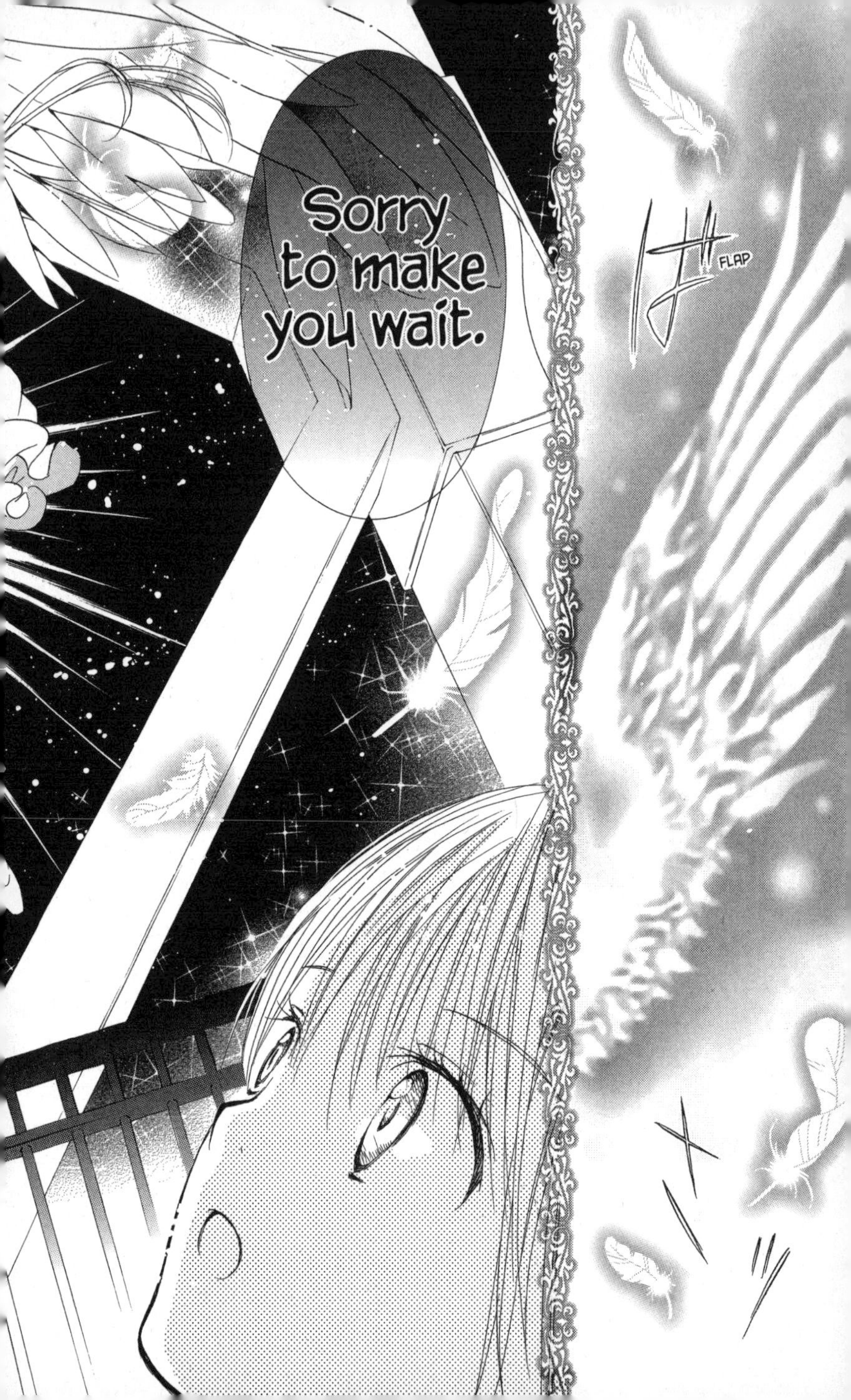
Sorry to make you wait.
FLAP

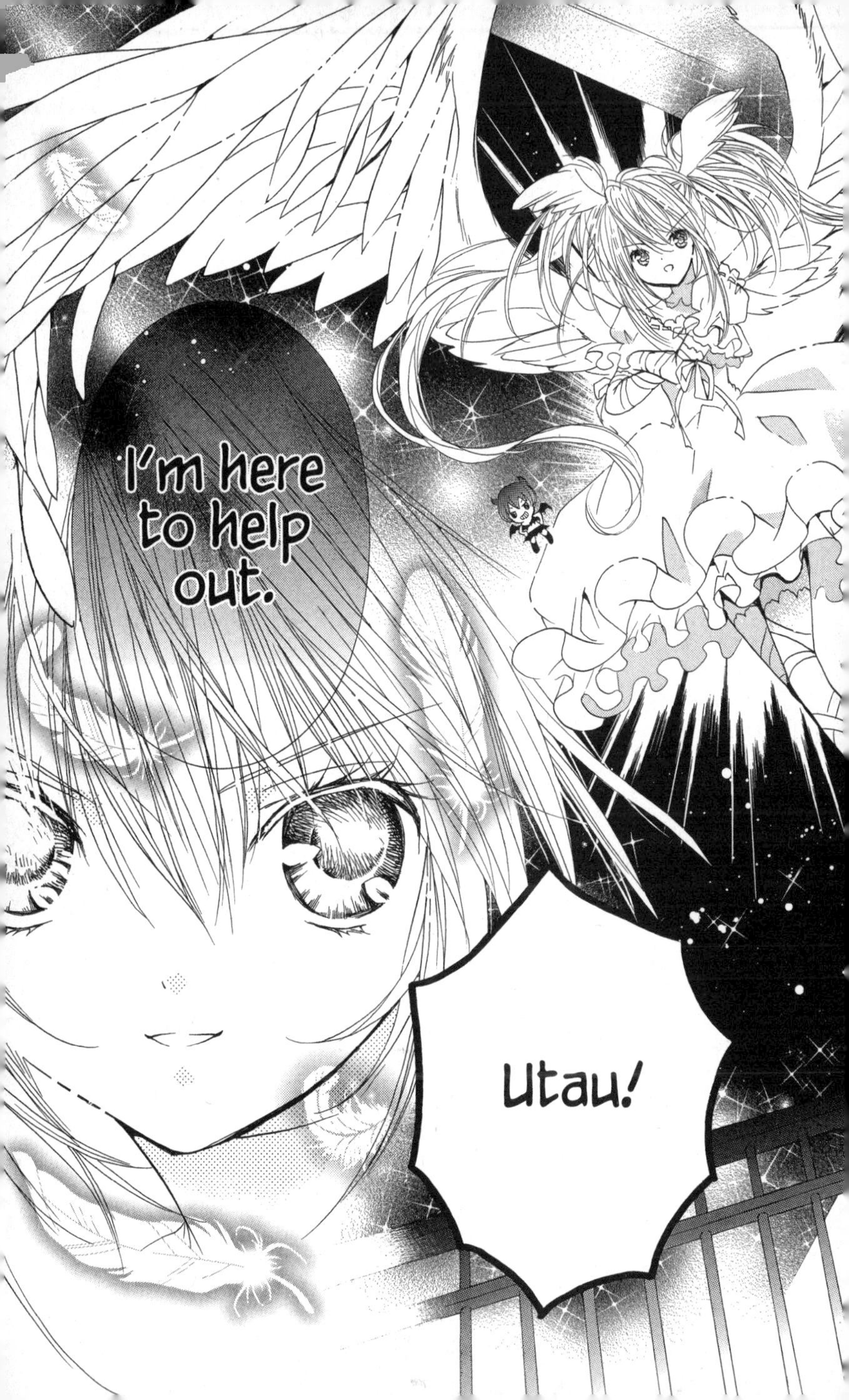
I'm here to help out.
Utau!

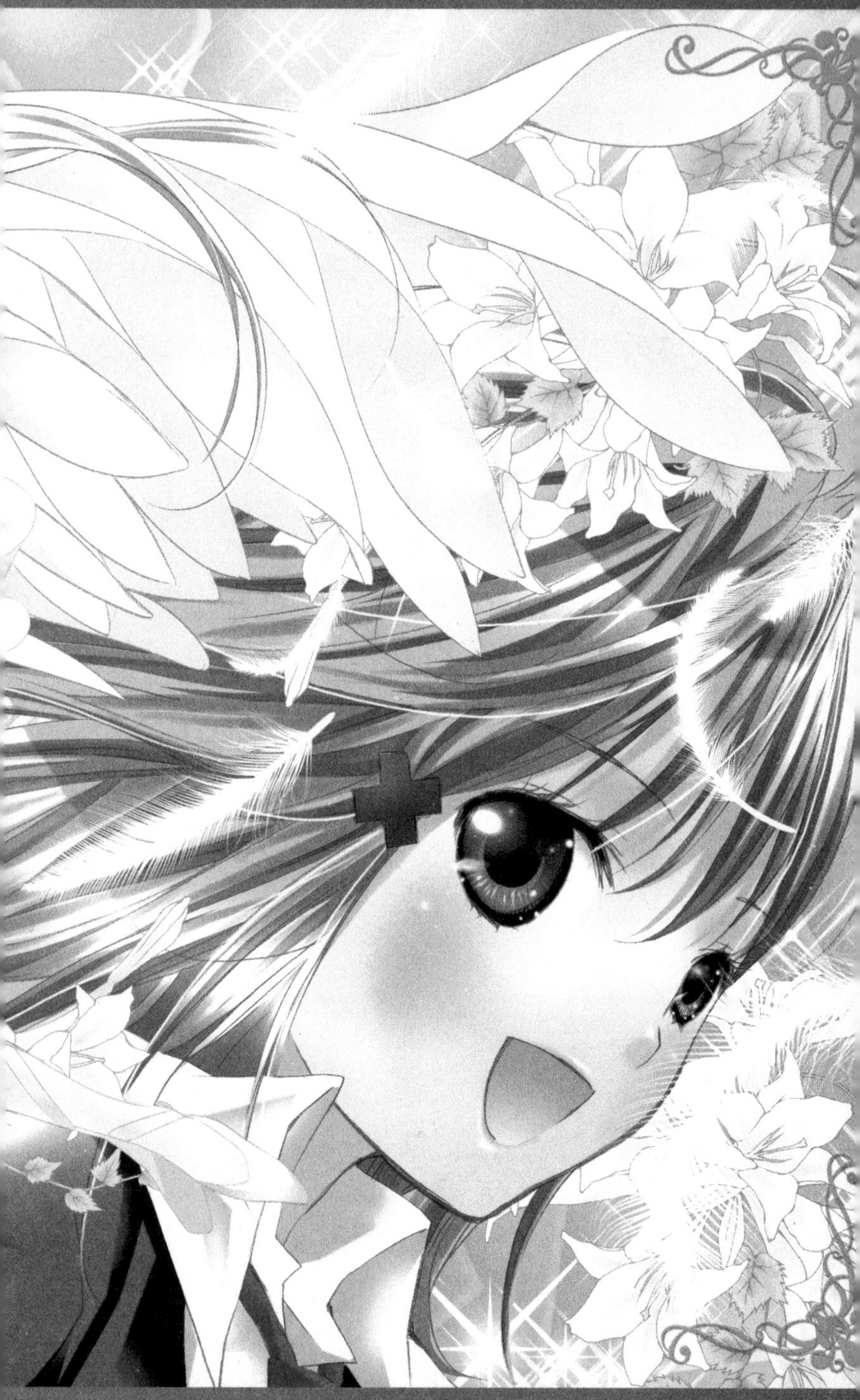

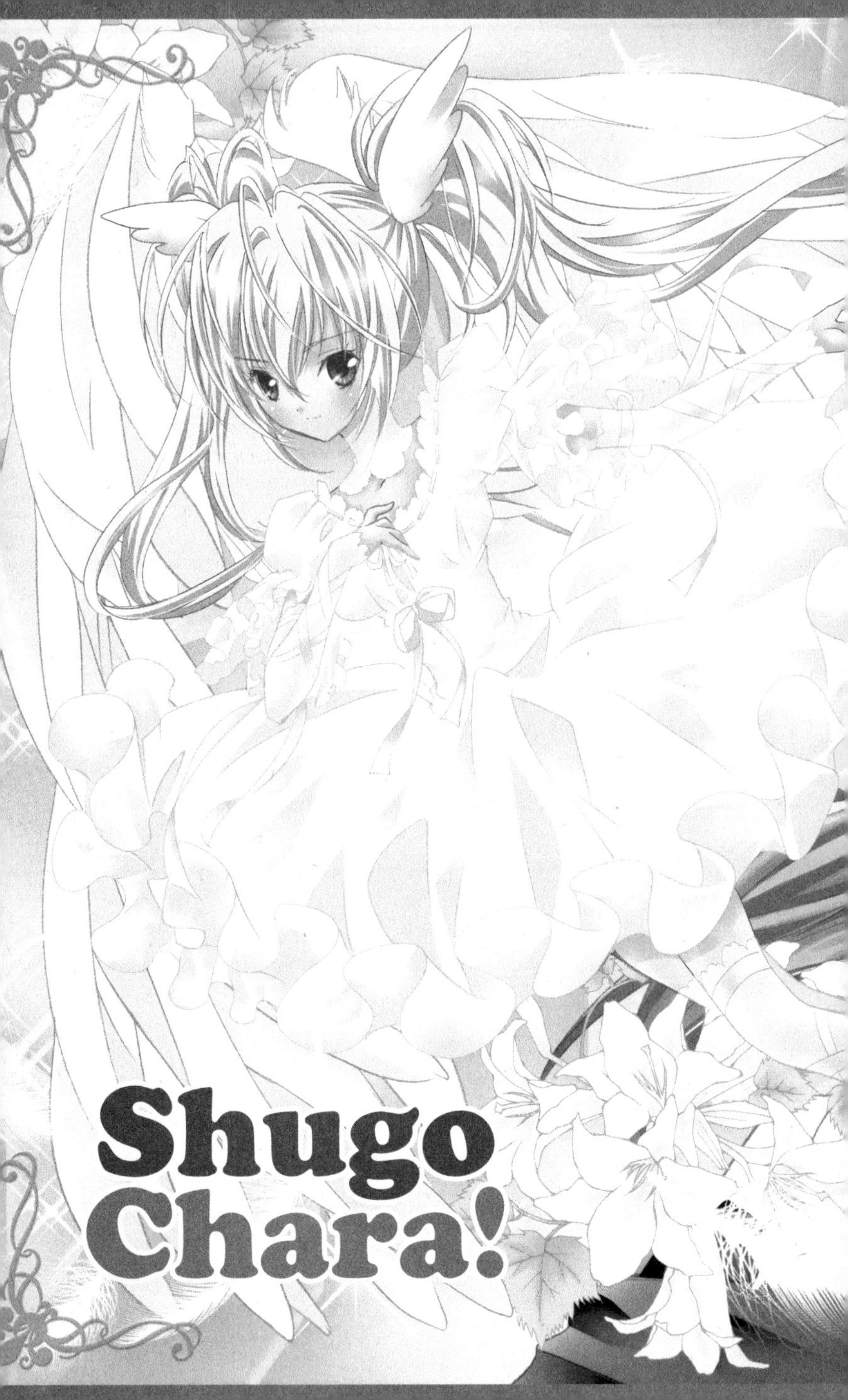
Shugo
Chara!

Shugo
Chara!

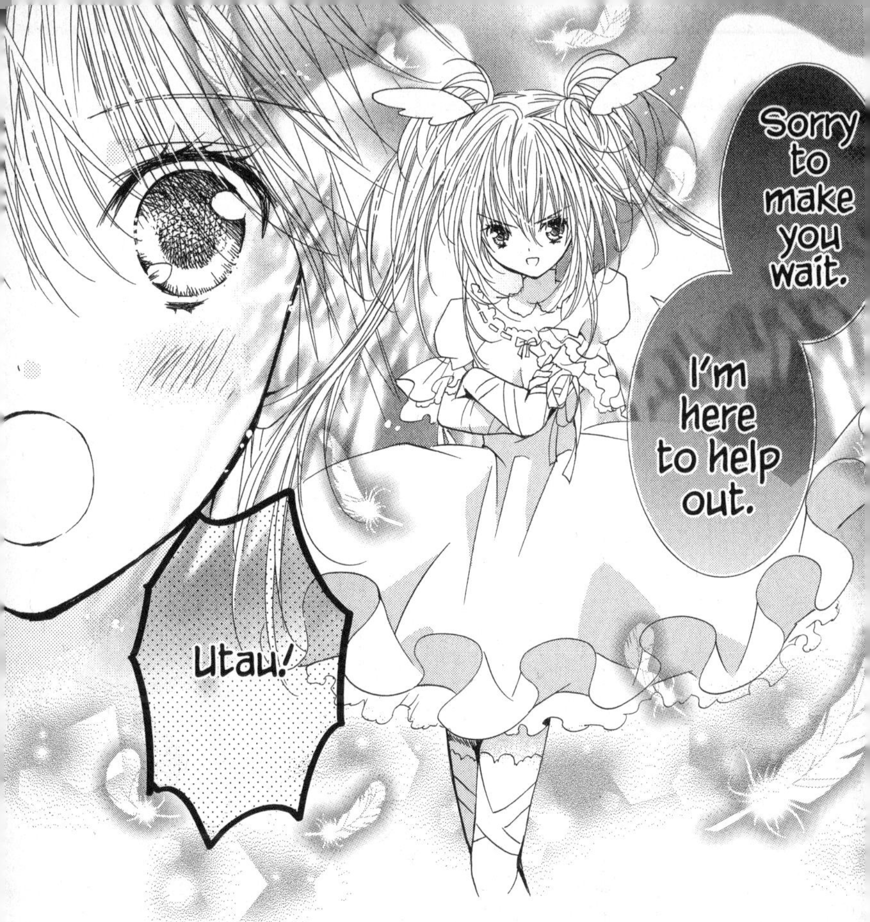
Sorry to make you wait.
I'm here to help out.
Utau!

Hey!

Hello ♥ This is Shibuko Ebara. Wow, wow! It's already Volume 9! So that means next is Volume 10!? That's amazing ♥ Clap, clap! Okay, time for more questions♥

Q1: How do you come up with the names for Character Transformations and moves?

A1: We both throw out some words and we put them together!

Q2: Is it fun to be a manga artist with your friend?

A2: It's very fun!! Lately, in our fan mail, we have had people say, "I am working on becoming a manga artist with my best friend."

To be continued!

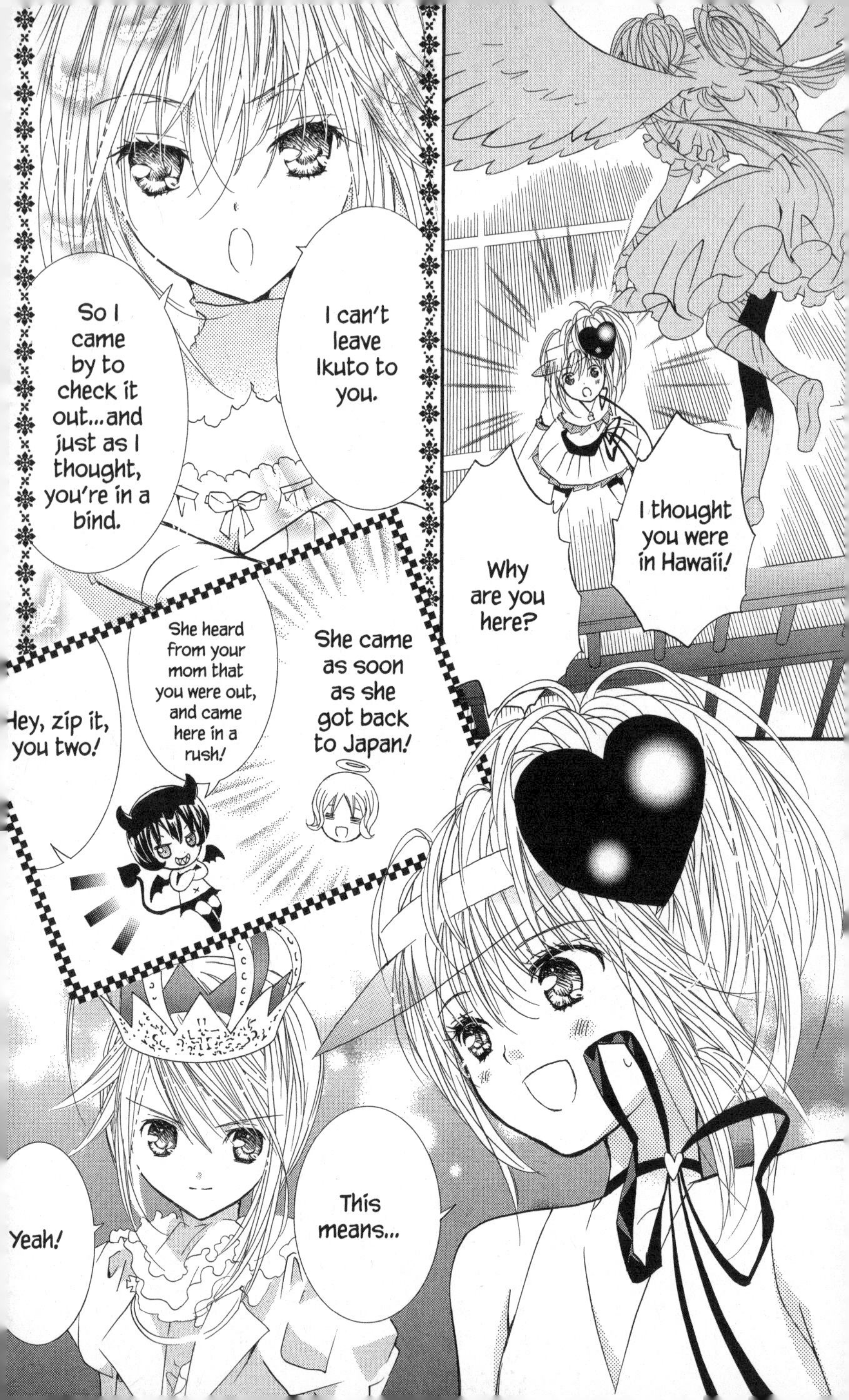
I thought you were in Hawaii!
Why are you here?
I can't leave Ikuto to you.
So I came by to check it out...and just as I thought, you're in a bind.
She came as soon as she got back to Japan!
She heard from your mom that you were out, and came here in a rush!
Hey, zip it, you two!
This means...
Yeah!

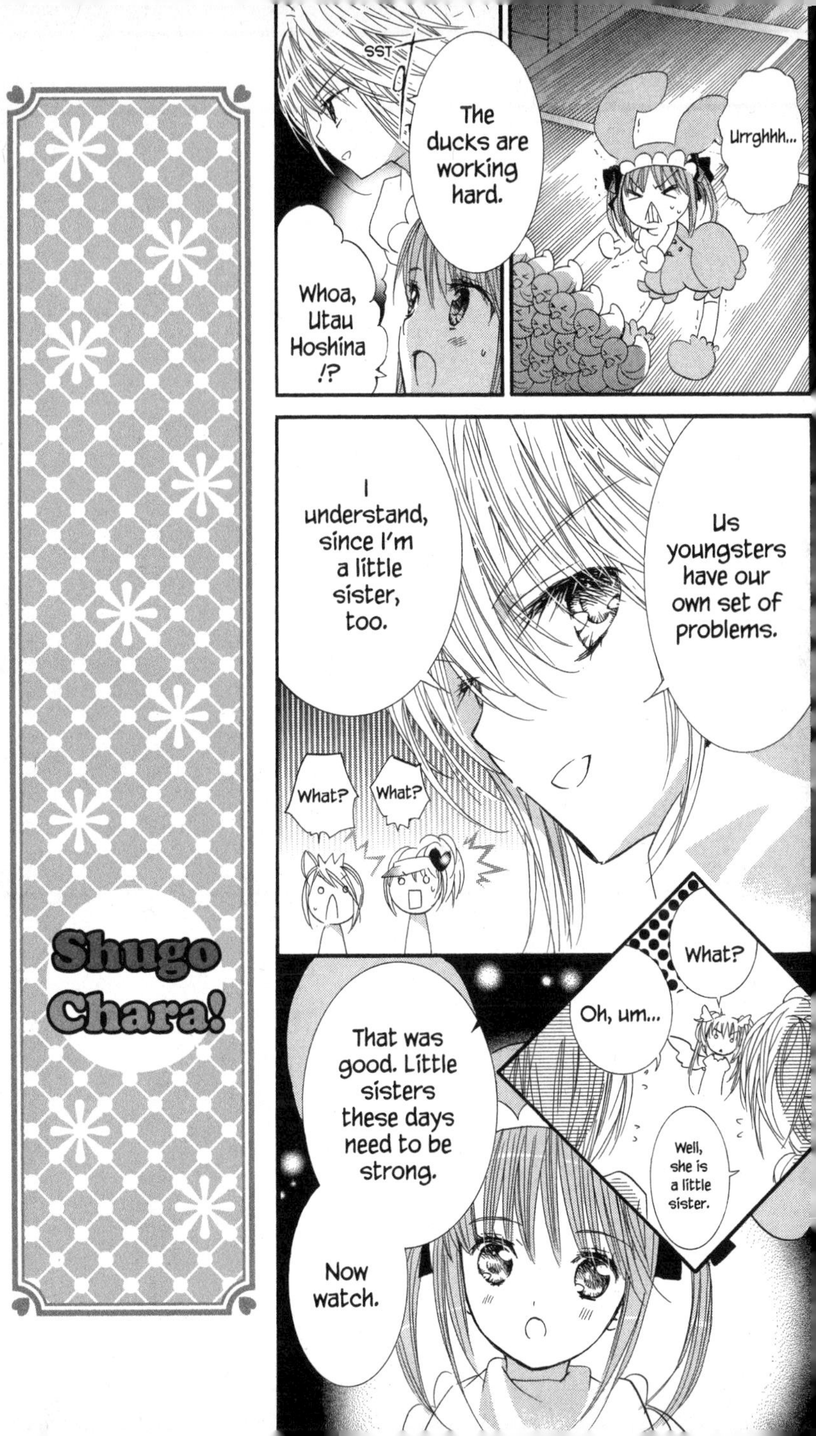
Urrghhh...
SST
The ducks are working hard.
Whoa, Utau Hoshina!?
Us youngsters have our own set of problems.
I understand, since I'm a little sister, too.
What?
What?
What?
Oh, um...
Well, she is a little sister.
That was good. Little sisters these days need to be strong.
Now watch.

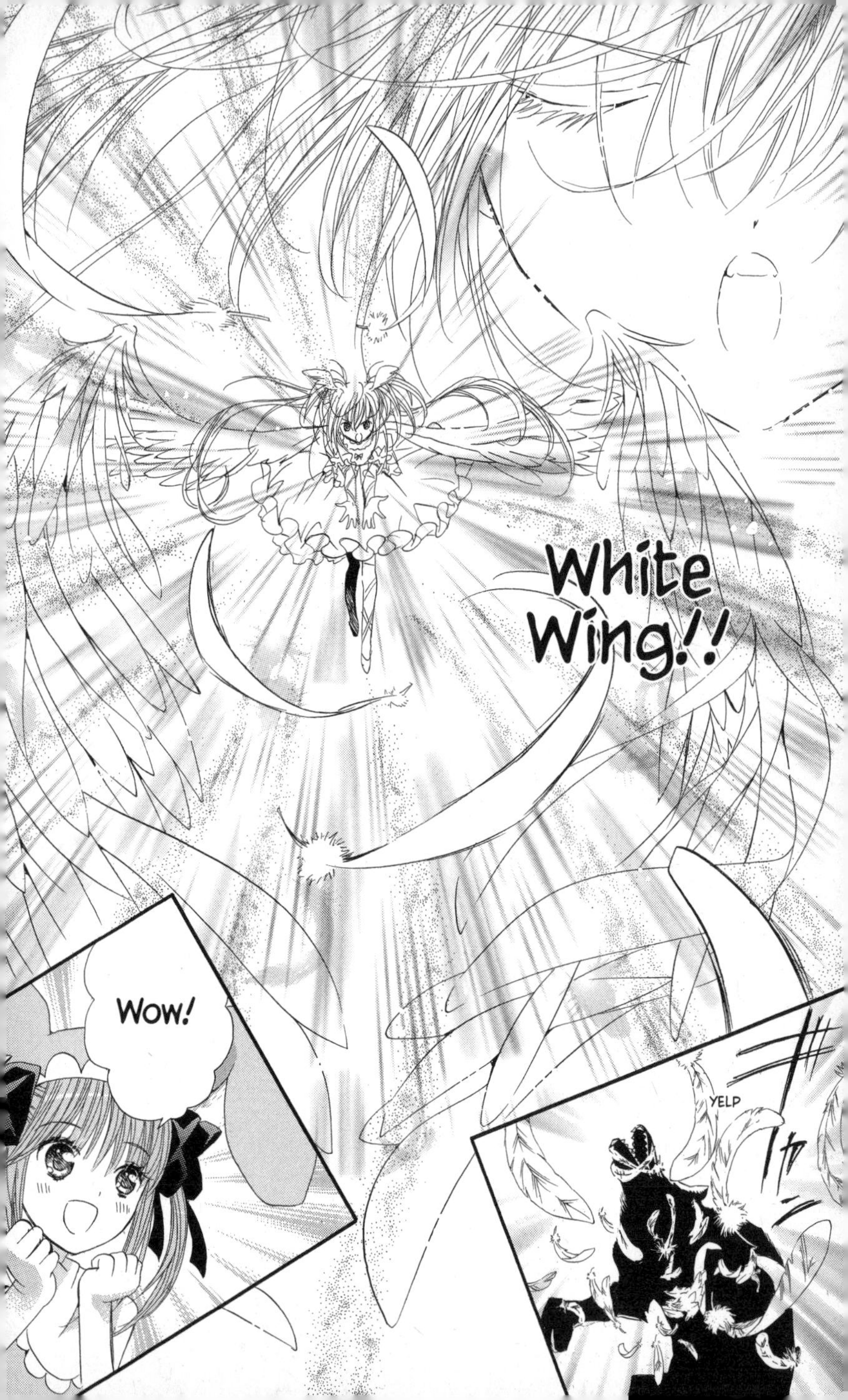
White Wing!!
YELP
Wow!

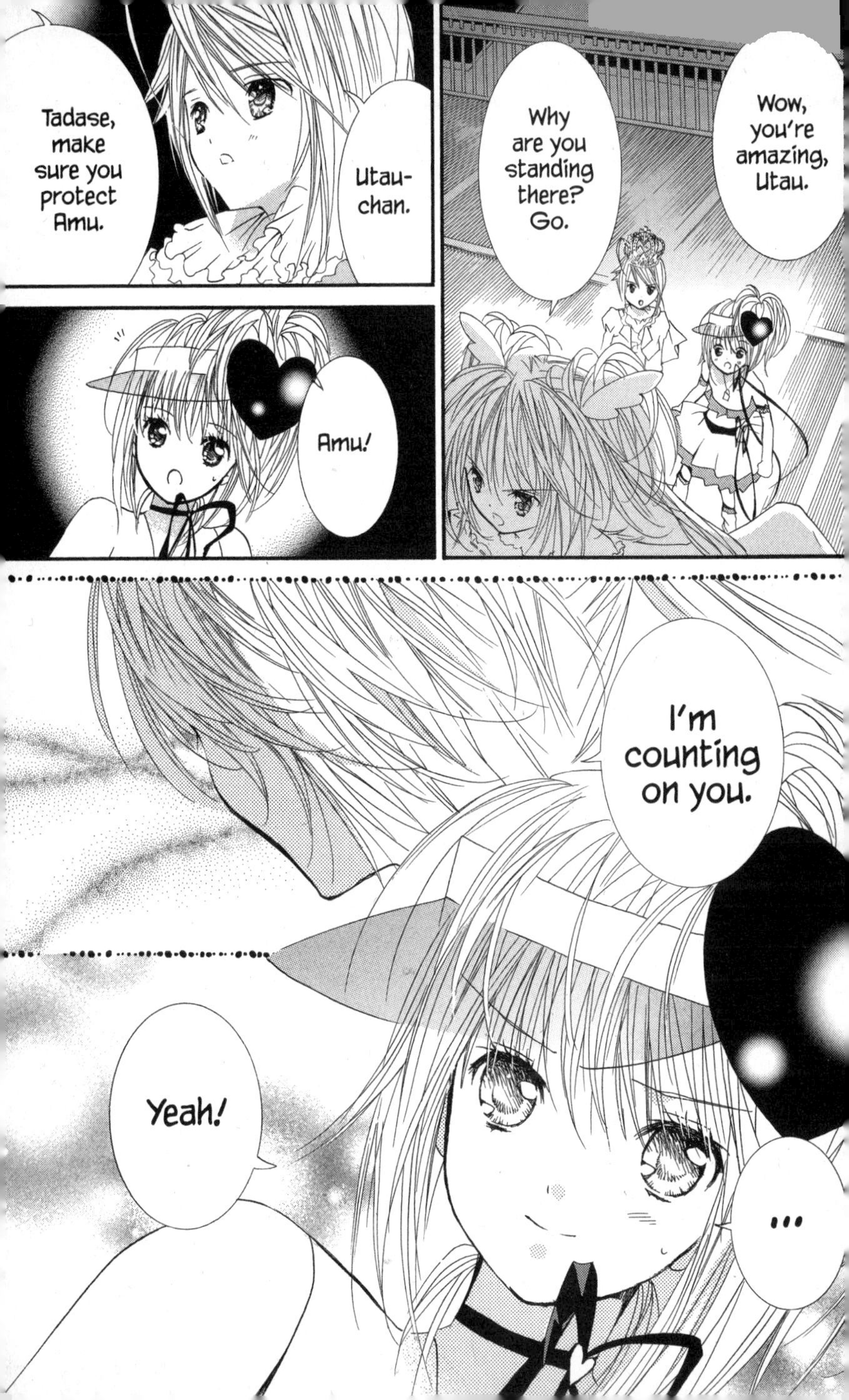
Wow, you're amazing, Utau.
Why are you standing there? Go.
Utau-chan.
Tadase, make sure you protect Amu.
Amu!
I'm counting on you.
...
Yeah!

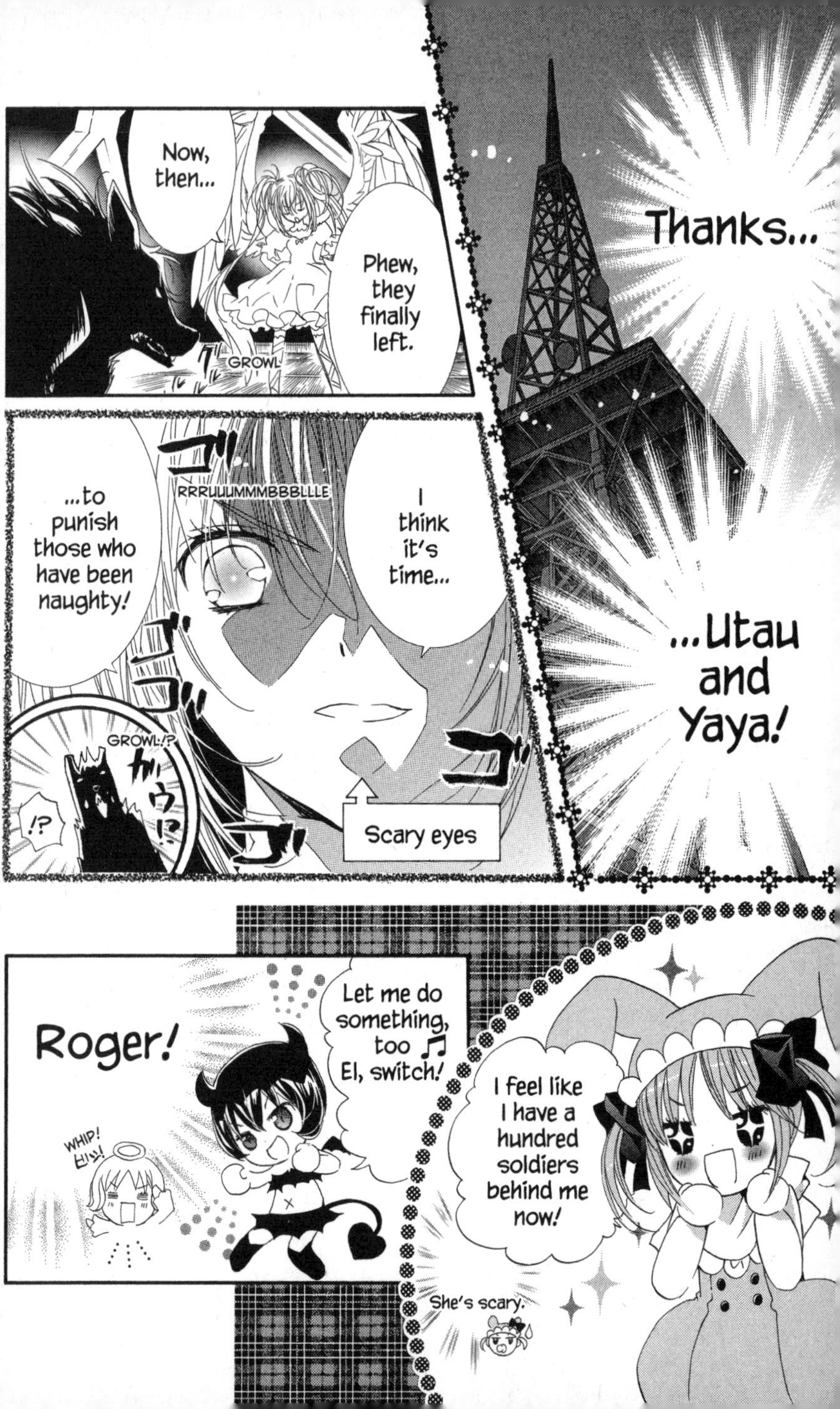
Thanks...
...Utau and Yaya!
Phew, they finally left.
Now, then...
GROWL
I think it's time...
...to punish those who have been naughty!
RRRUUUMMMBBBLLLE
Scary eyes
GROWL!?
!?
I feel like I have a hundred soldiers behind me now!
She's scary.
Let me do something, too ♫ El, switch!
Roger!
WHIP!

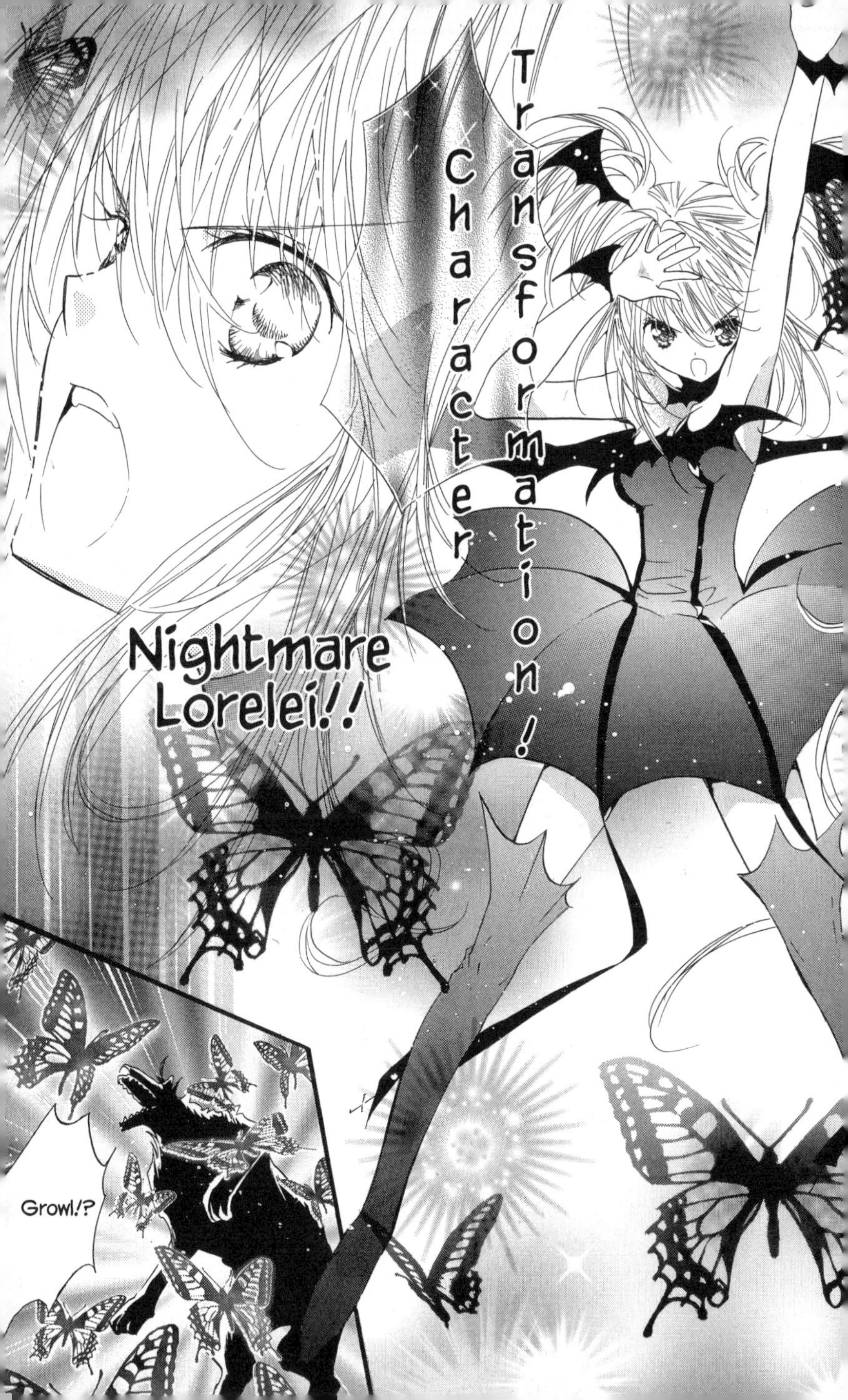
Character Transformation!
Nightmare Lorelei!!
Growl!?

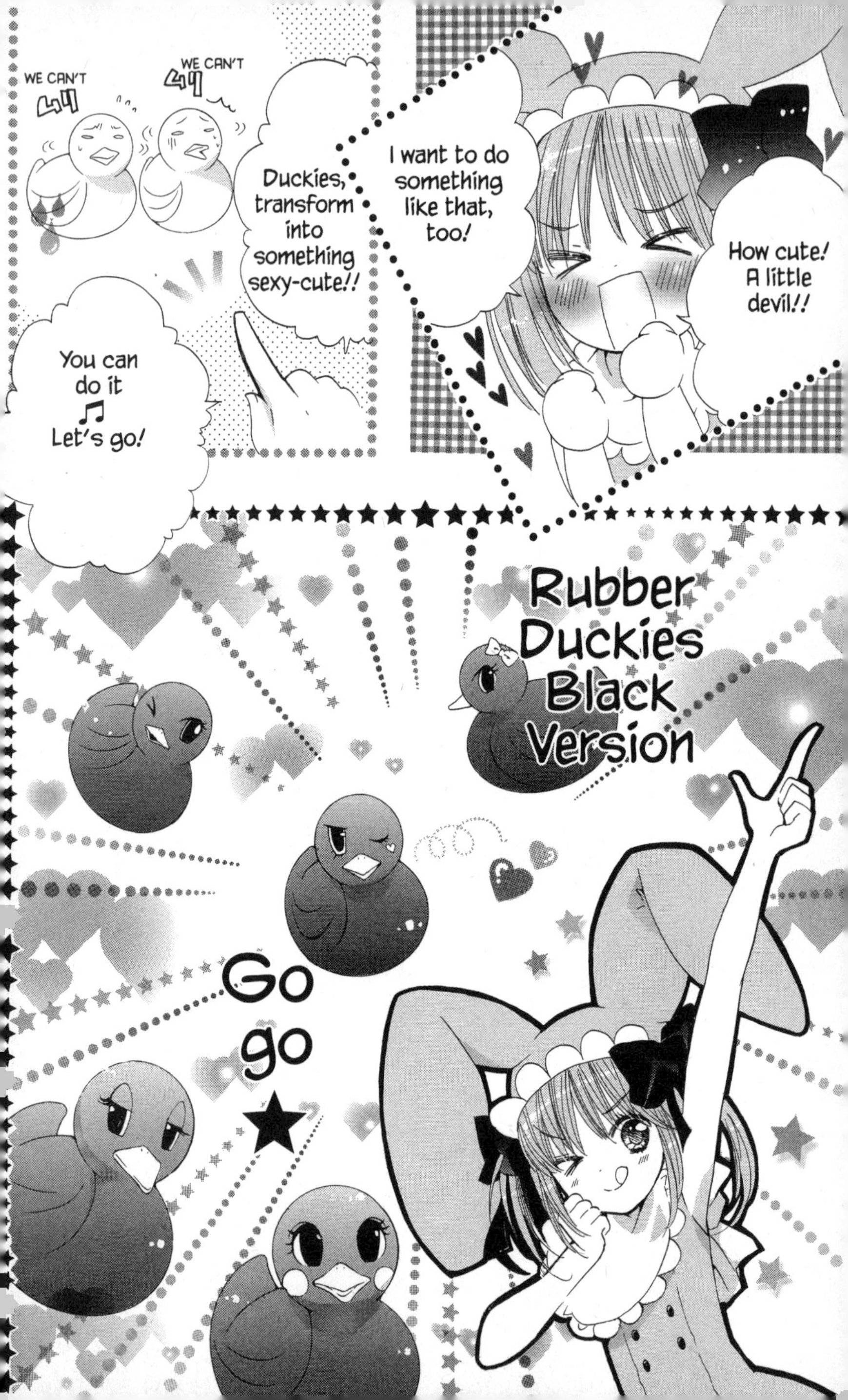
How cute! A little devil!!
I want to do something like that, too!
Duckies, transform into something sexy-cute!!
WE CAN'T
WE CAN'T
You can do it ♫ Let's go!
Rubber Duckies Black Version
Go go ★

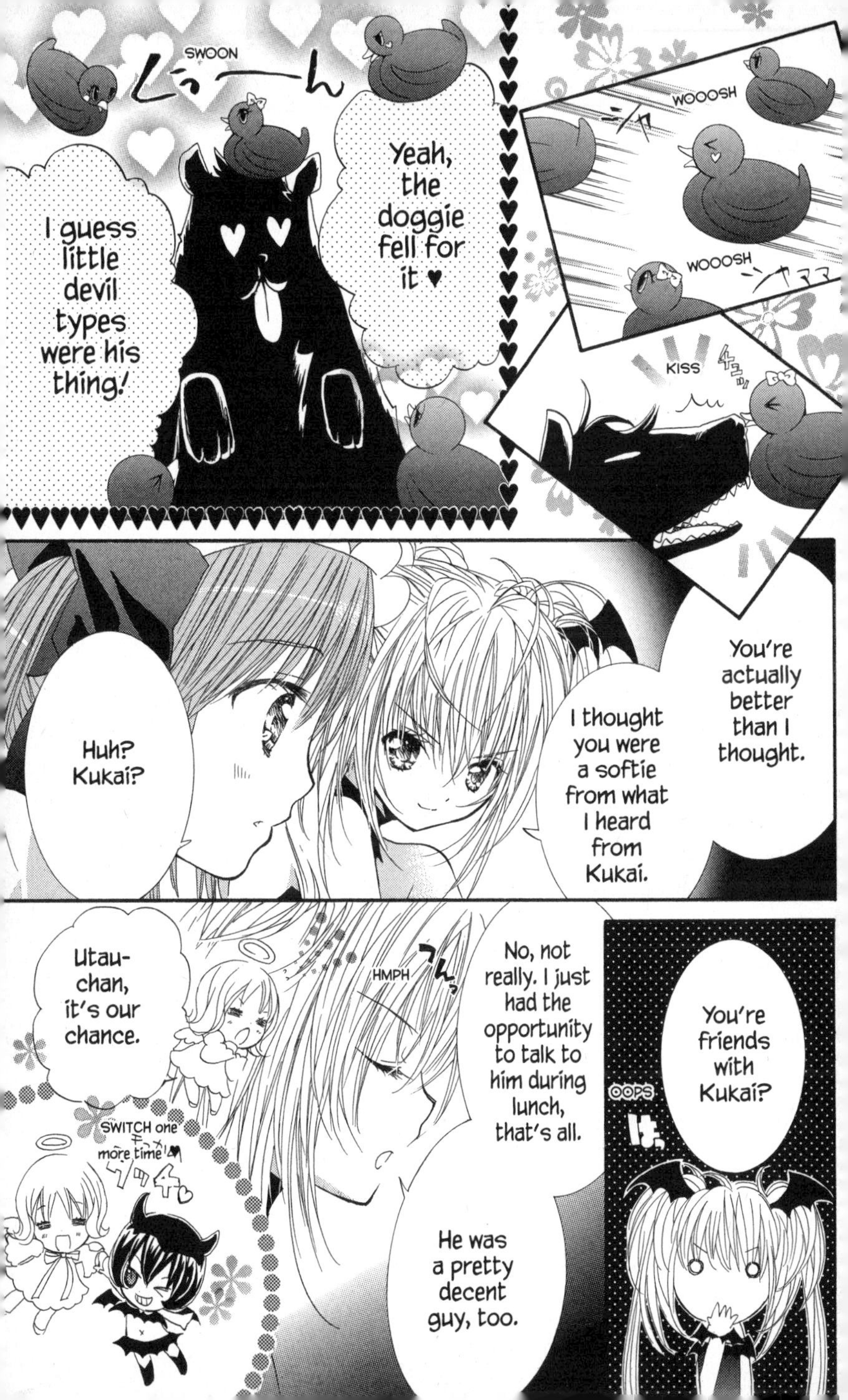
WOOOSH
WOOOSH
KISS
SWOON
Yeah, the doggie fell for it ♥
I guess little devil types were his thing!
You're actually better than I thought.
I thought you were a softie from what I heard from Kukai.
Huh? Kukai?
You're friends with Kukai?
OOPS
No, not really. I just had the opportunity to talk to him during lunch, that's all.
HMPH
He was a pretty decent guy, too.
Utau-chan, it's our chance.
SWITCH one more time!

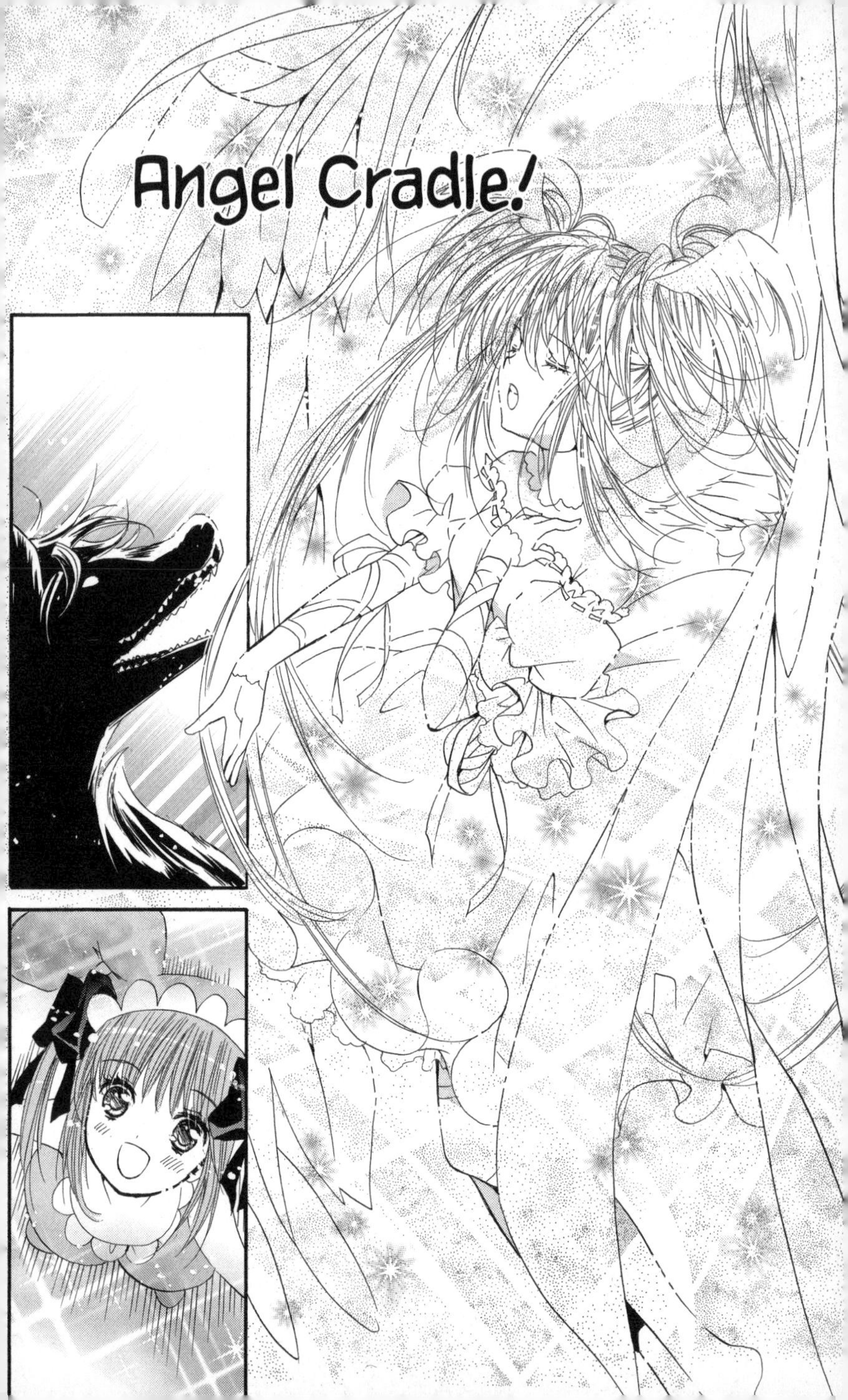
Angel Cradle!

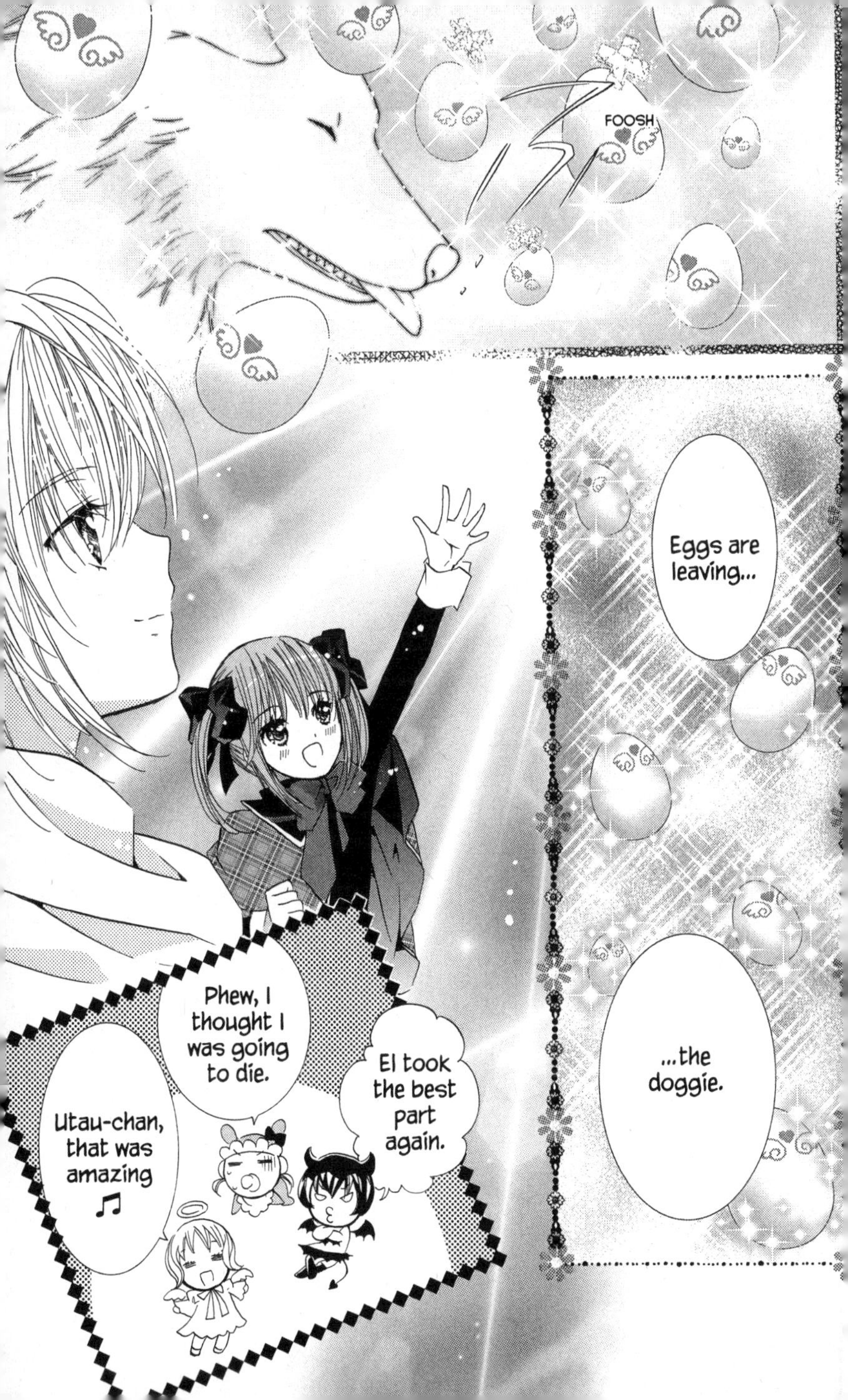
FOOSH
Eggs are leaving...
...the doggie.
Phew, I thought I was going to die.
El took the best part again.
Utau-chan, that was amazing ♫

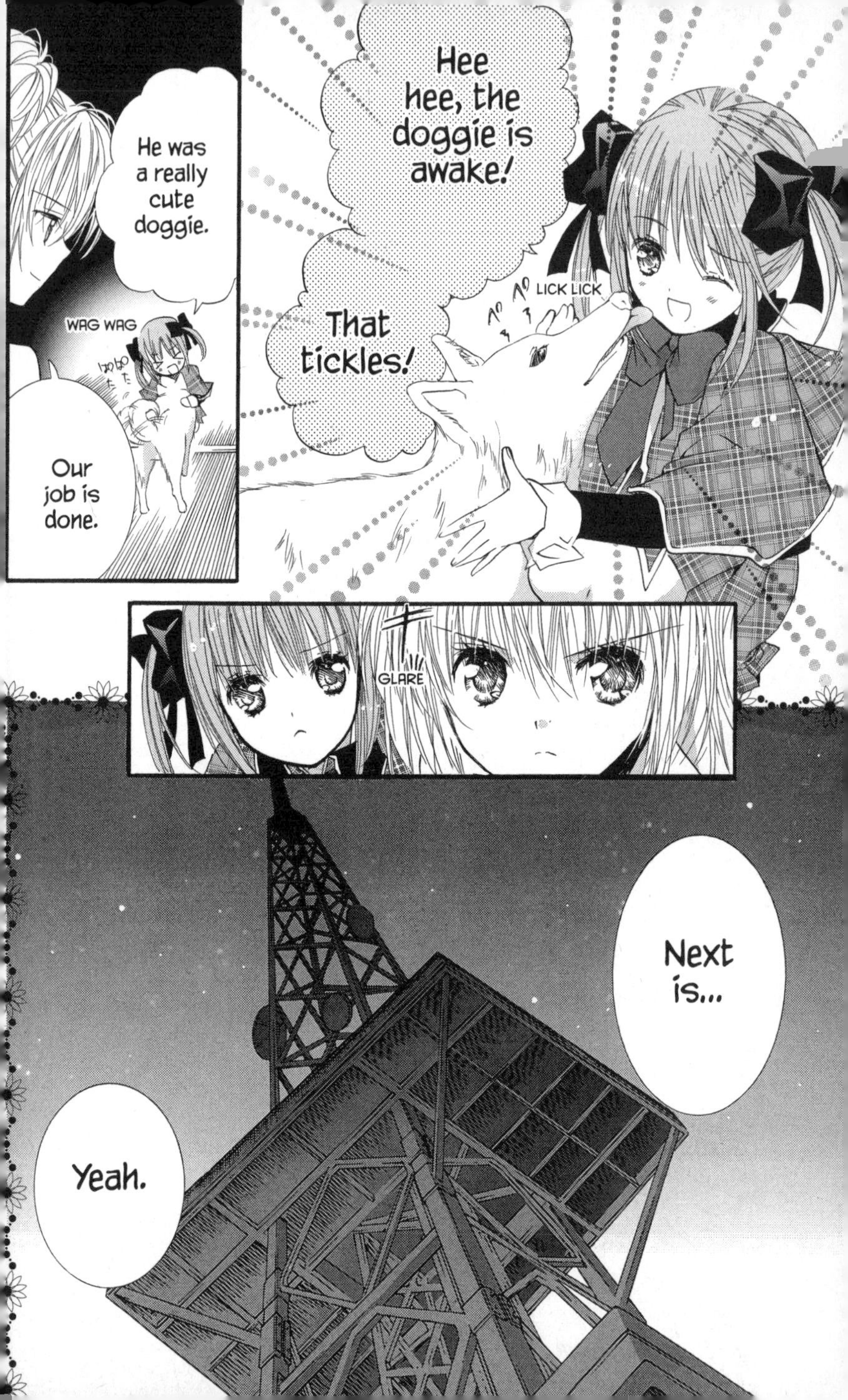
Hee hee, the doggie is awake!
LICK LICK
That tickles!
He was a really cute doggie.
WAG WAG
Our job is done.
GLARE
Next is...
Yeah.

Amu-chi!
Tadase!

Ikuto!

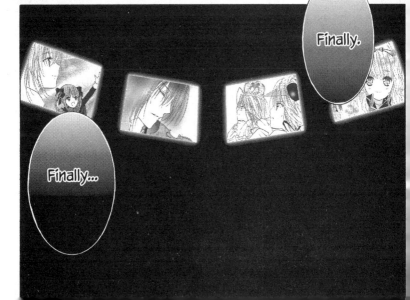

Finally.

Finally...

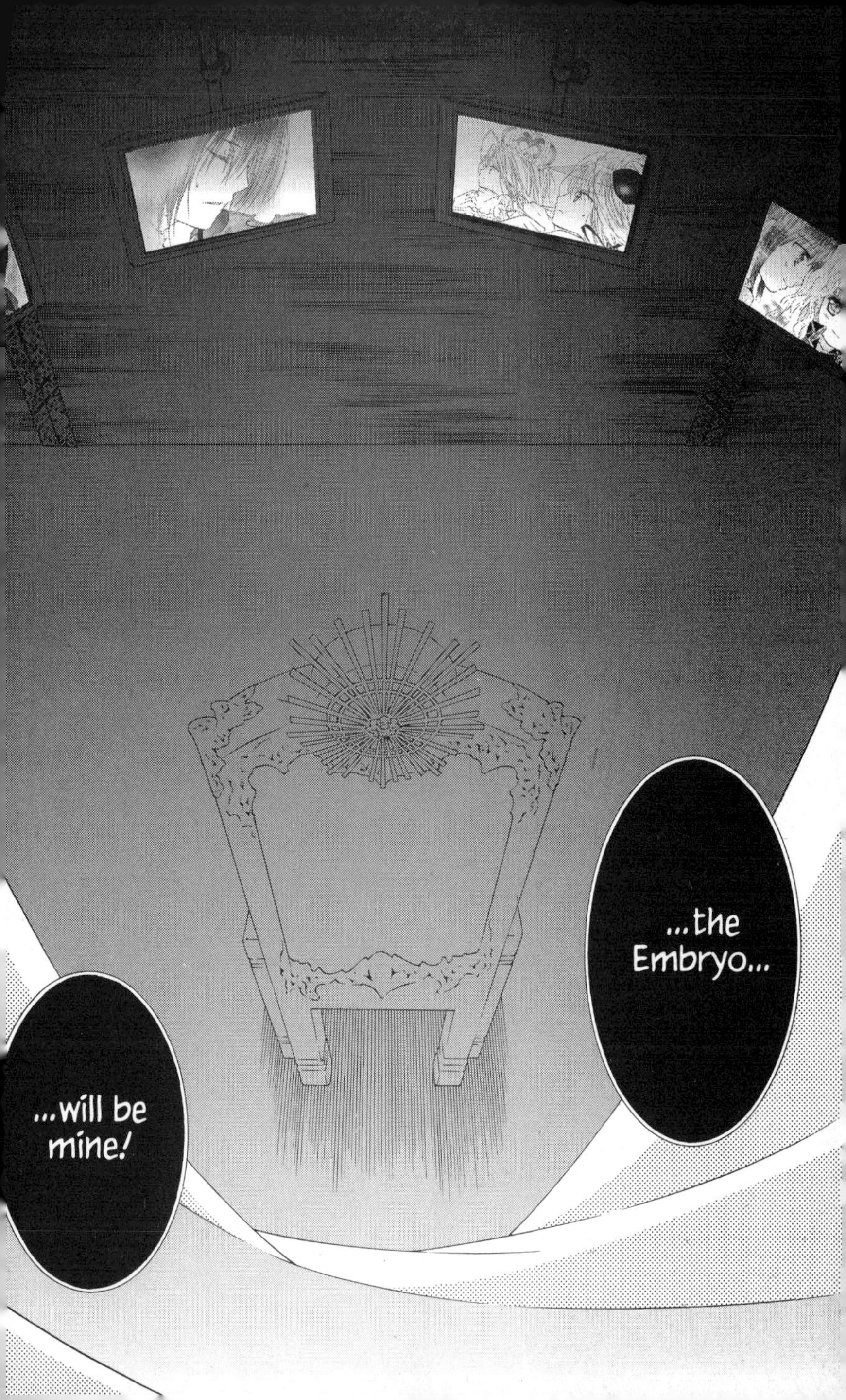
...the Embryo...
...will be mine!

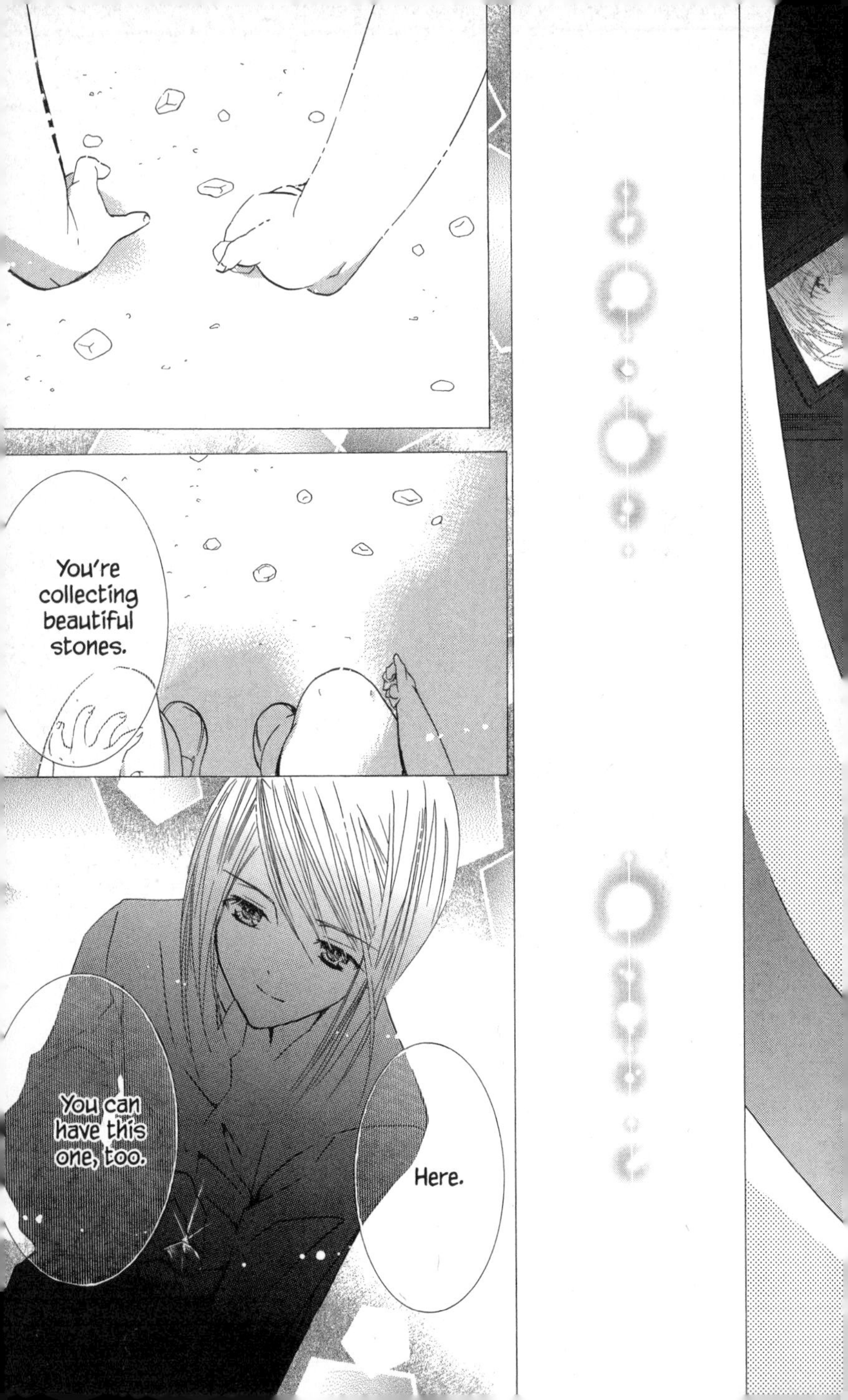
You're collecting beautiful stones.
Here.
You can have this one, too.

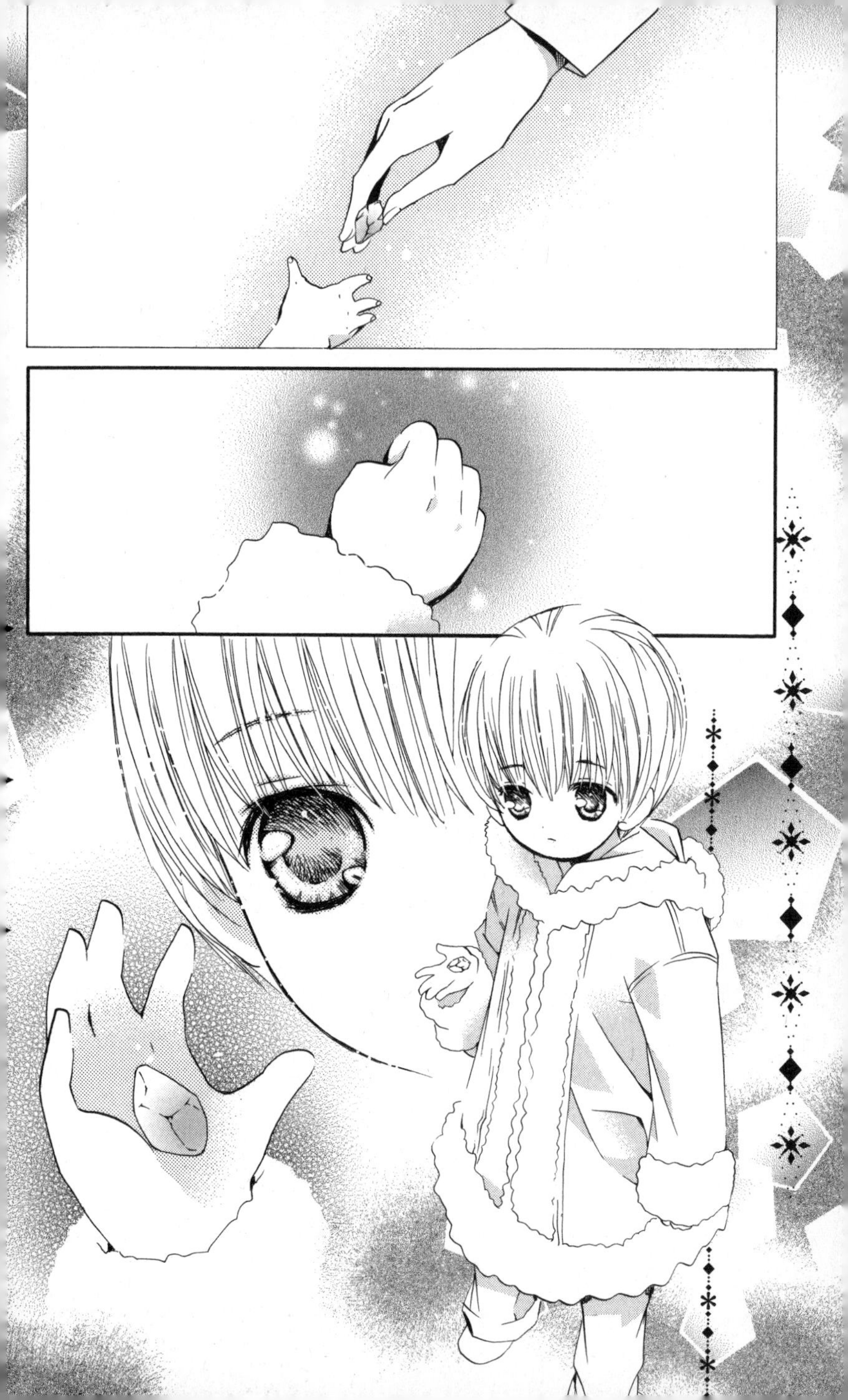

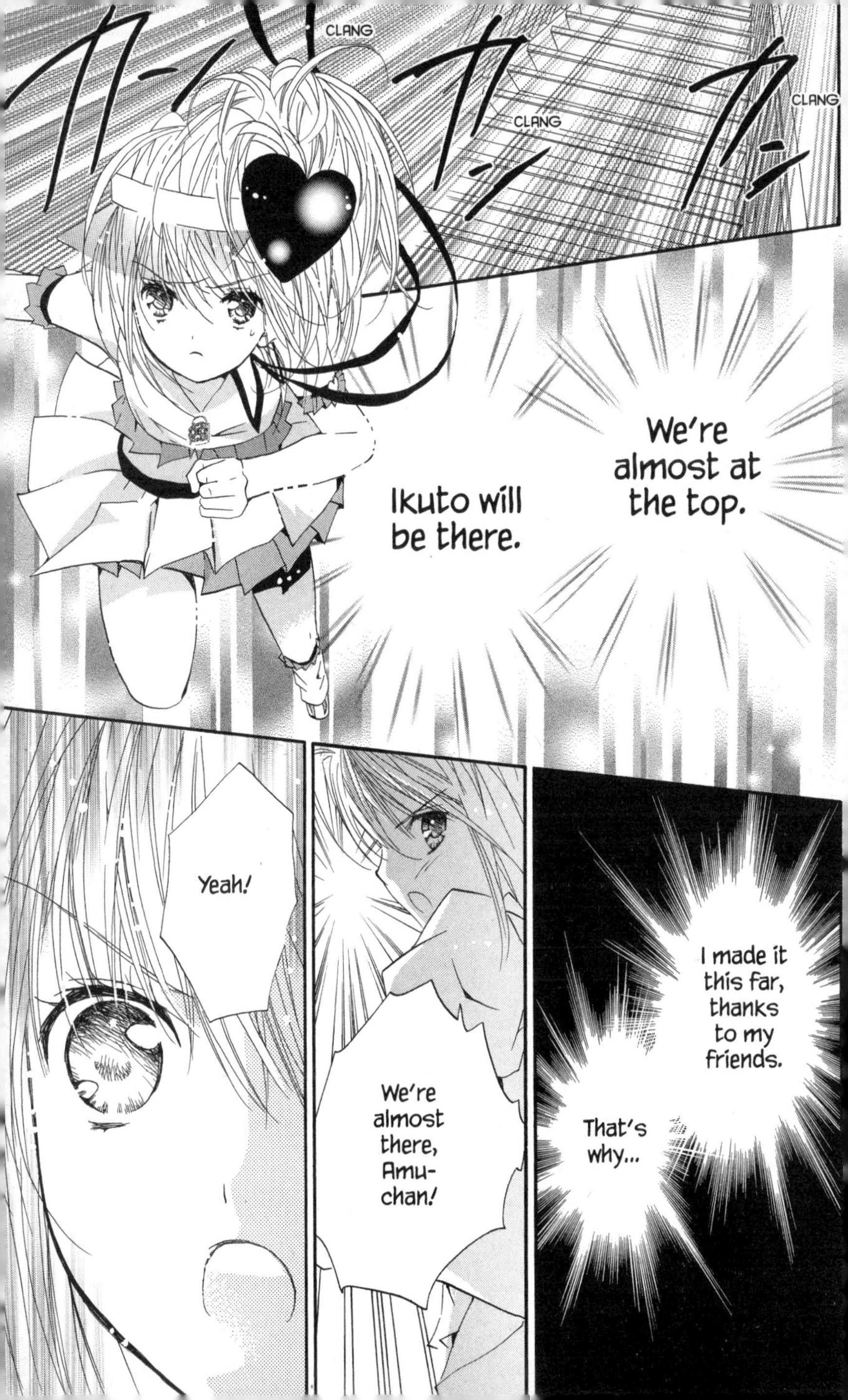
CLANG
CLANG
CLANG
We're almost at the top.
Ikuto will be there.
I made it this far, thanks to my friends.
That's why...
We're almost there, Amu-chan!
Yeah!

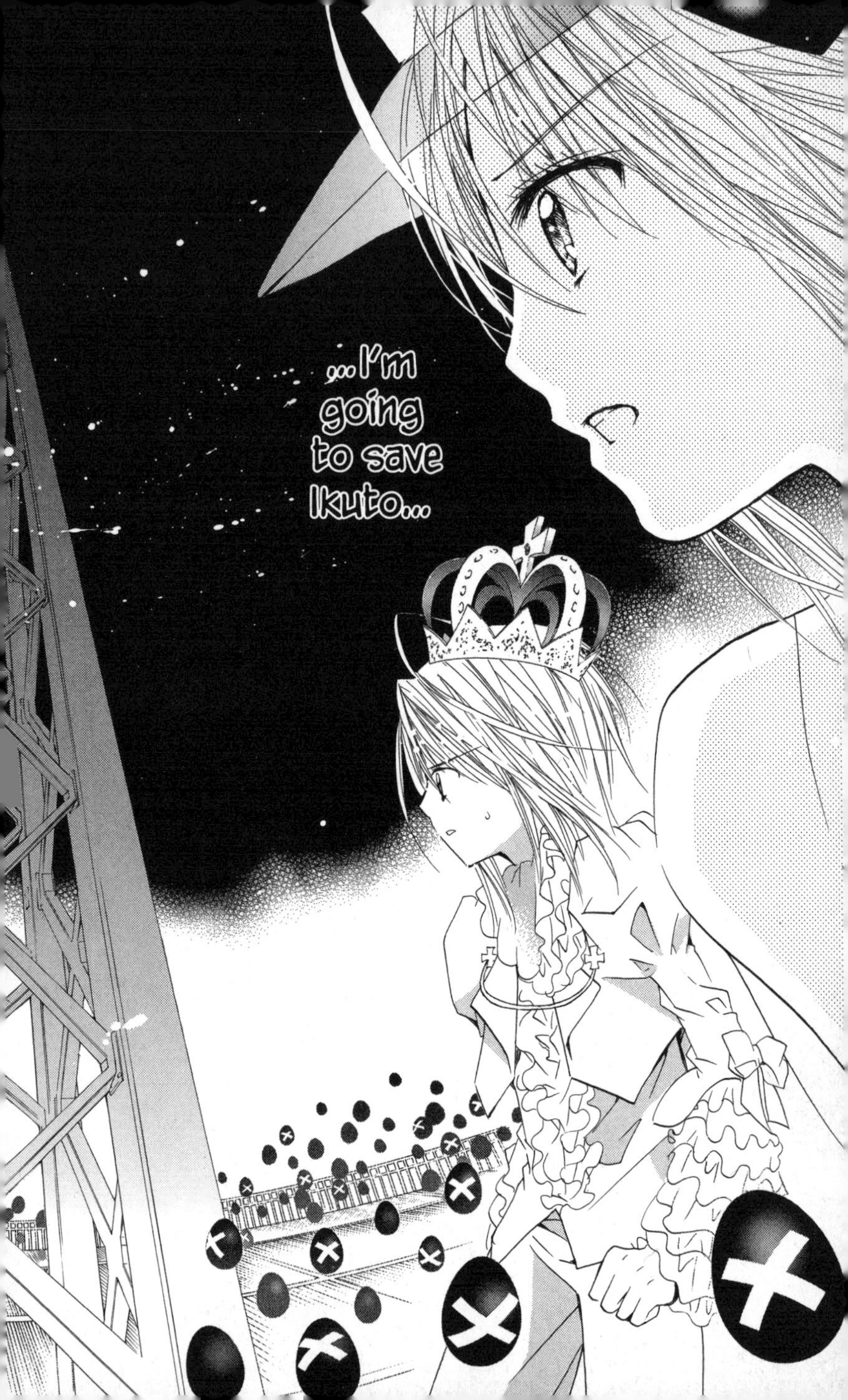
...I'm going to save Ikuto...

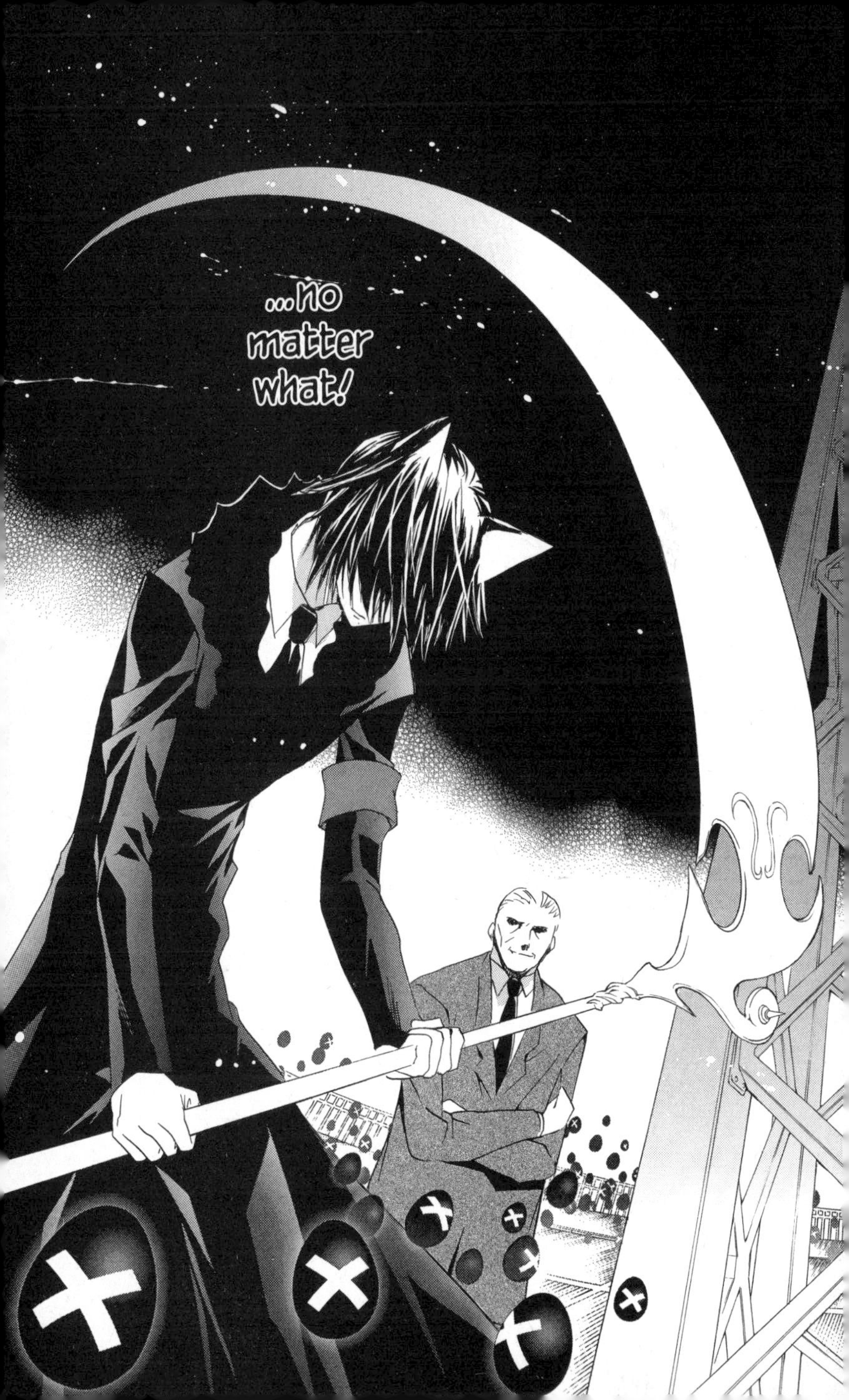
...no matter what!

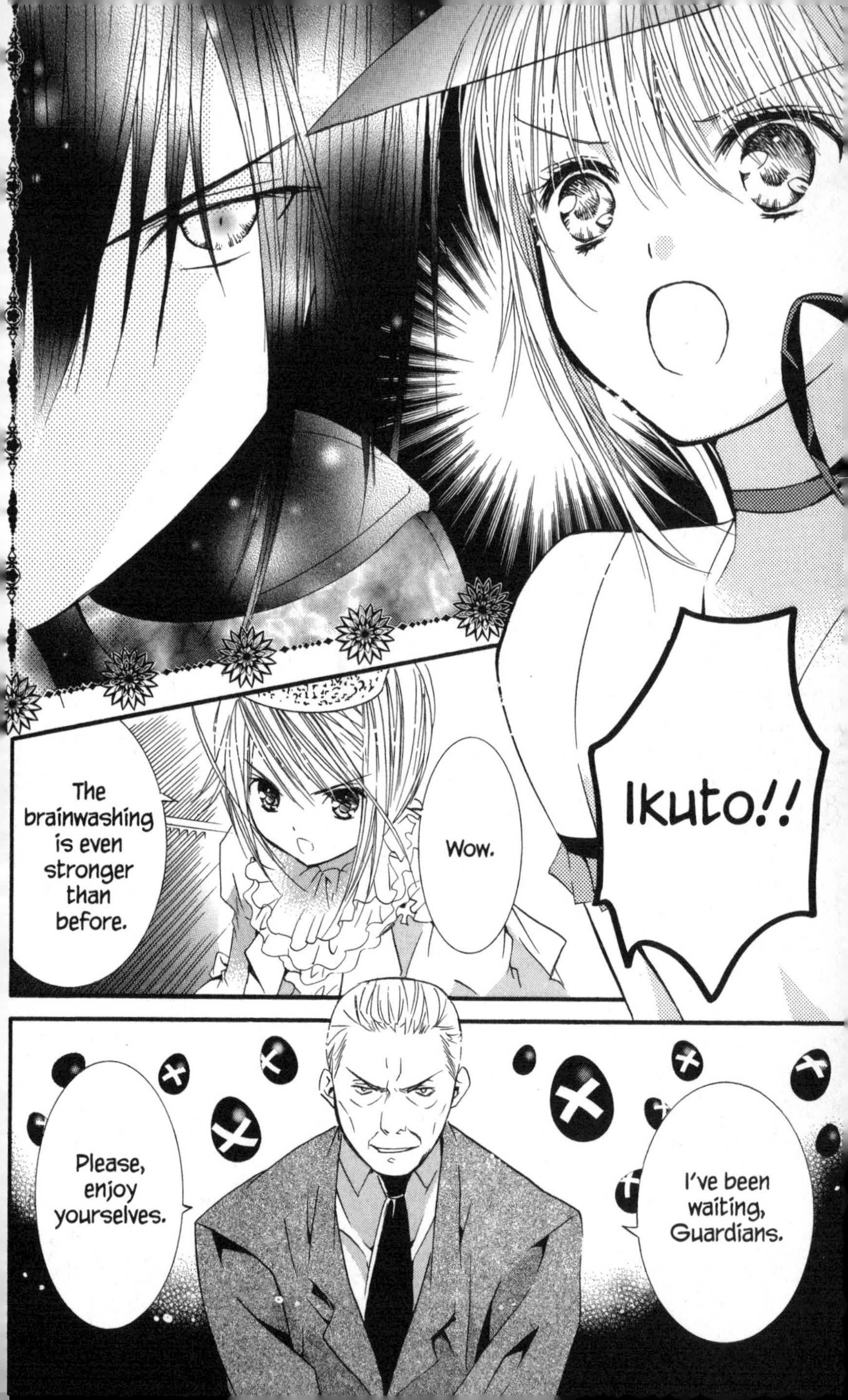
Ikuto!!
Wow.
The brainwashing is even stronger than before.
I've been waiting, Guardians.
Please, enjoy yourselves.

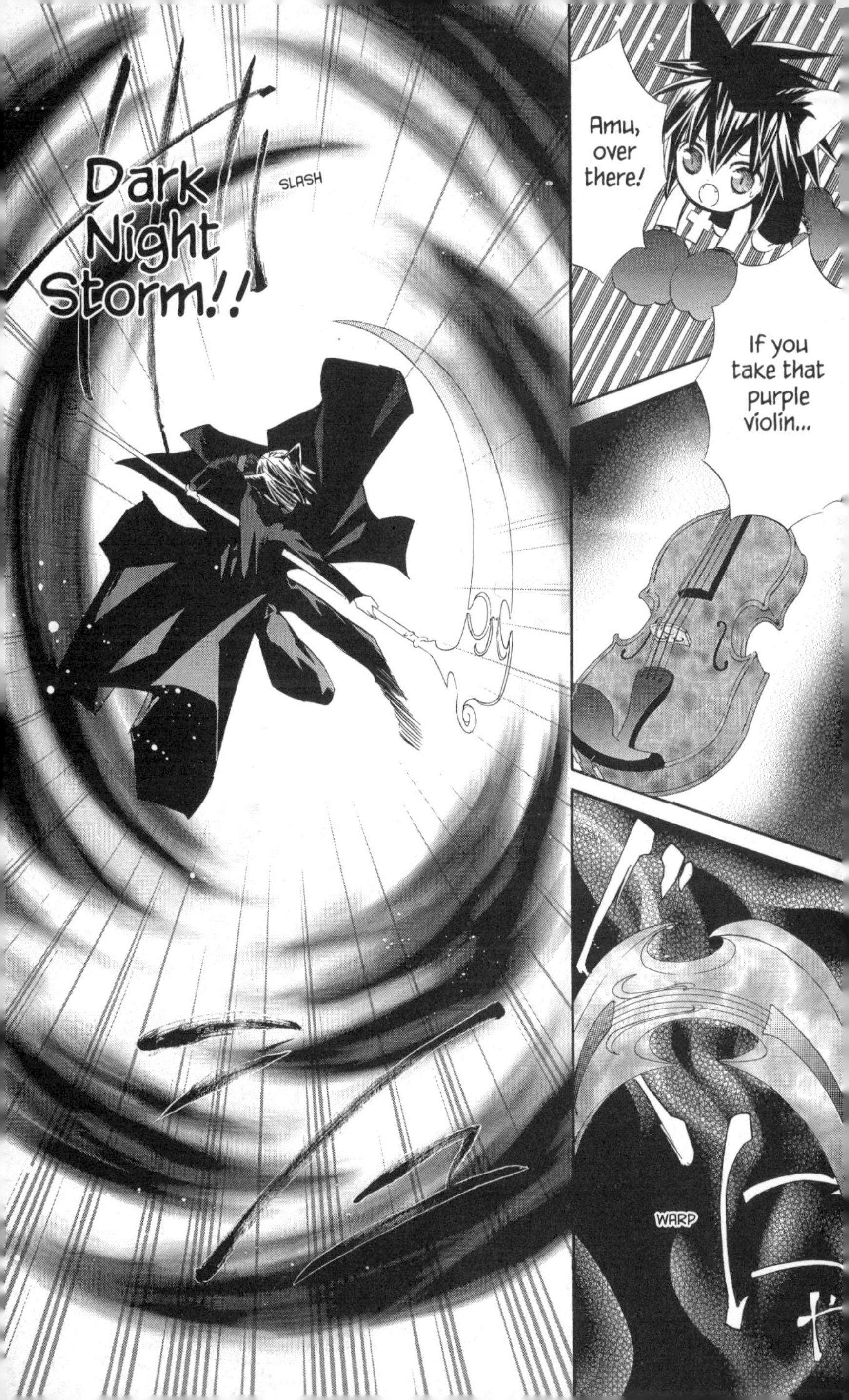
Amu, over there!
If you take that purple violin...
WARP
Dark Night Storm!!
SLASH

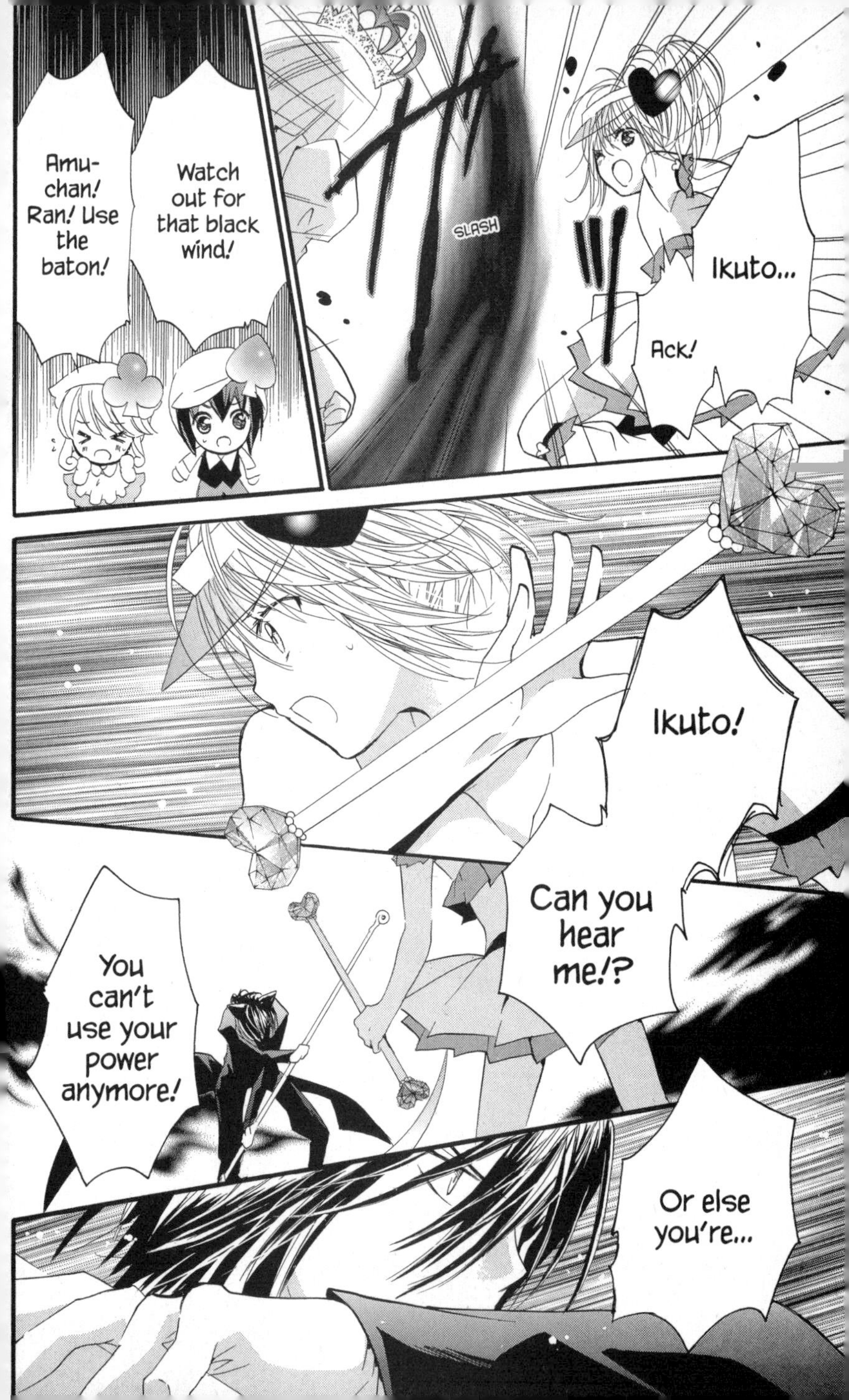
Ikuto...
Ack!
SLASH
Watch out for that black wind!
Amu-chan! Ran! Use the baton!
Ikuto!
Can you hear me!?
You can't use your power anymore!
Or else you're...

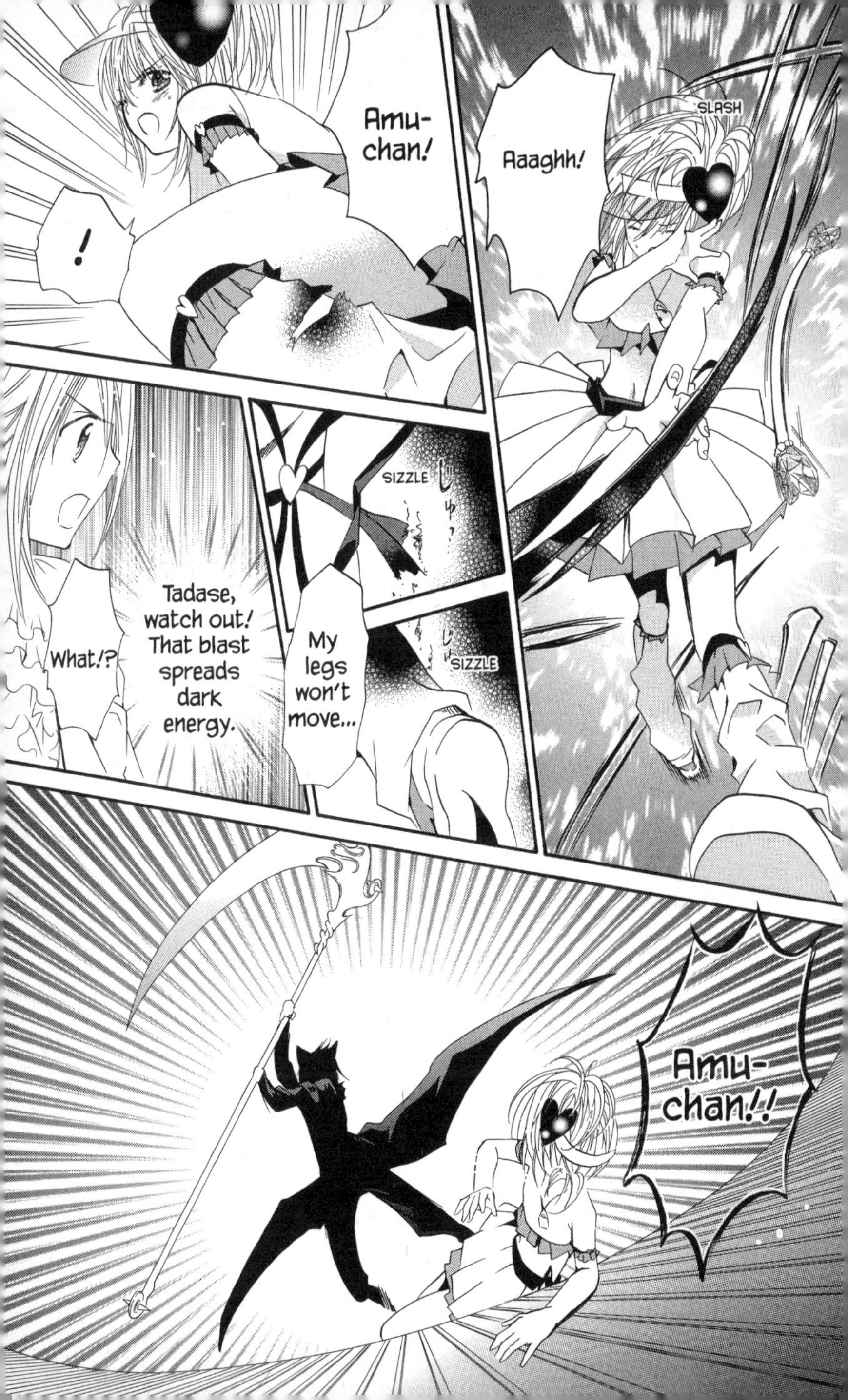
SLASH
Aaaghh!
Amu-chan!
!
SIZZLE
SIZZLE
My legs won't move...
Tadase, watch out! That blast spreads dark energy.
What!?
Amu-chan!!

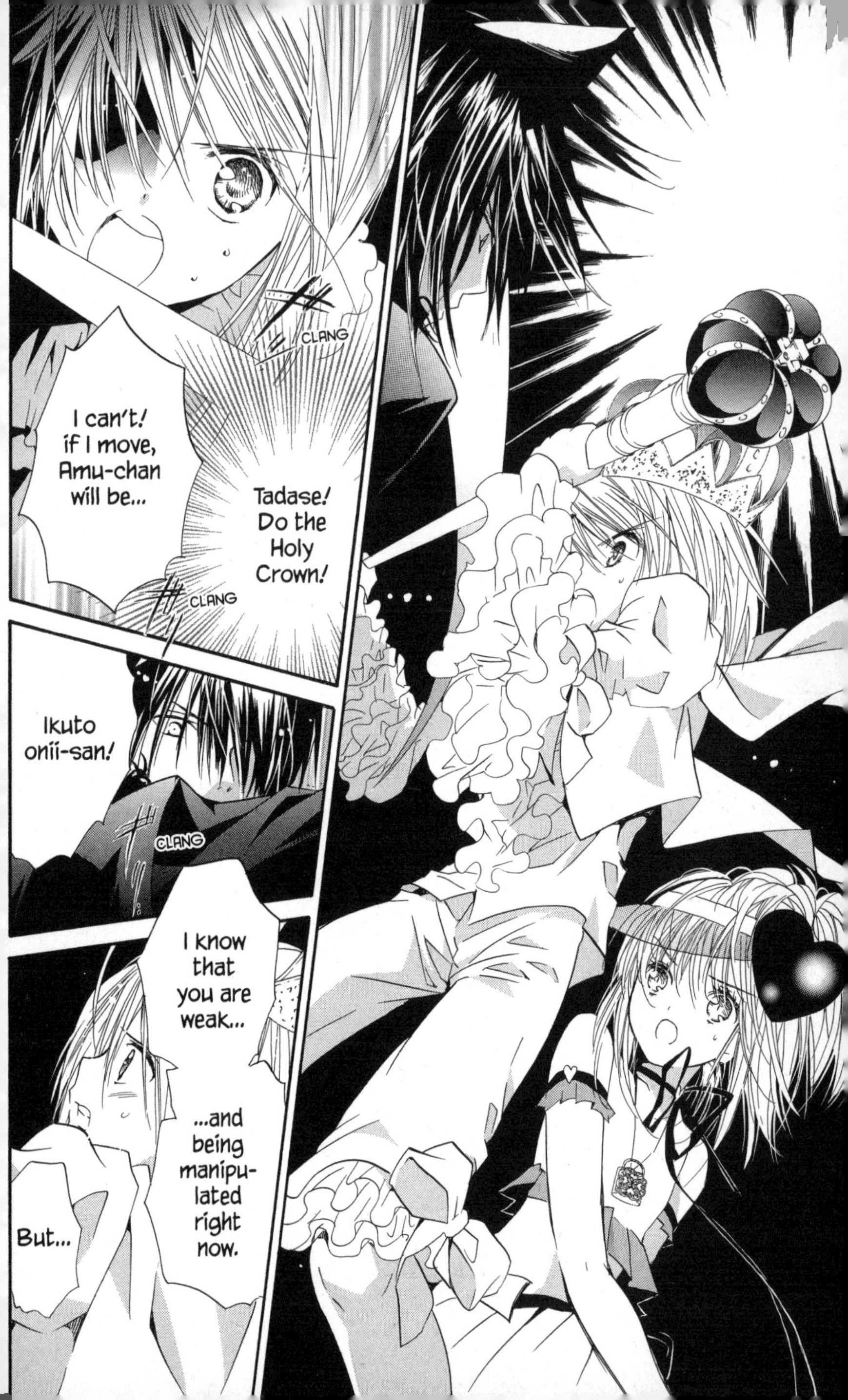
CLANG
Tadase! Do the Holy Crown!
I can't! if I move, Amu-chan will be...
CLANG
Ikuto onii-san!
CLANG
I know that you are weak...
...and being manipulated right now.
But...

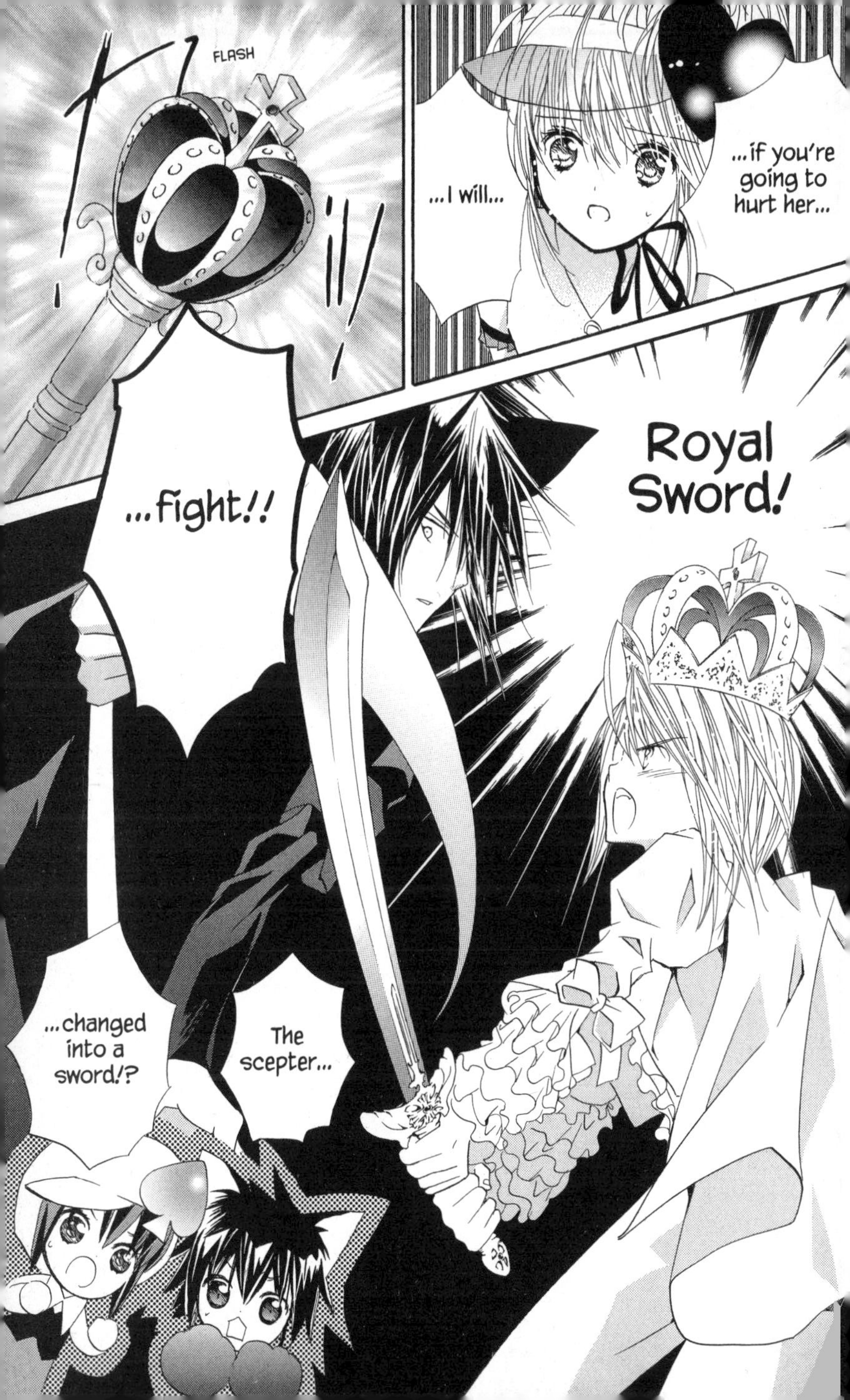
...if you're going to hurt her...
...I will...
FLASH
...fight!!
Royal Sword!
The scepter...
...changed into a sword!?

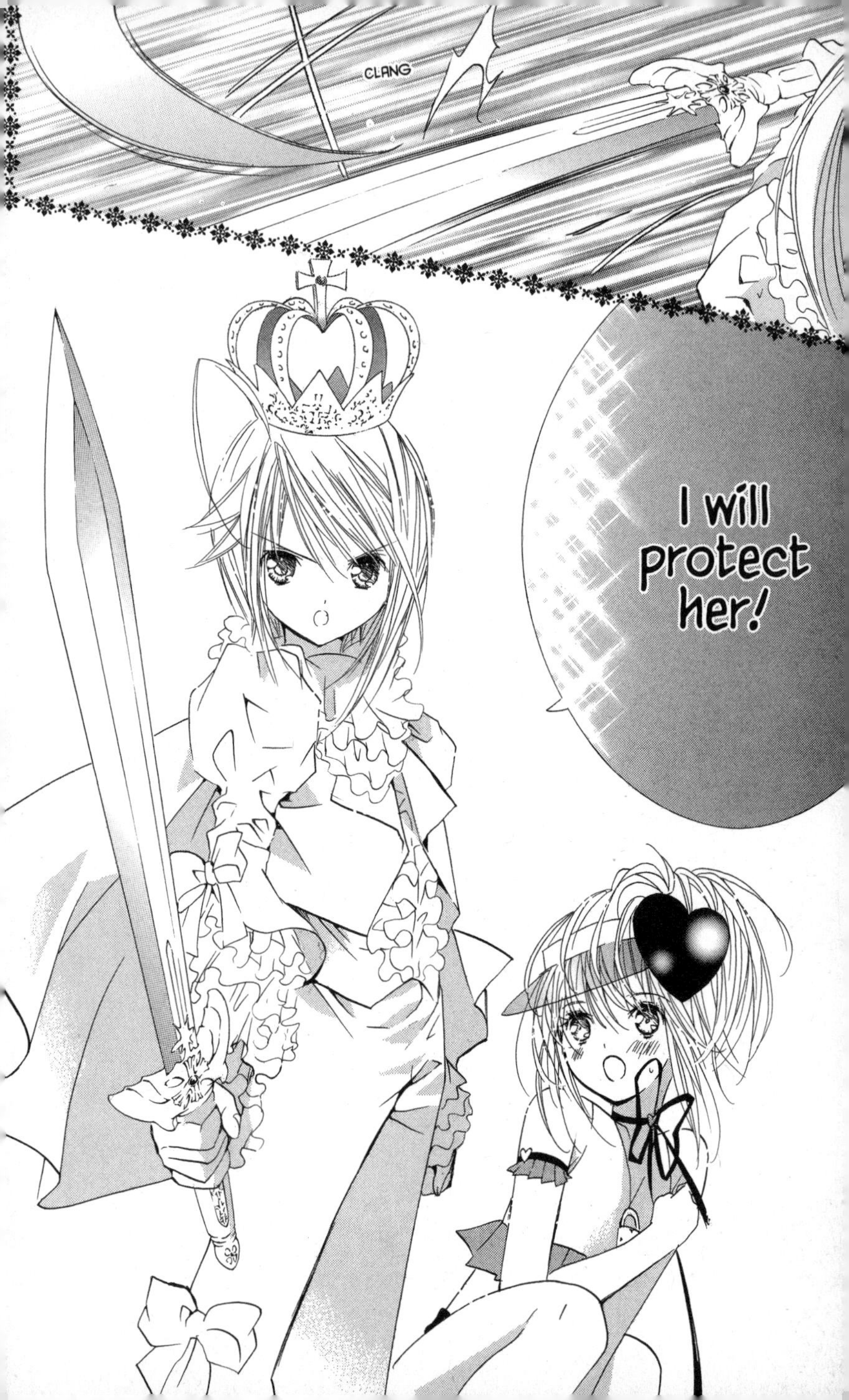
CLANG
I will protect her!

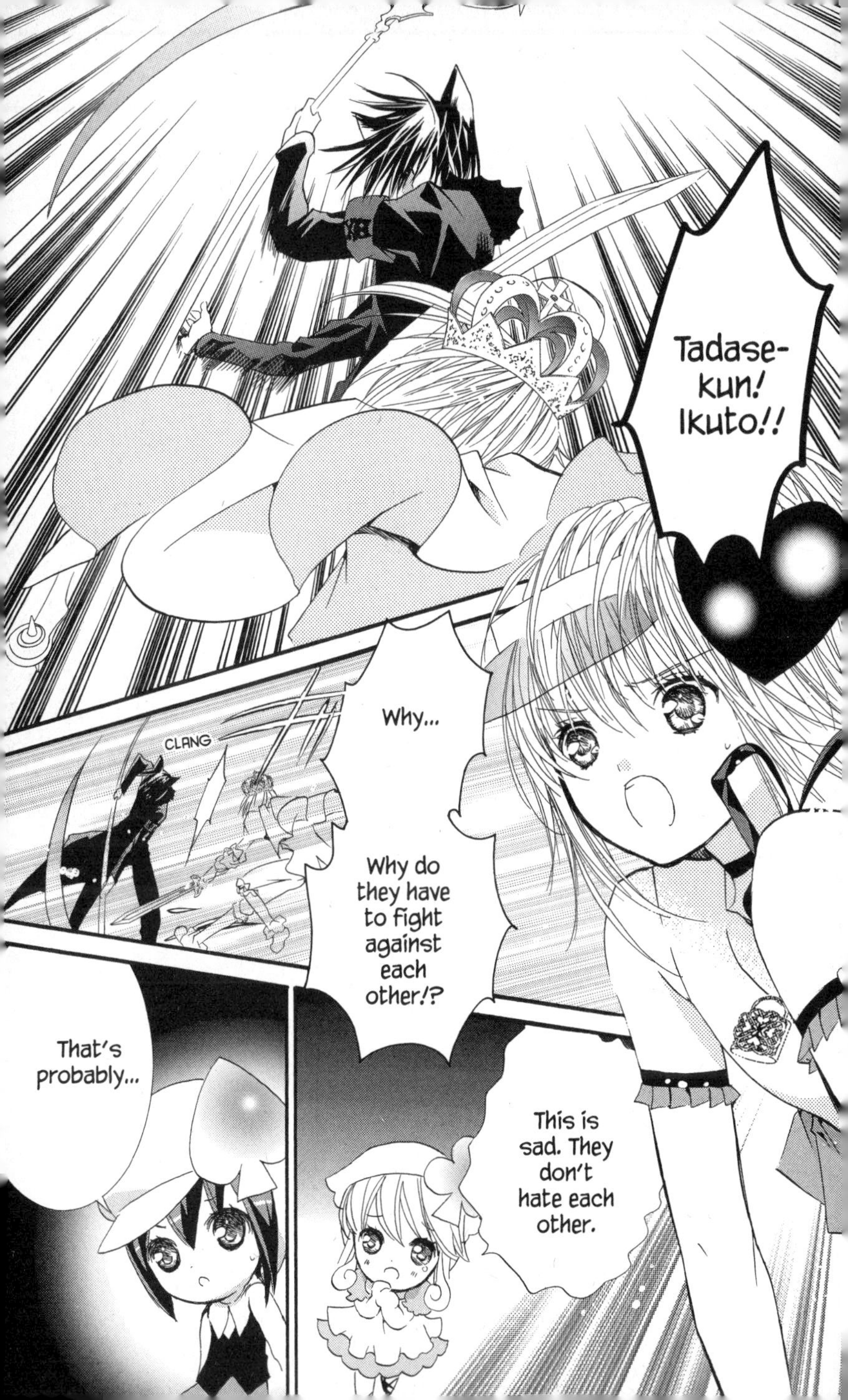
Tadase-kun! Ikuto!!
Why...
Why do they have to fight against each other!?
CLANG
This is sad. They don't hate each other.
That's probably...

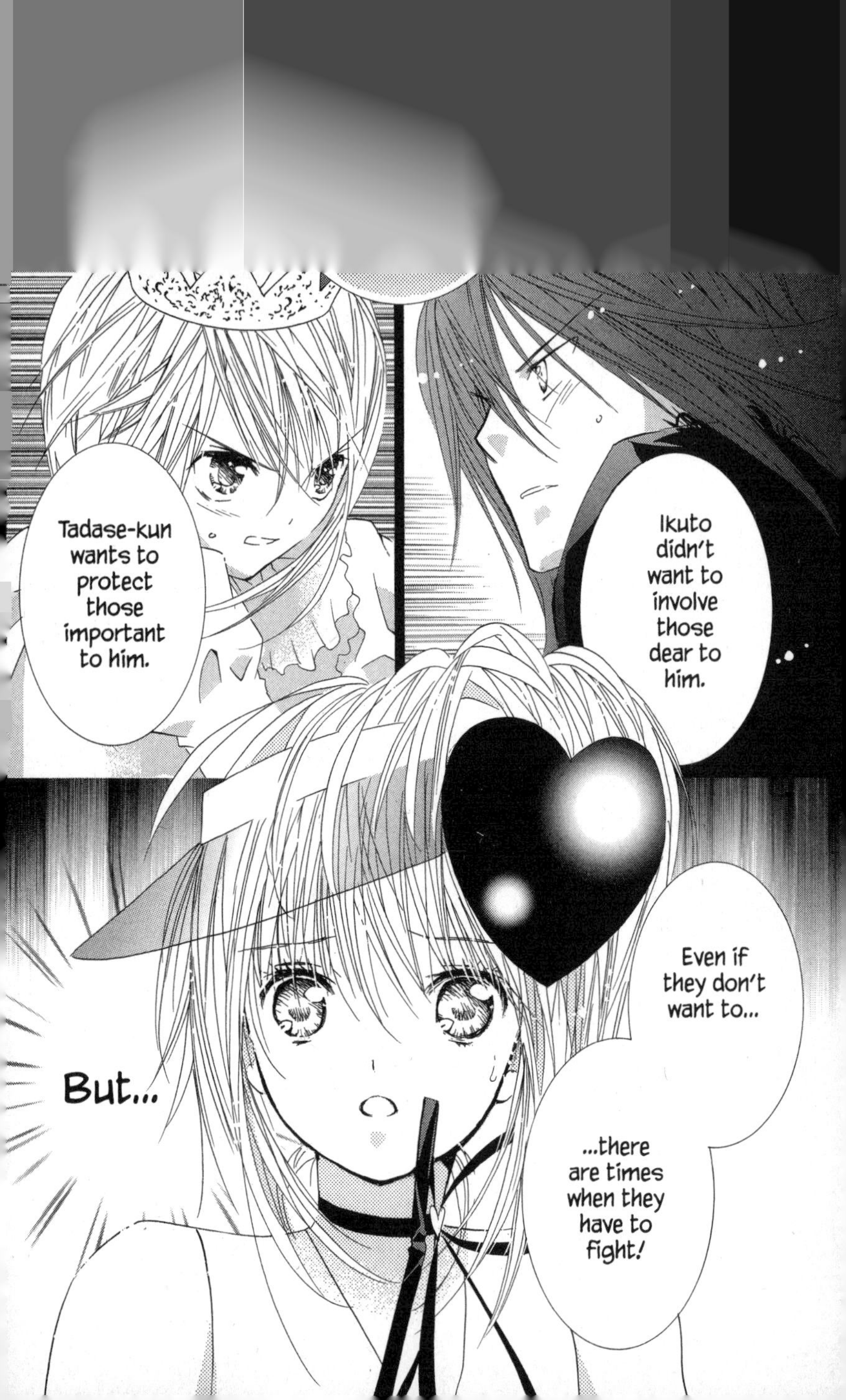
Ikuto didn't want to involve those dear to him.
Tadase-kun wants to protect those important to him.
But...
Even if they don't want to...
...there are times when they have to fight!

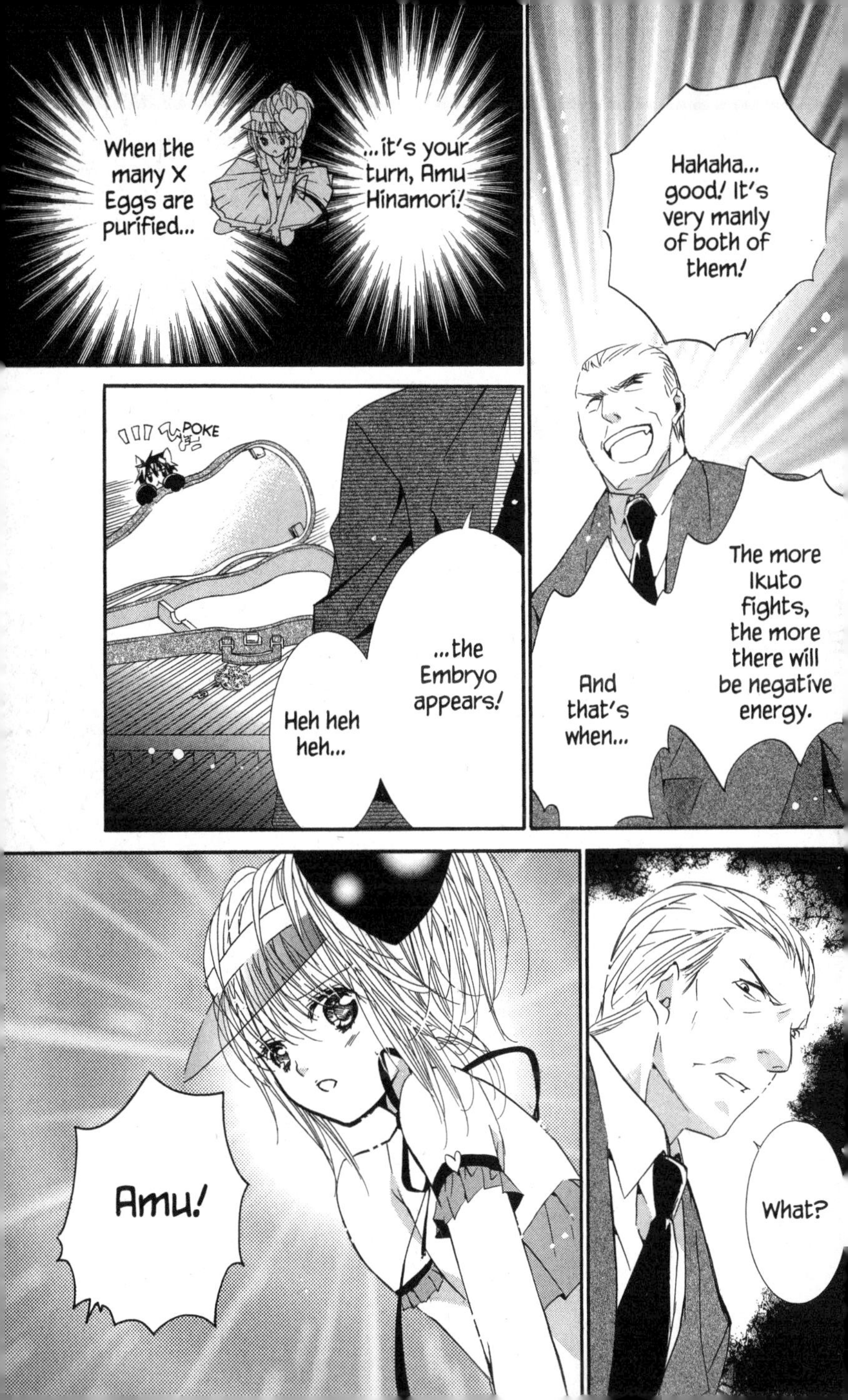

Hahaha... good! It's very manly of both of them!
The more Ikuto fights, the more there will be negative energy.
And that's when...
When the many X Eggs are purified...
...it's your turn, Amu Hinamori!
...the Embryo appears!
Heh heh heh...
POKE
What?
Amu!

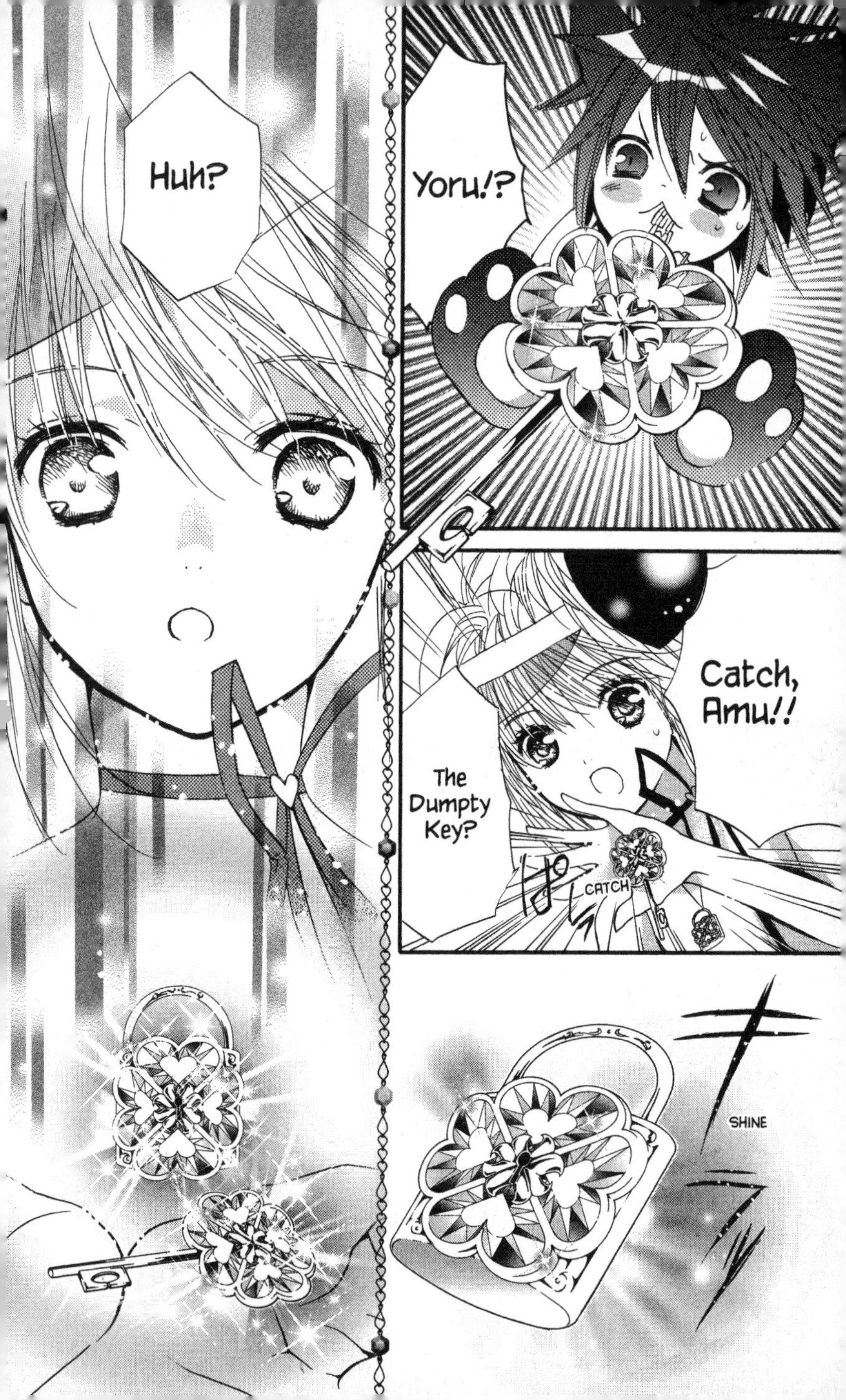
Yoru!?
Catch, Amu!!
The Dumpty Key?
CATCH
SHINE
Huh?

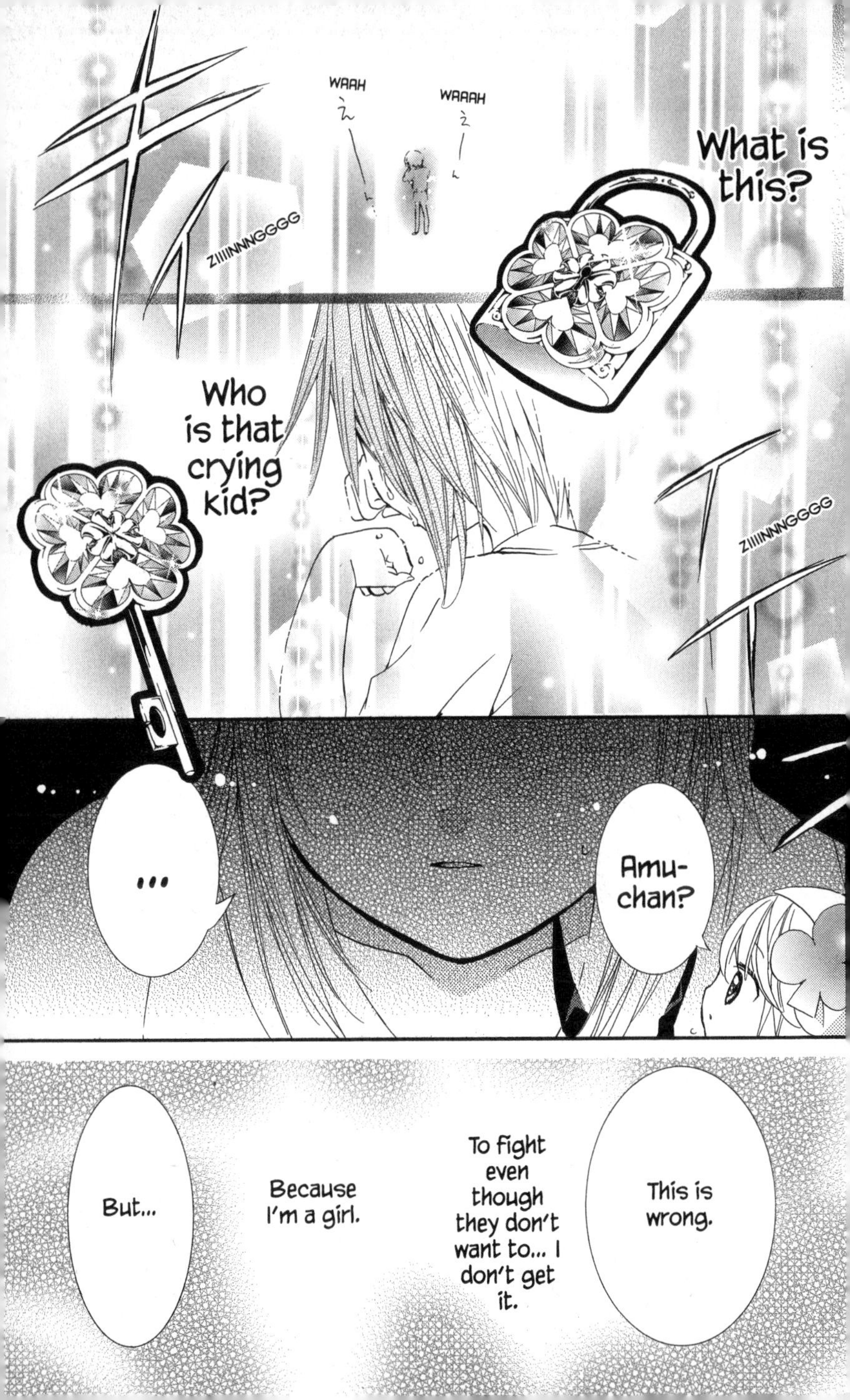
What is this?
ZIIIINNNGGGG
WAAAH
WAAH
Who is that crying kid?
ZIIIINNNGGGG
Amu-chan?
...
This is wrong.
To fight even though they don't want to... I don't get it.
Because I'm a girl.
But...

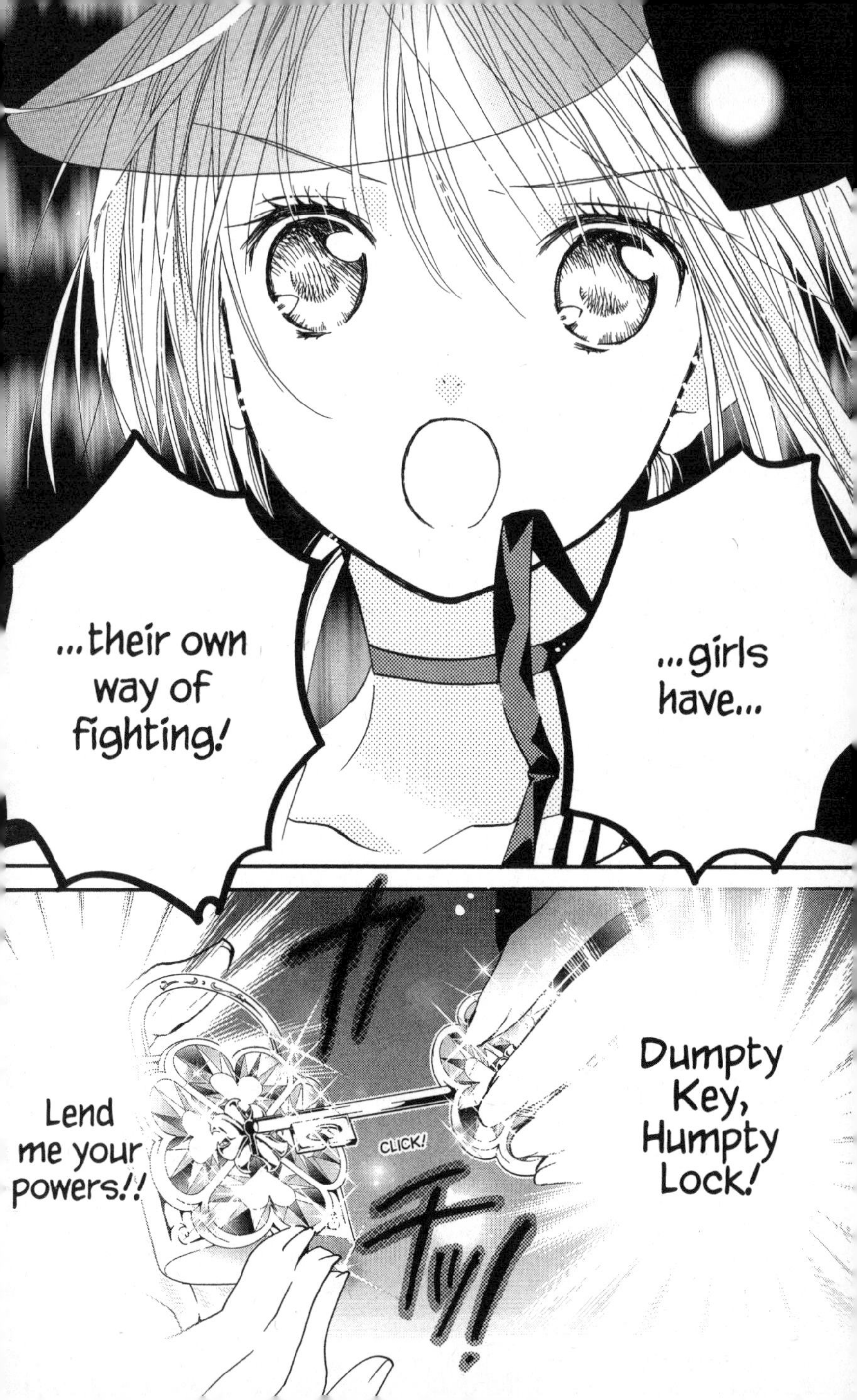
...girls have...
...their own way of fighting!
Dumpty Key, Humpty Lock!
CLICK!
Lend me your powers!!

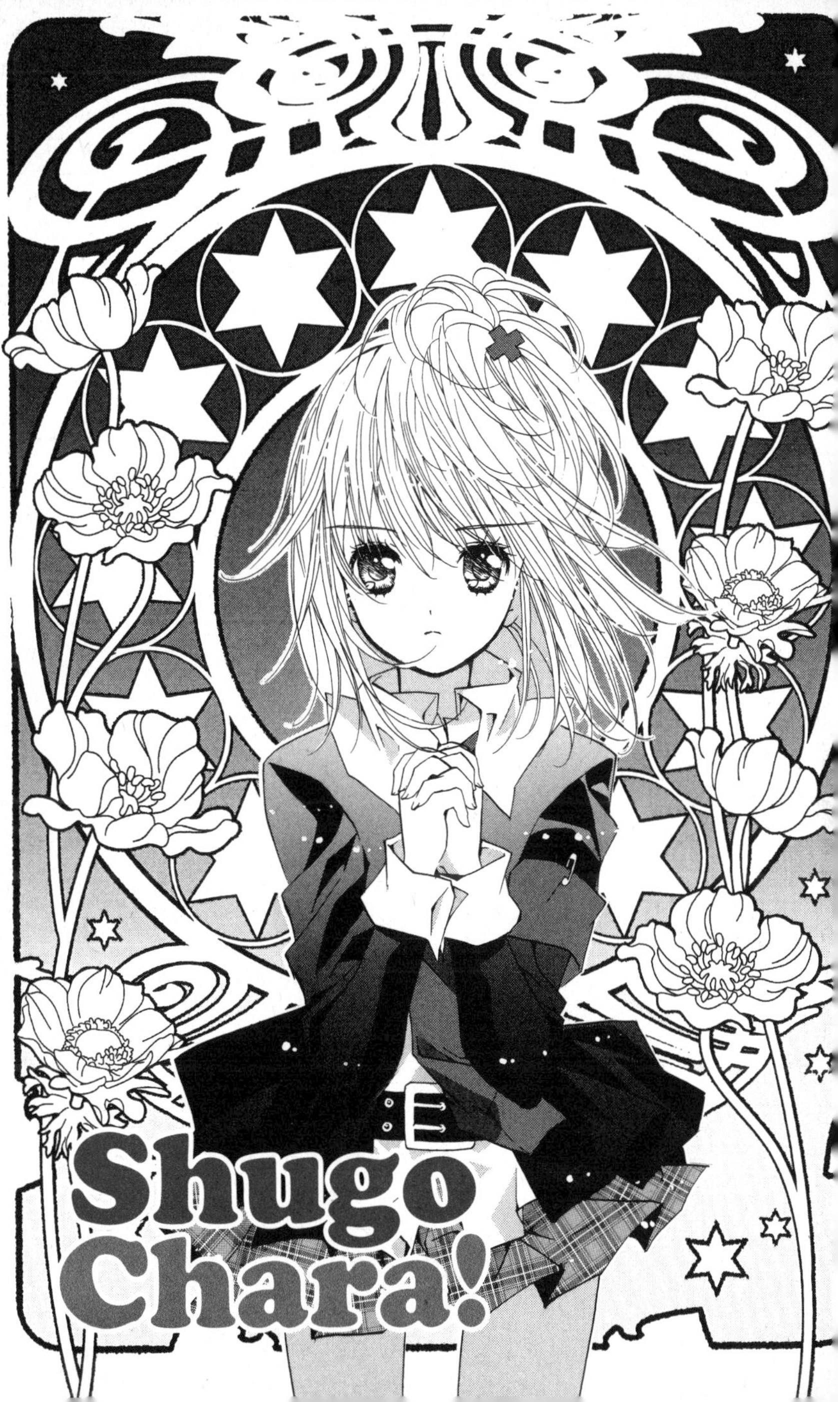
Shugo Chara!

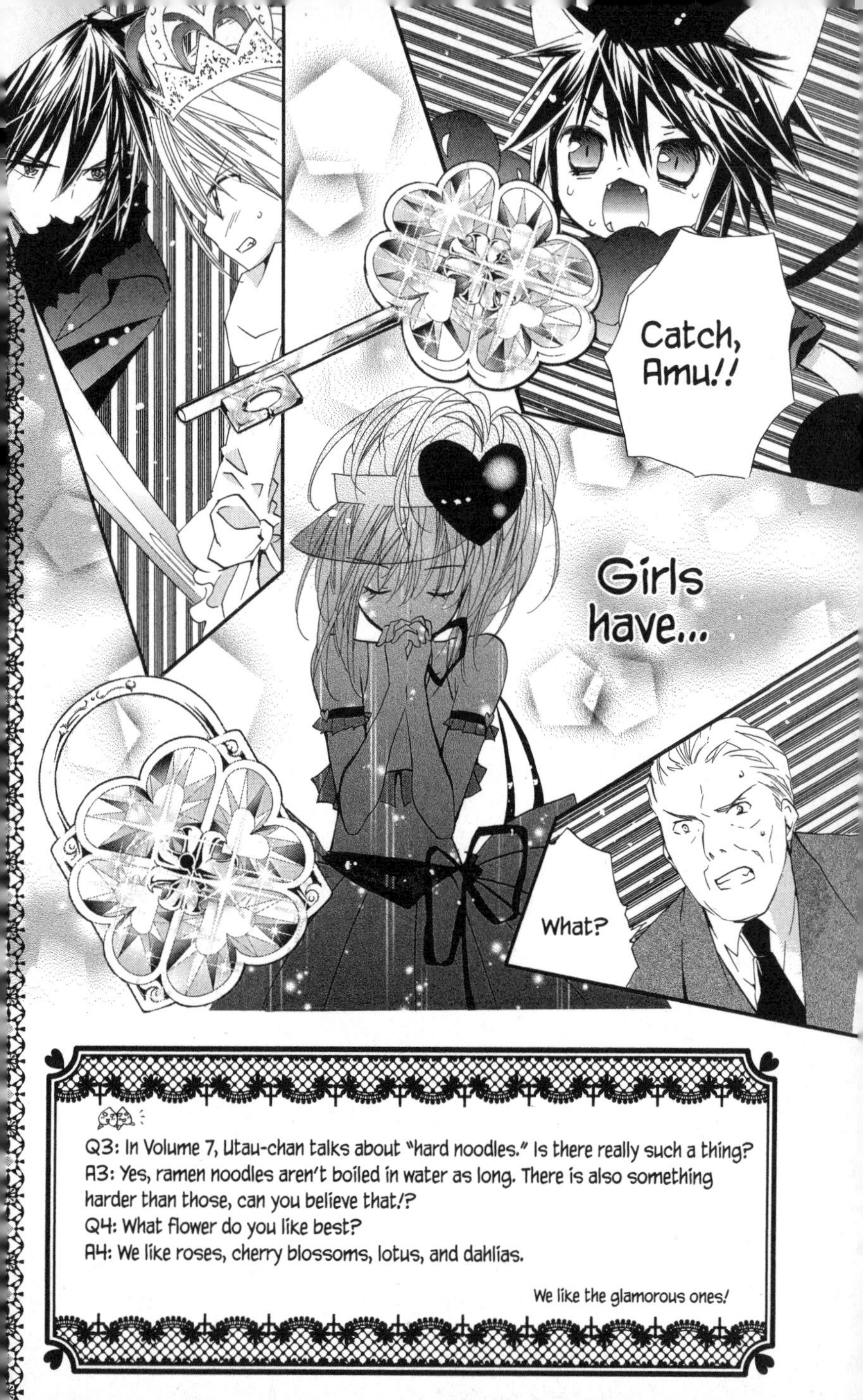
Catch, Amu!!
Girls have...
What?

Q3: In Volume 7, Utau-chan talks about "hard noodles." Is there really such a thing?
A3: Yes, ramen noodles aren't boiled in water as long. There is also something harder than those, can you believe that!?
Q4: What flower do you like best?
A4: We like roses, cherry blossoms, lotus, and dahlias.

We like the glamorous ones!

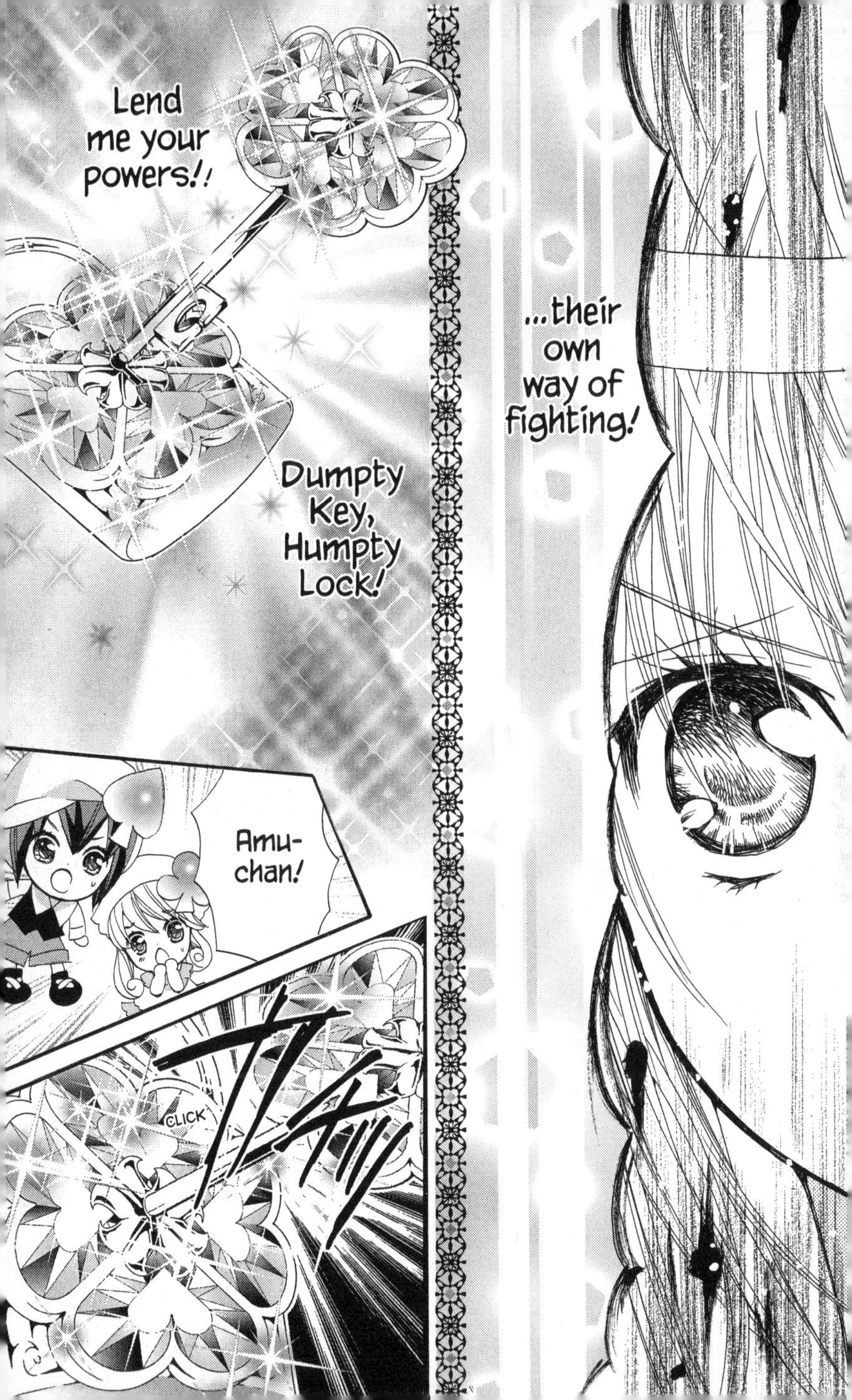
...their own way of fighting!
Lend me your powers!!
Dumpty Key, Humpty Lock!
Amu-chan!
CLICK

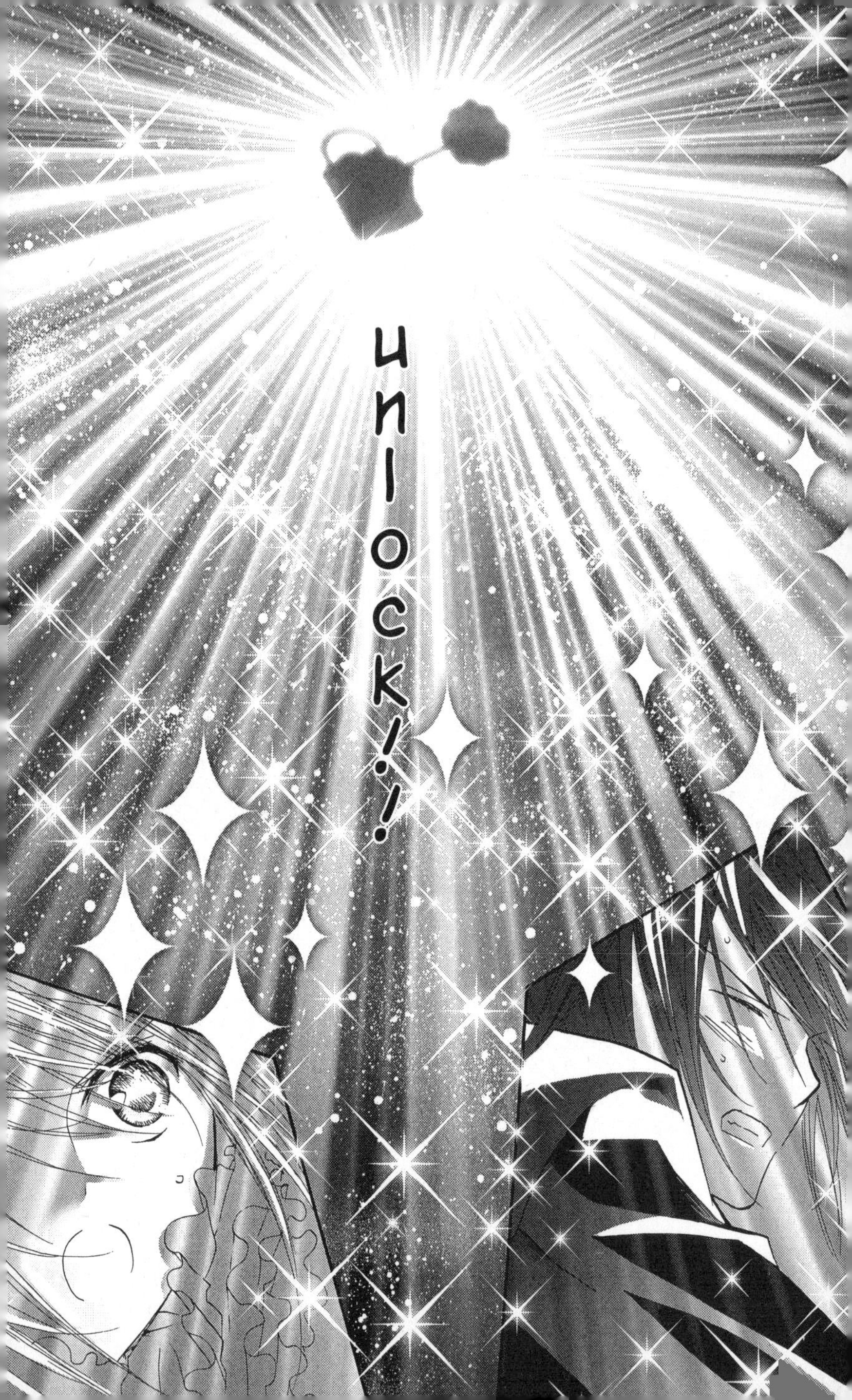
Unlock!!

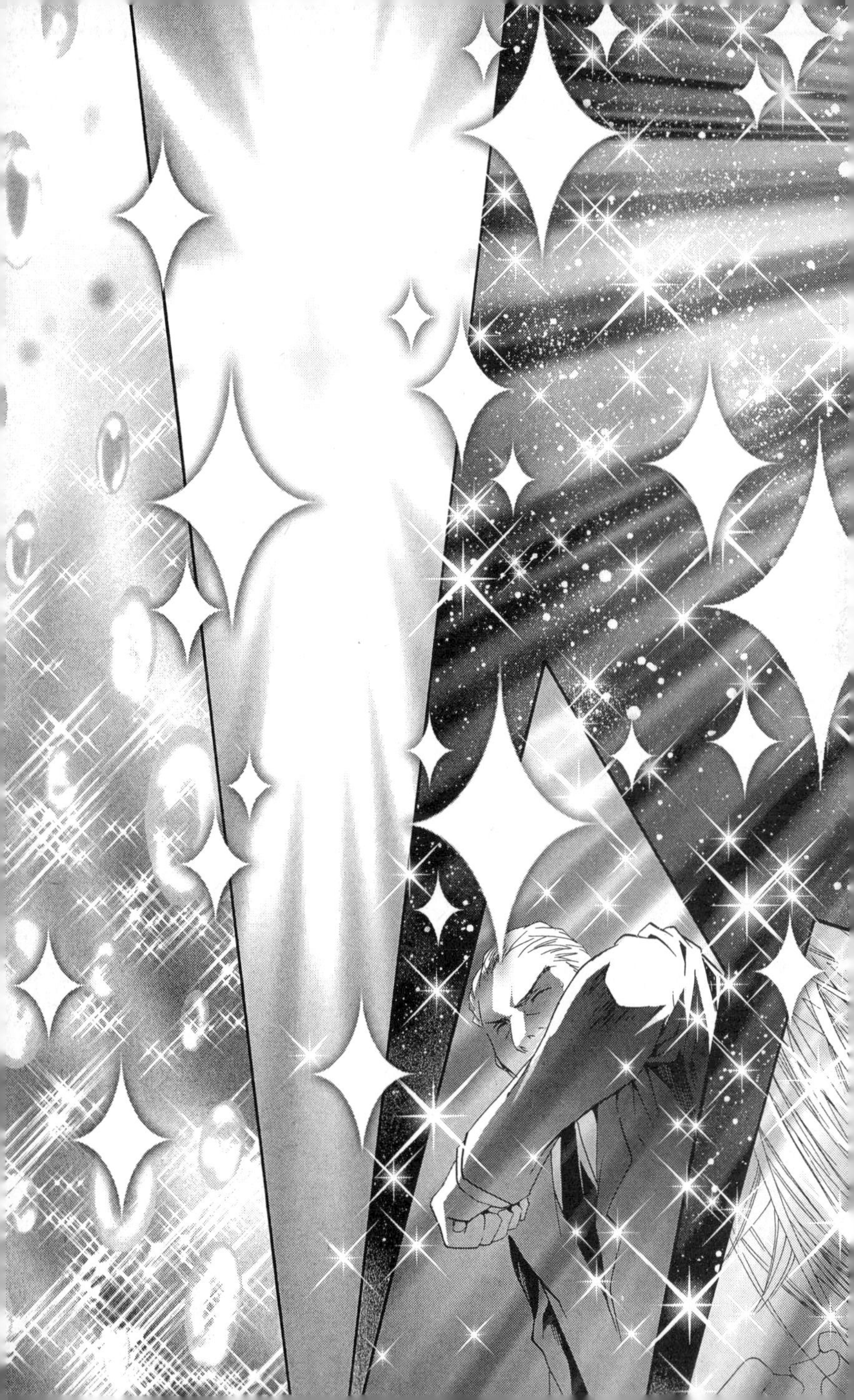

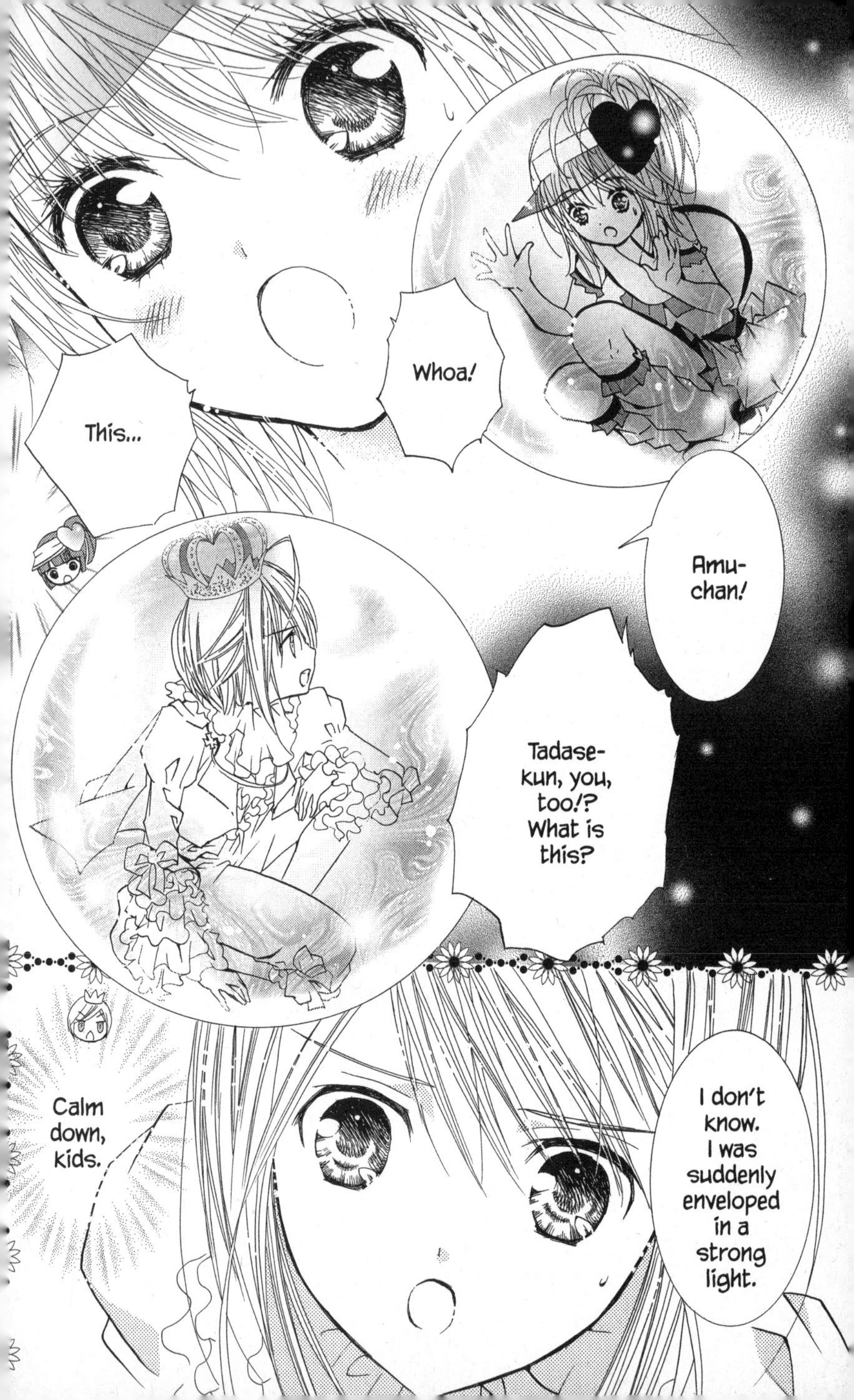
Whoa!
This...
Amu-chan!
Tadase-kun, you, too!? What is this?
I don't know. I was suddenly enveloped in a strong light.
Calm down, kids.

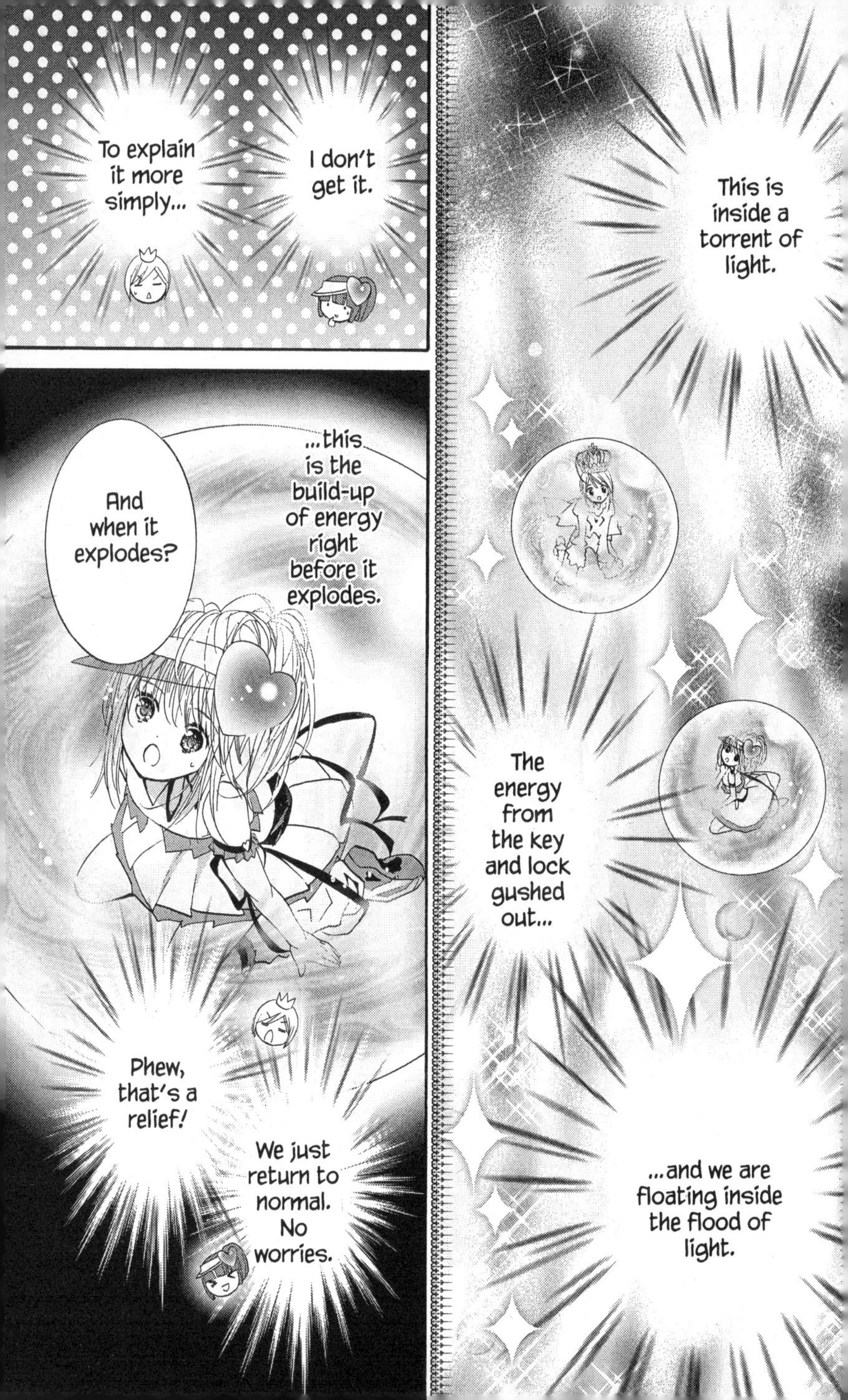
This is inside a torrent of light.
The energy from the key and lock gushed out...
...and we are floating inside the flood of light.
I don't get it.
To explain it more simply...
...this is the build-up of energy right before it explodes.
And when it explodes?
We just return to normal. No worries.
Phew, that's a relief!

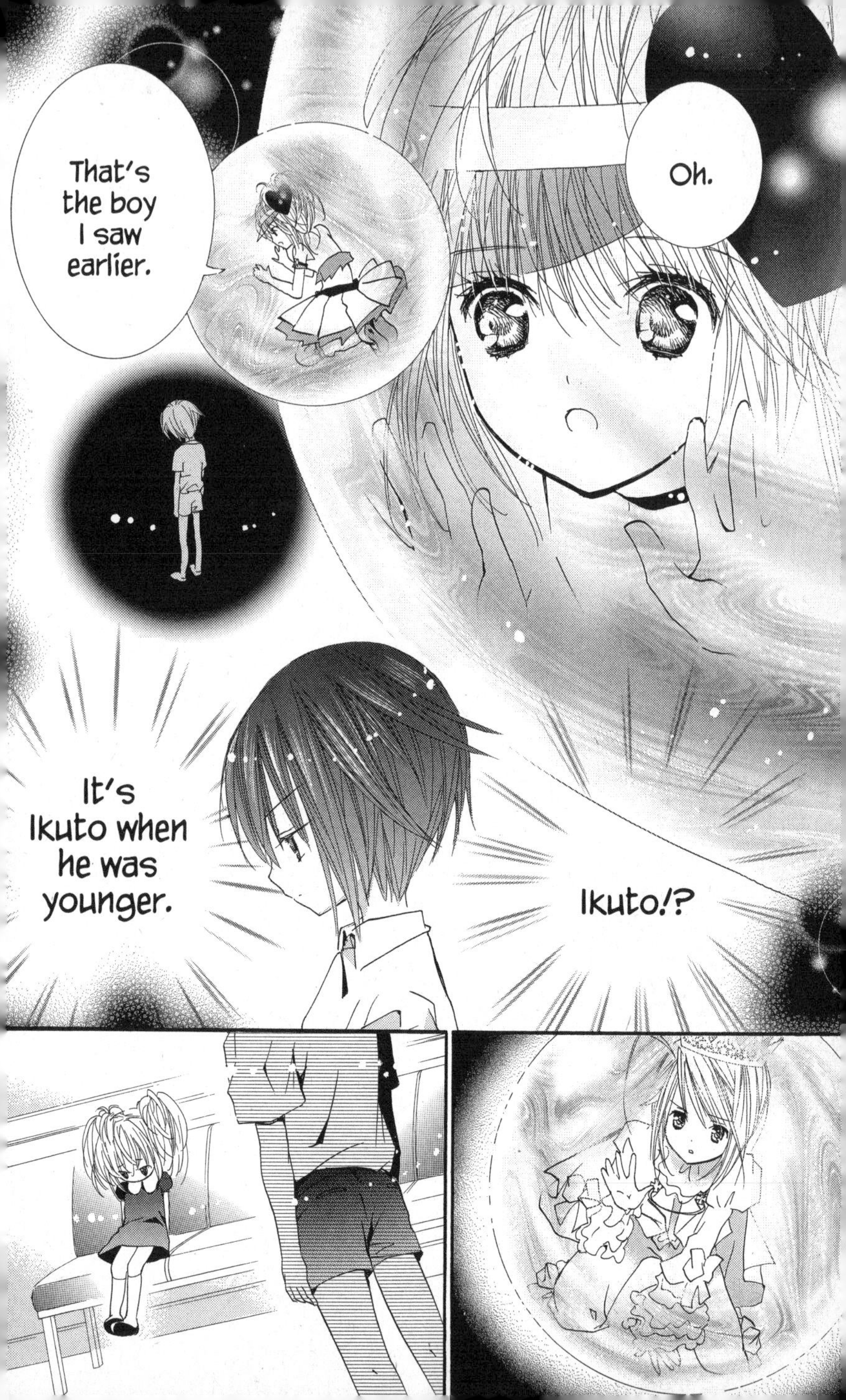
Oh.
That's the boy I saw earlier.
Ikuto!?
It's Ikuto when he was younger.

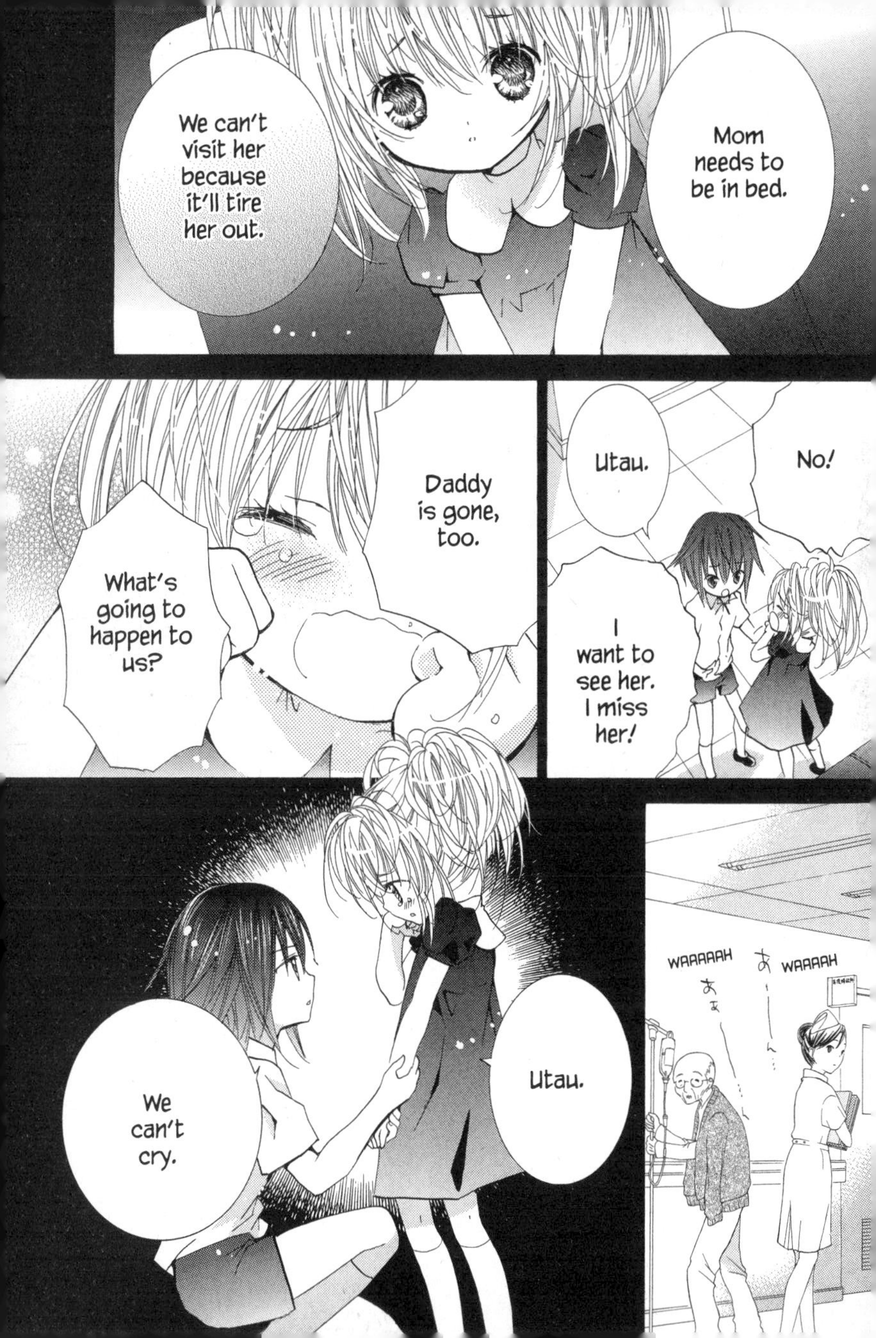

Mom needs to be in bed.
We can't visit her because it'll tire her out.
No!
Utau.
I want to see her. I miss her!
Daddy is gone, too.
What's going to happen to us?
WAAAAH
あーん…
あぁ
WAAAAAH
Utau.
We can't cry.

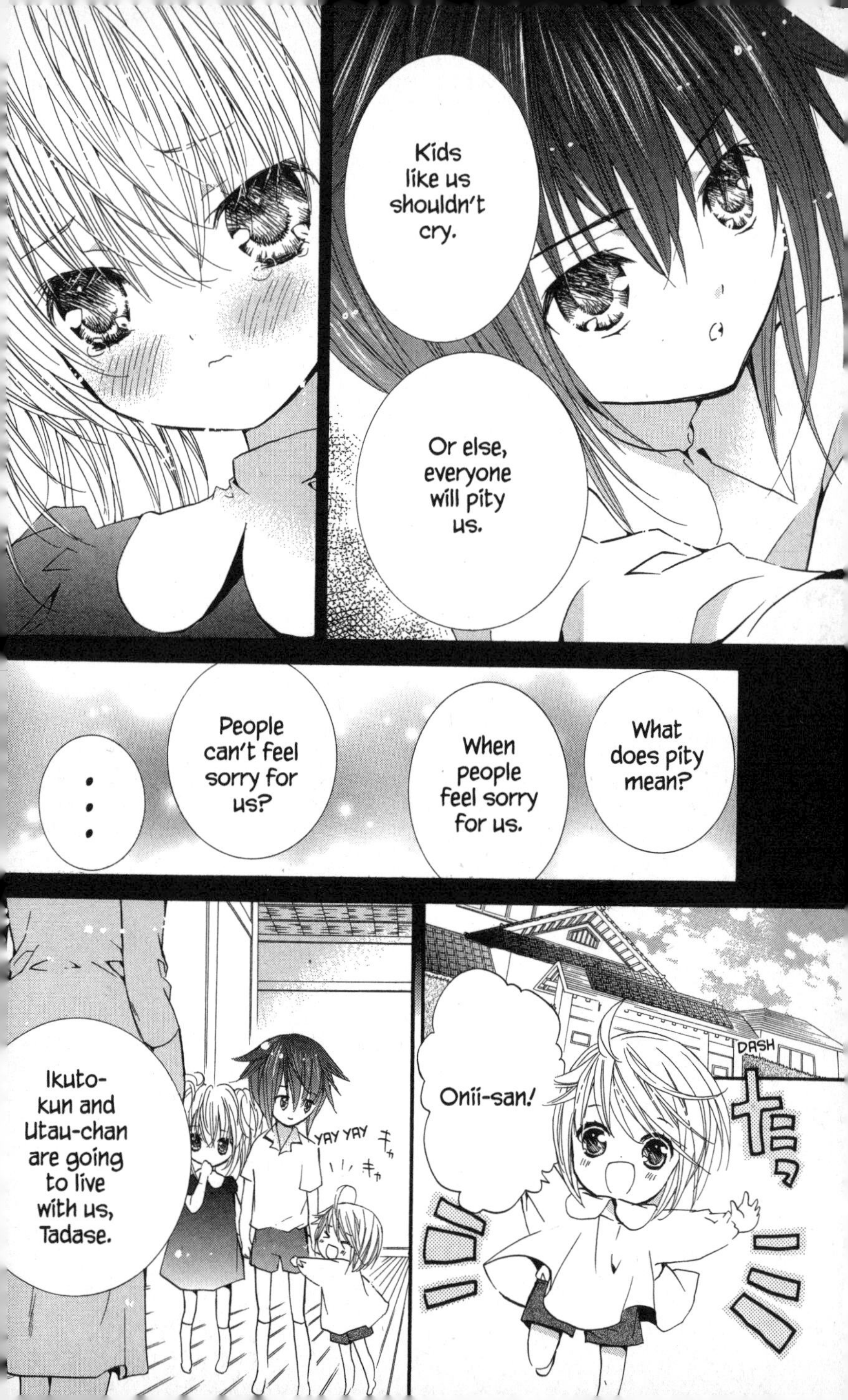
Kids like us shouldn't cry.
Or else, everyone will pity us.
What does pity mean?
When people feel sorry for us.
People can't feel sorry for us?
. . .
Onii-san!
DASH
Ikuto-kun and Utau-chan are going to live with us, Tadase.
YAY YAY

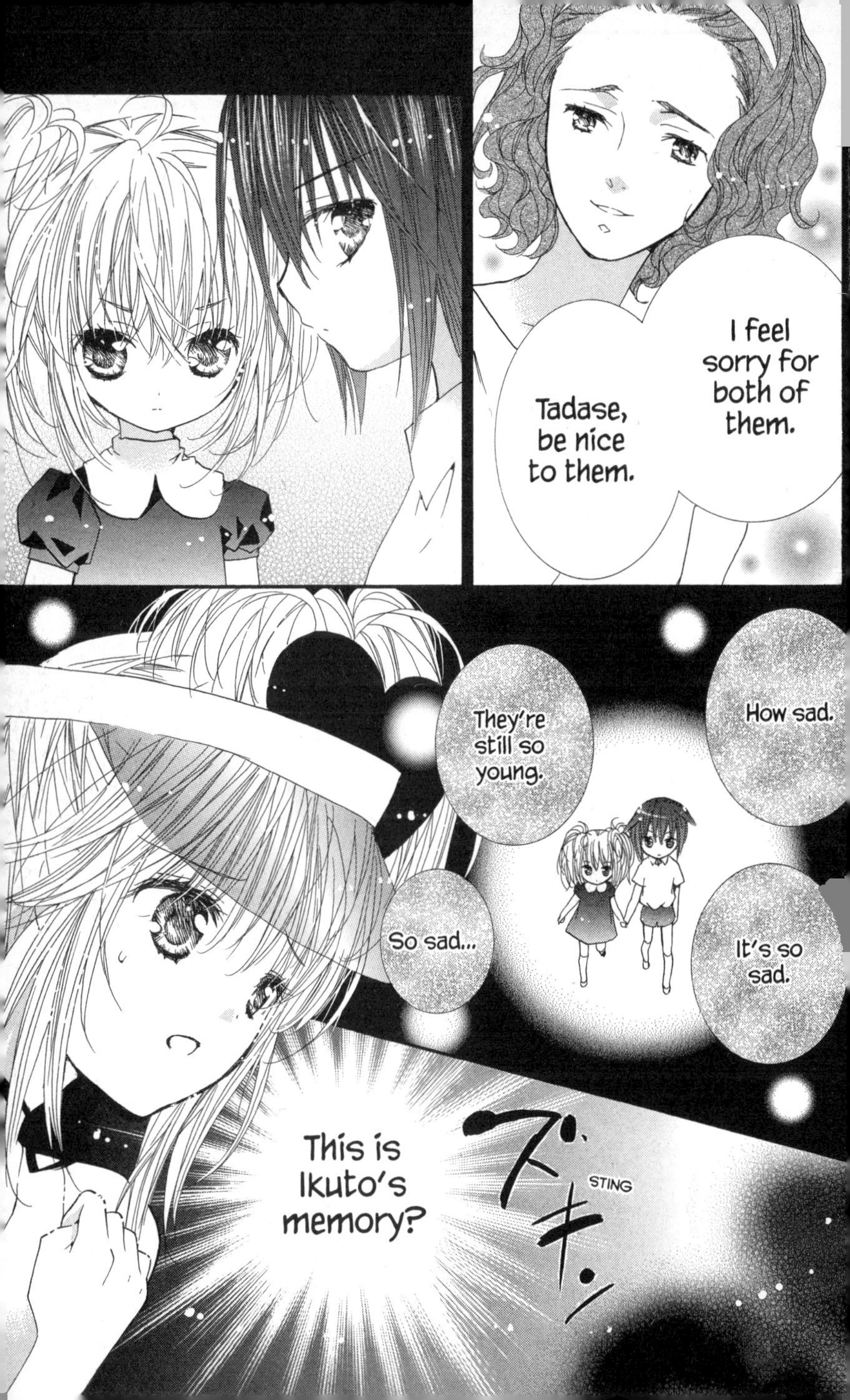
I feel sorry for both of them.
Tadase, be nice to them.
How sad.
They're still so young.
It's so sad.
So sad...
STING
This is Ikuto's memory?

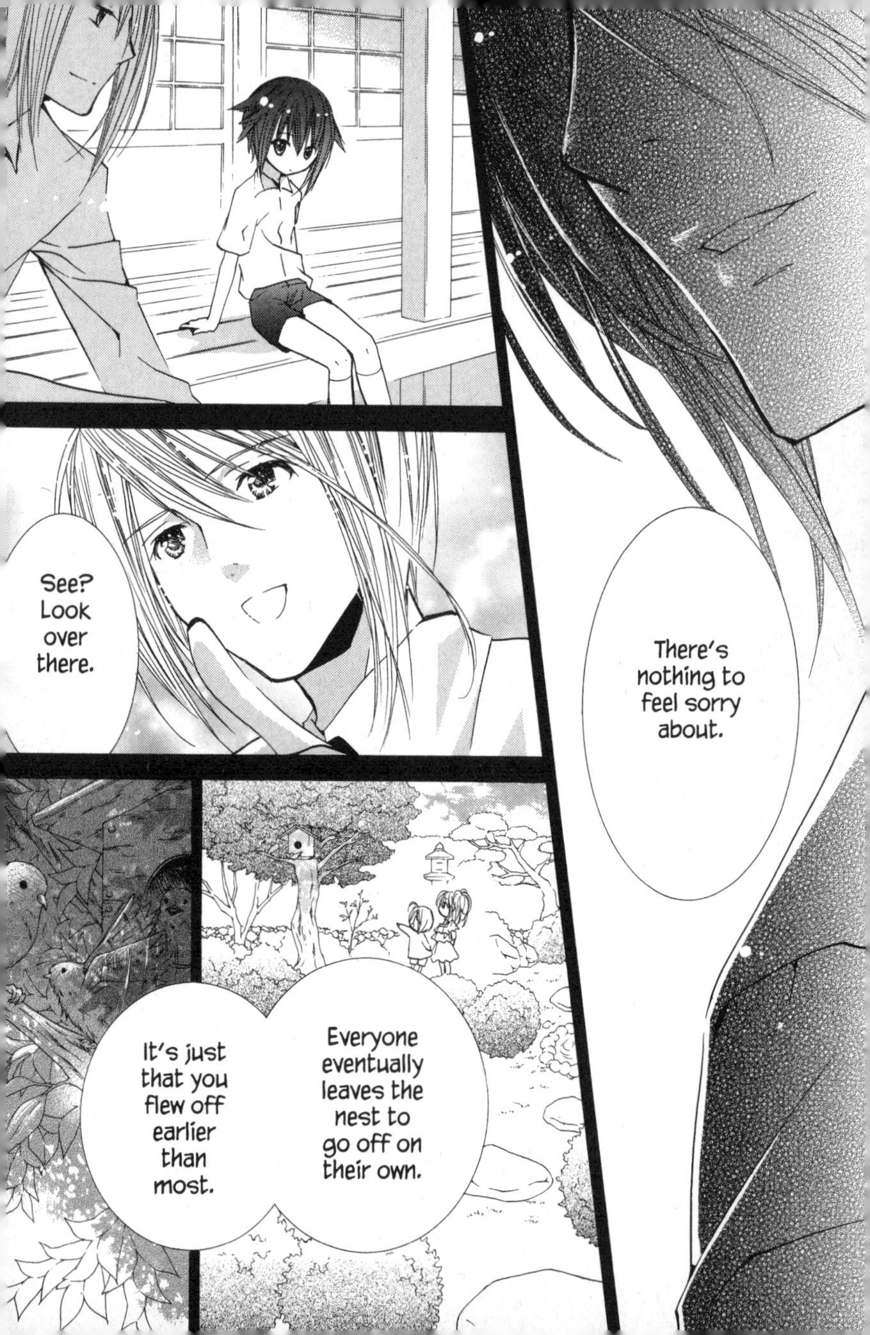
There's nothing to feel sorry about.
See? Look over there.
Everyone eventually leaves the nest to go off on their own.
It's just that you flew off earlier than most.

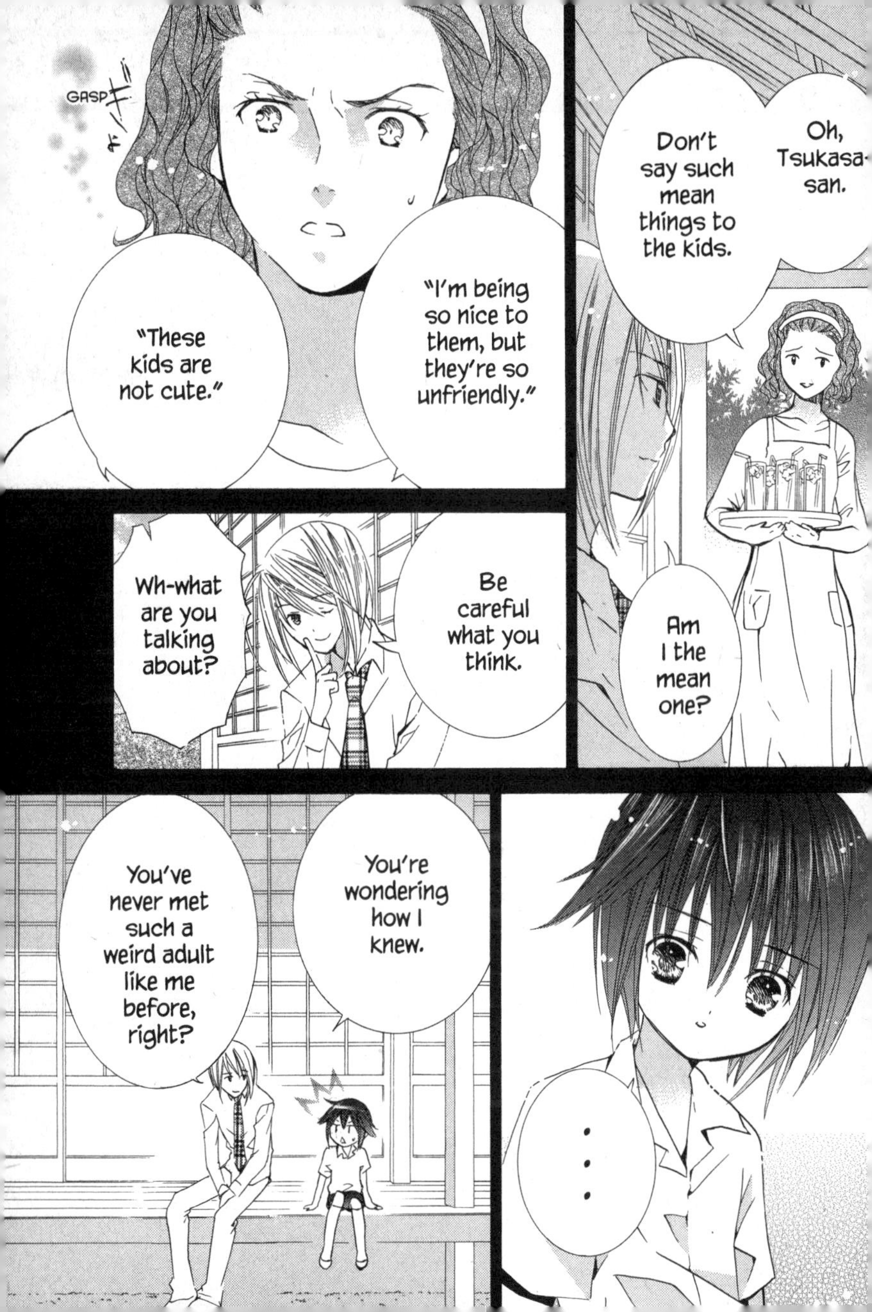
Oh, Tsukasa-san.
Don't say such mean things to the kids.
Am I the mean one?
GASP
"I'm being so nice to them, but they're so unfriendly."
"These kids are not cute."
Be careful what you think.
Wh-what are you talking about?
...
You're wondering how I knew.
You've never met such a weird adult like me before, right?

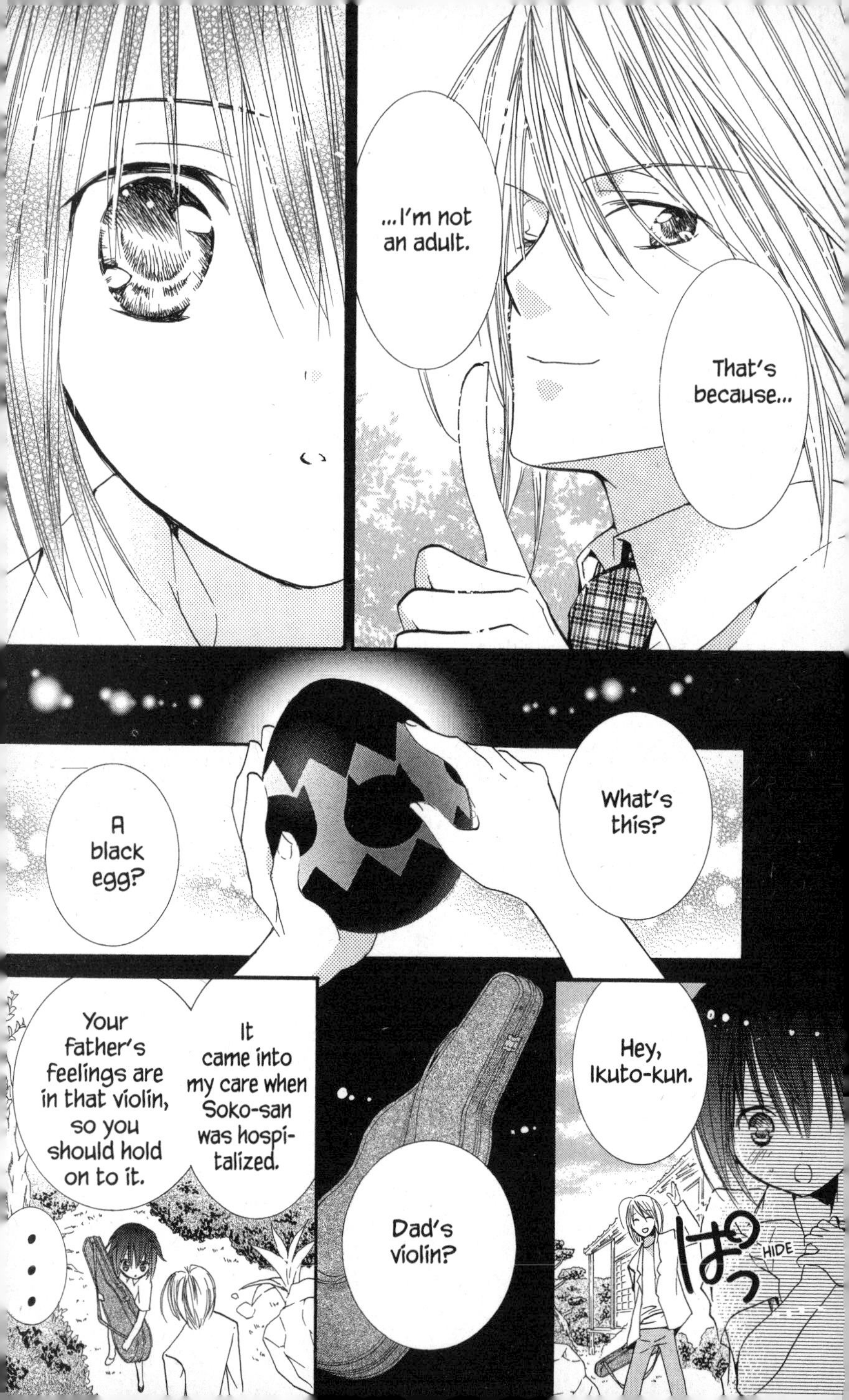
That's because...
...I'm not an adult.
What's this?
A black egg?
Hey, Ikuto-kun.
ぱっ
HIDE
Dad's violin?
It came into my care when Soko-san was hospitalized.
Your father's feelings are in that violin, so you should hold on to it.
...

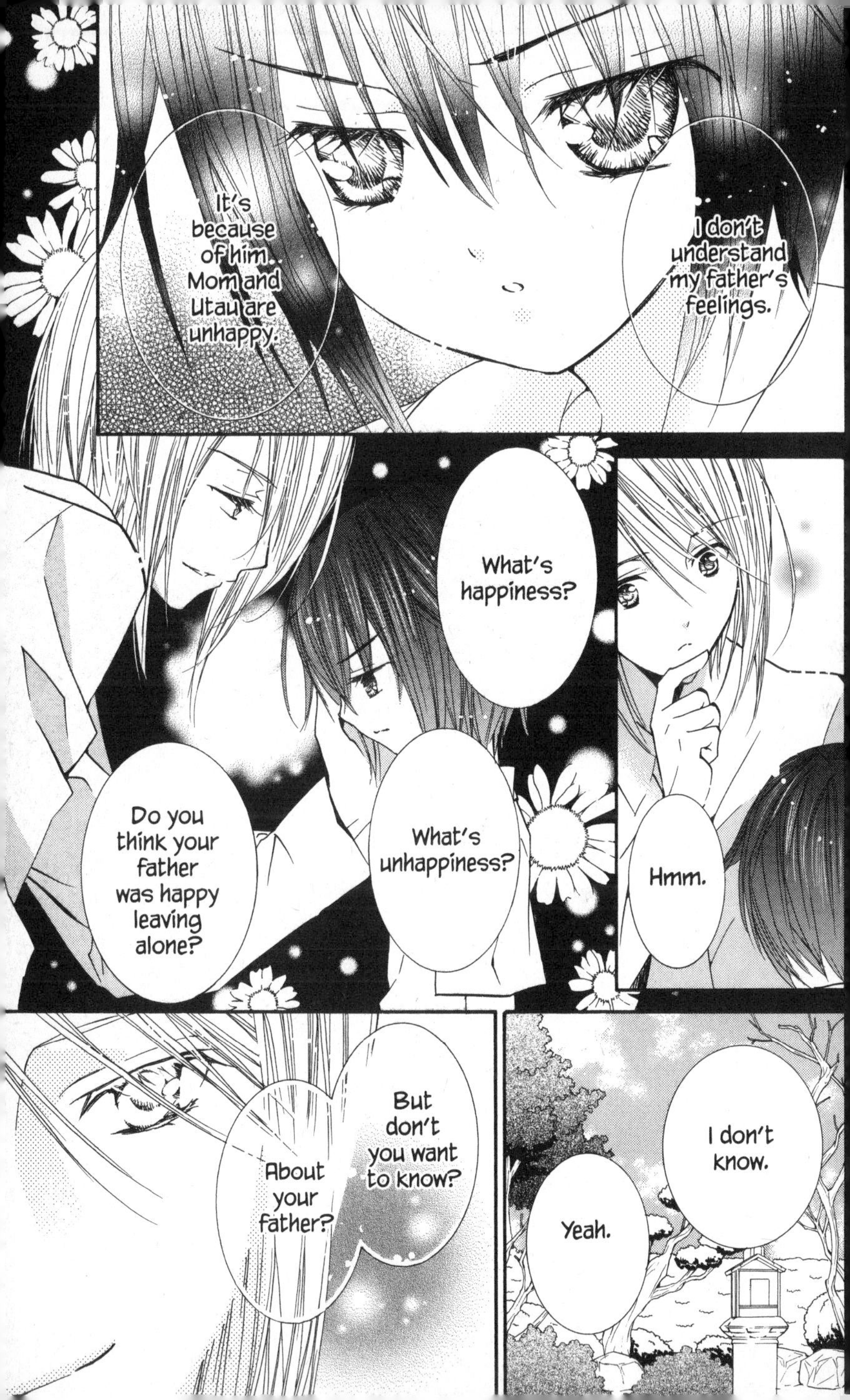
I don't understand my father's feelings.
It's because of him Mom and Utau are unhappy.
Hmm.
What's happiness?
What's unhappiness?
Do you think your father was happy leaving alone?
I don't know.
Yeah.
But don't you want to know?
About your father?

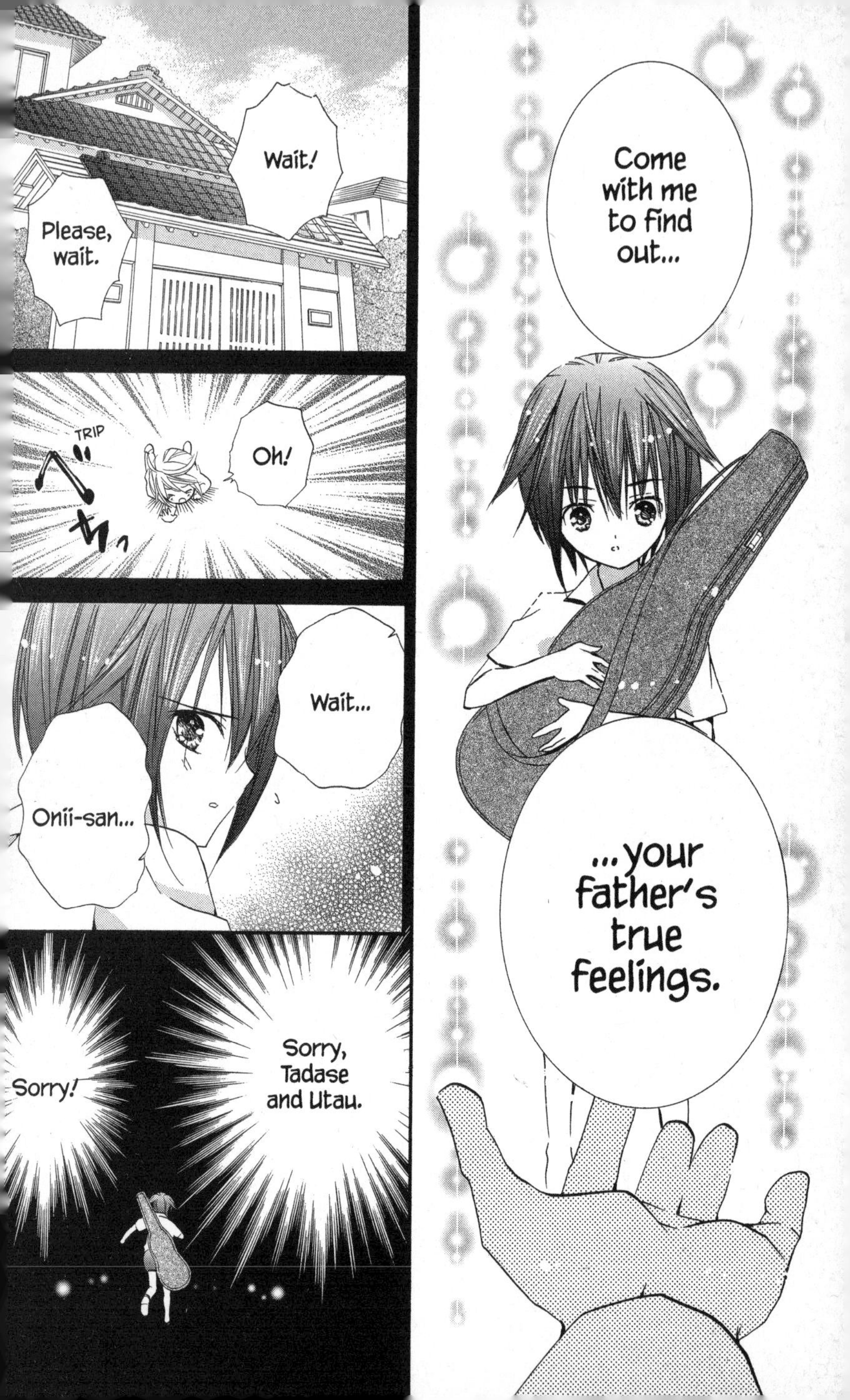
Come with me to find out...
...your father's true feelings.
Wait!
Please, wait.
Oh!
TRIP
Wait...
Onii-san...
Sorry, Tadase and Utau.
Sorry!

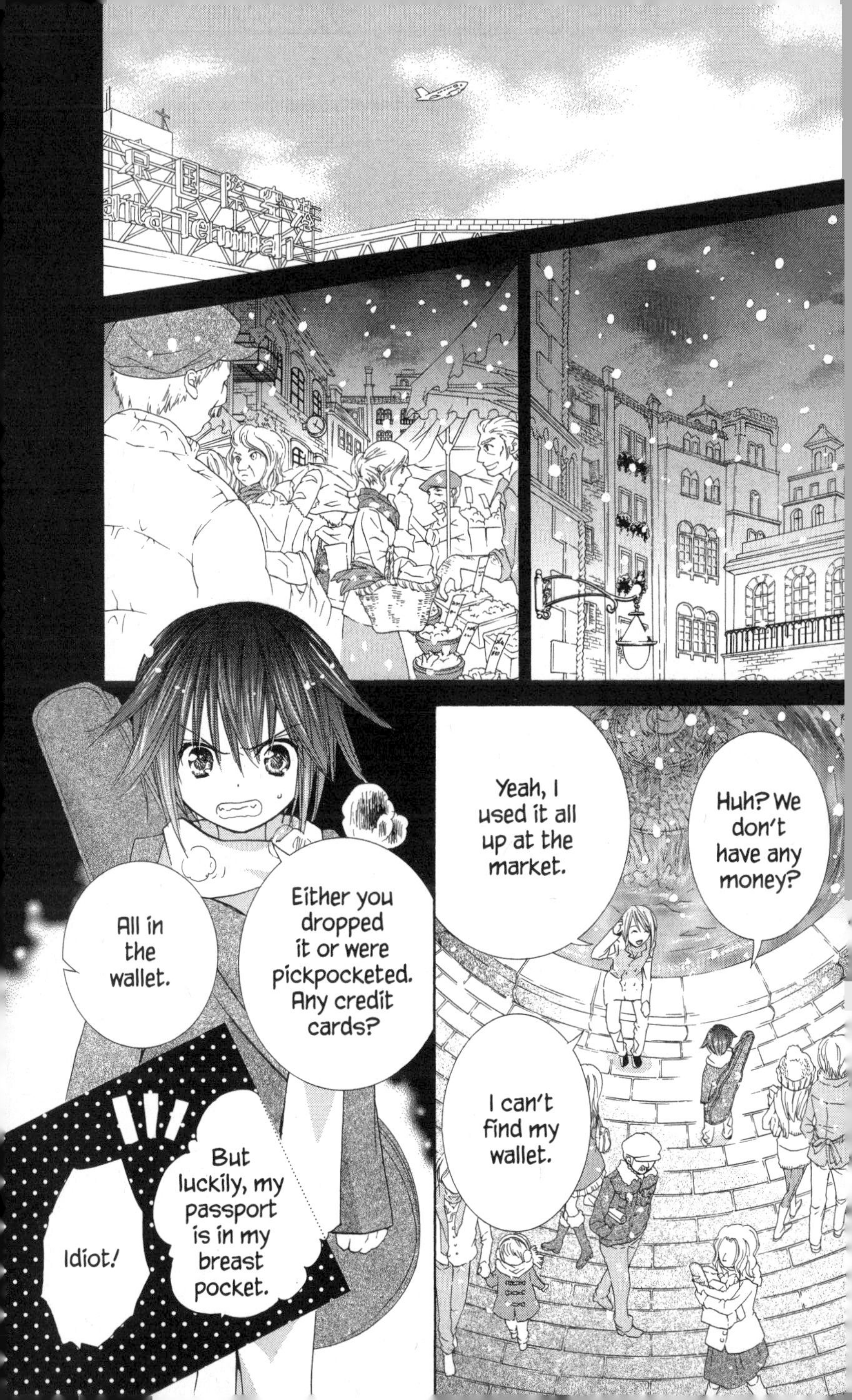
Huh? We don't have any money?
Yeah, I used it all up at the market.
I can't find my wallet.
Either you dropped it or were pickpocketed. Any credit cards?
All in the wallet.
But luckily, my passport is in my breast pocket.
Idiot!

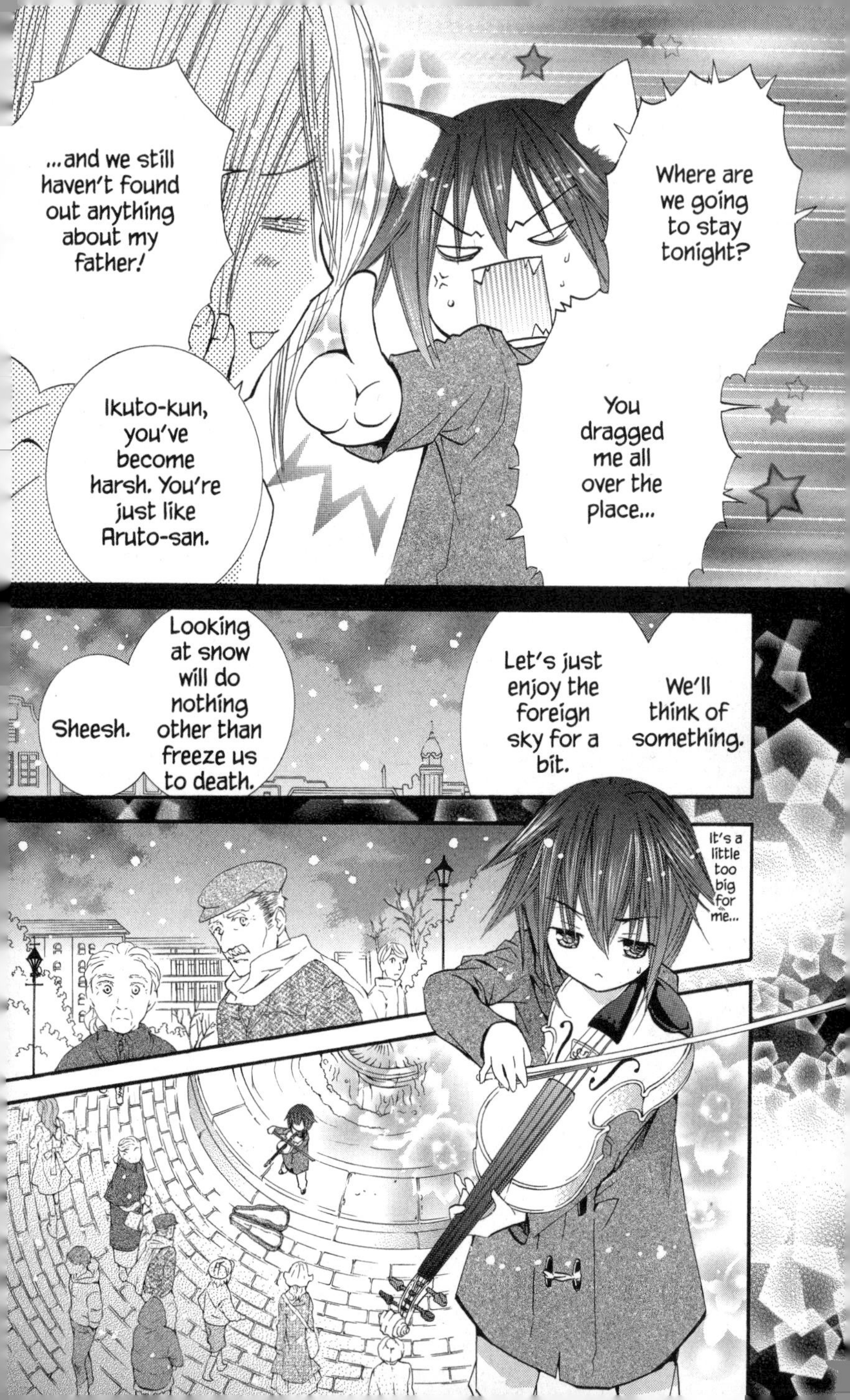
Where are we going to stay tonight?
You dragged me all over the place...
...and we still haven't found out anything about my father!
Ikuto-kun, you've become harsh. You're just like Aruto-san.
We'll think of something.
Let's just enjoy the foreign sky for a bit.
Looking at snow will do nothing other than freeze us to death.
Sheesh.
It's a little too big for me...

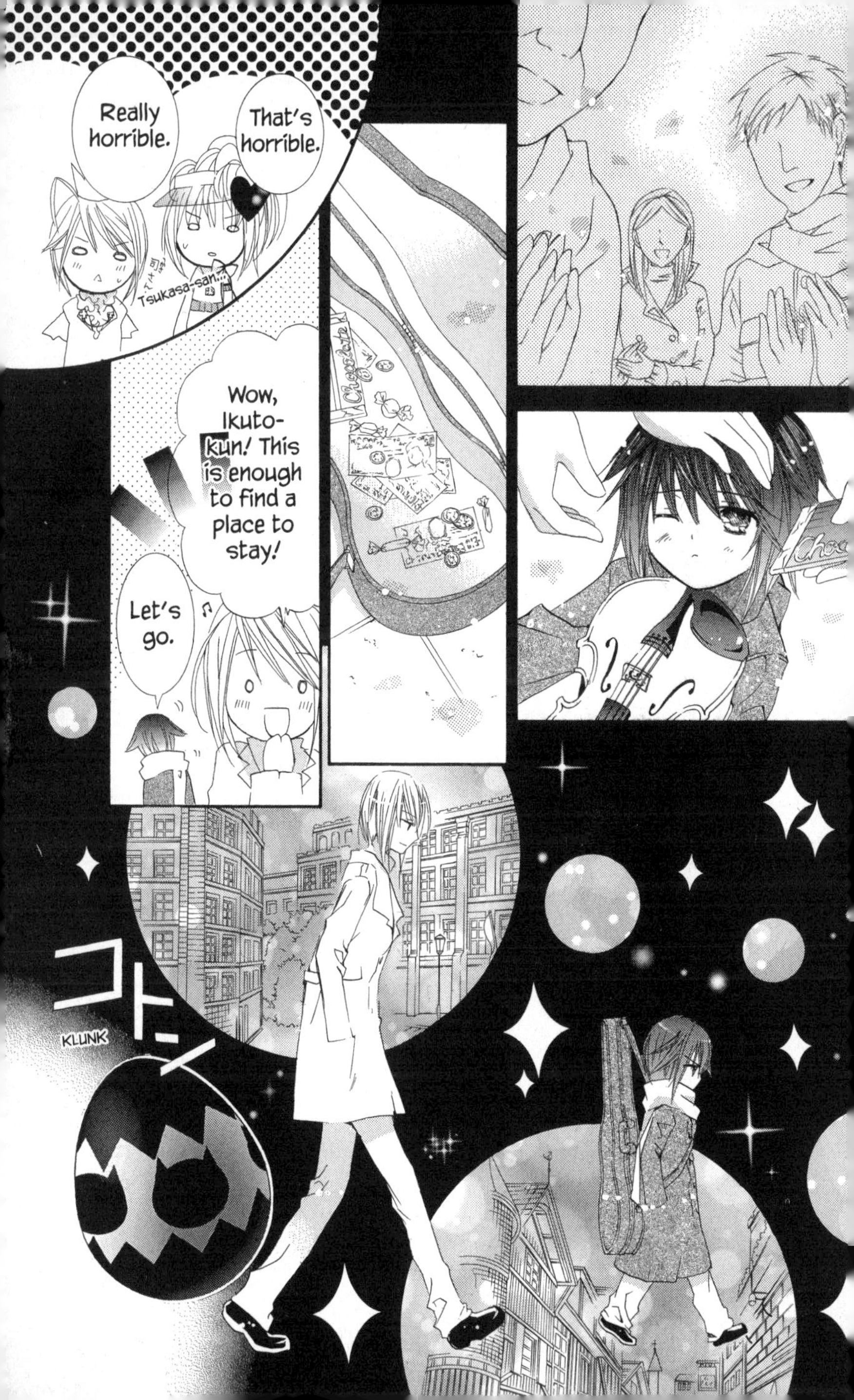

That's horrible.
Really horrible.
Tsukasa-san...
Wow, Ikuto-kun! This is enough to find a place to stay!
Let's go.
KLUNK

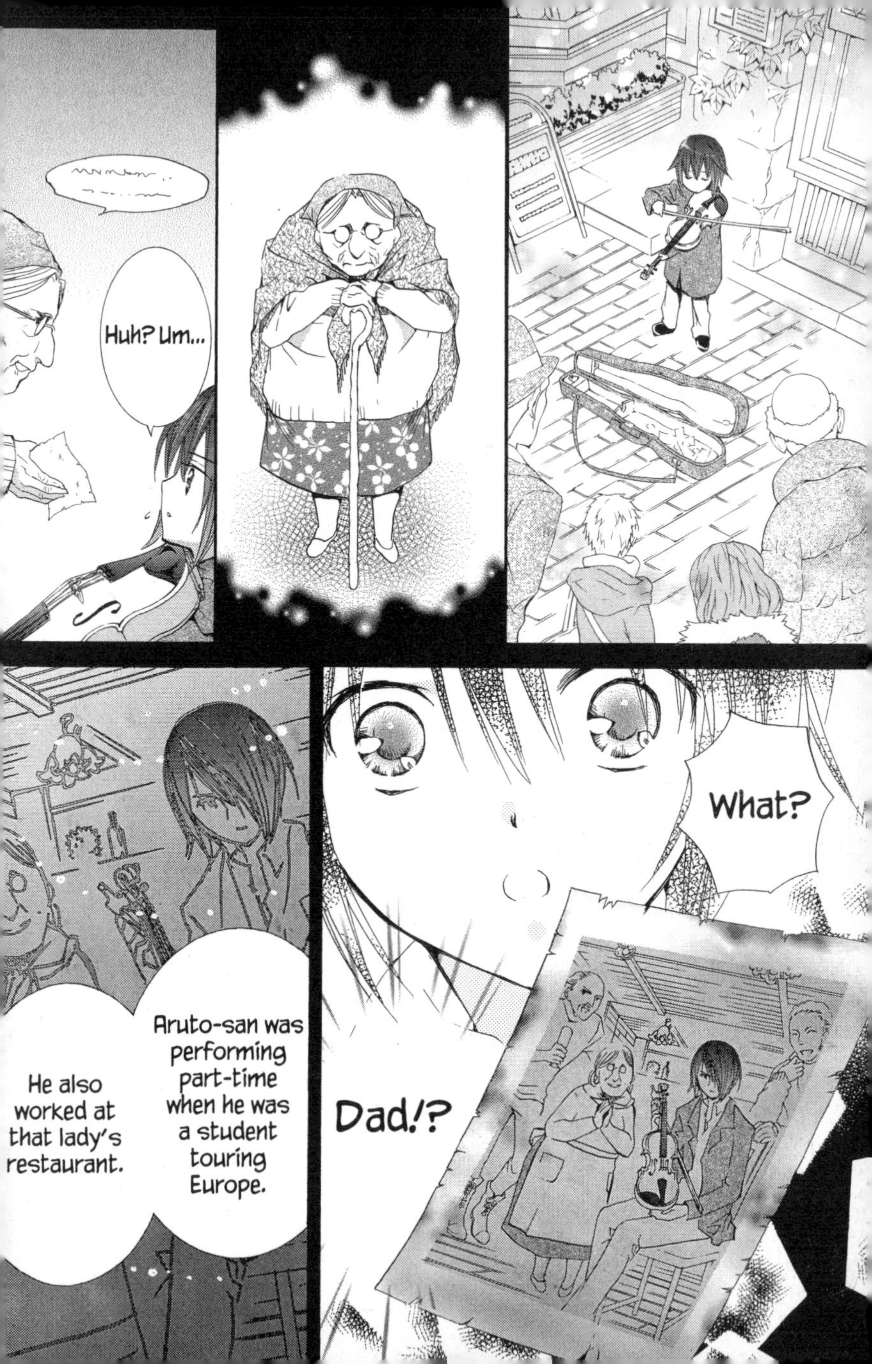
Huh? Um...
What?
Dad!?
Aruto-san was performing part-time when he was a student touring Europe.
He also worked at that lady's restaurant.

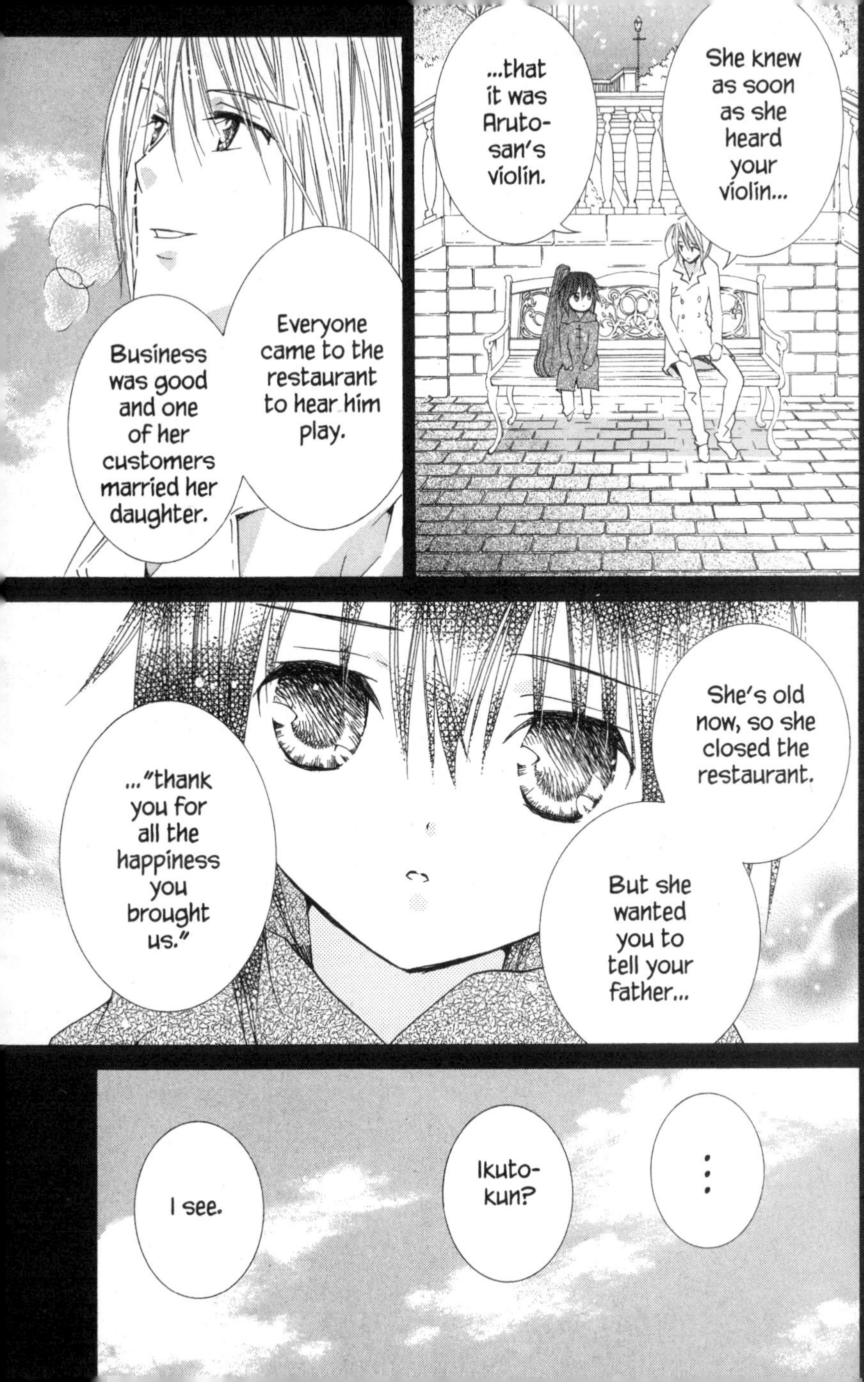
She knew as soon as she heard your violin...
...that it was Aruto-san's violin.
Everyone came to the restaurant to hear him play.
Business was good and one of her customers married her daughter.
She's old now, so she closed the restaurant.
But she wanted you to tell your father...
..."thank you for all the happiness you brought us."
...
Ikuto-kun?
I see.

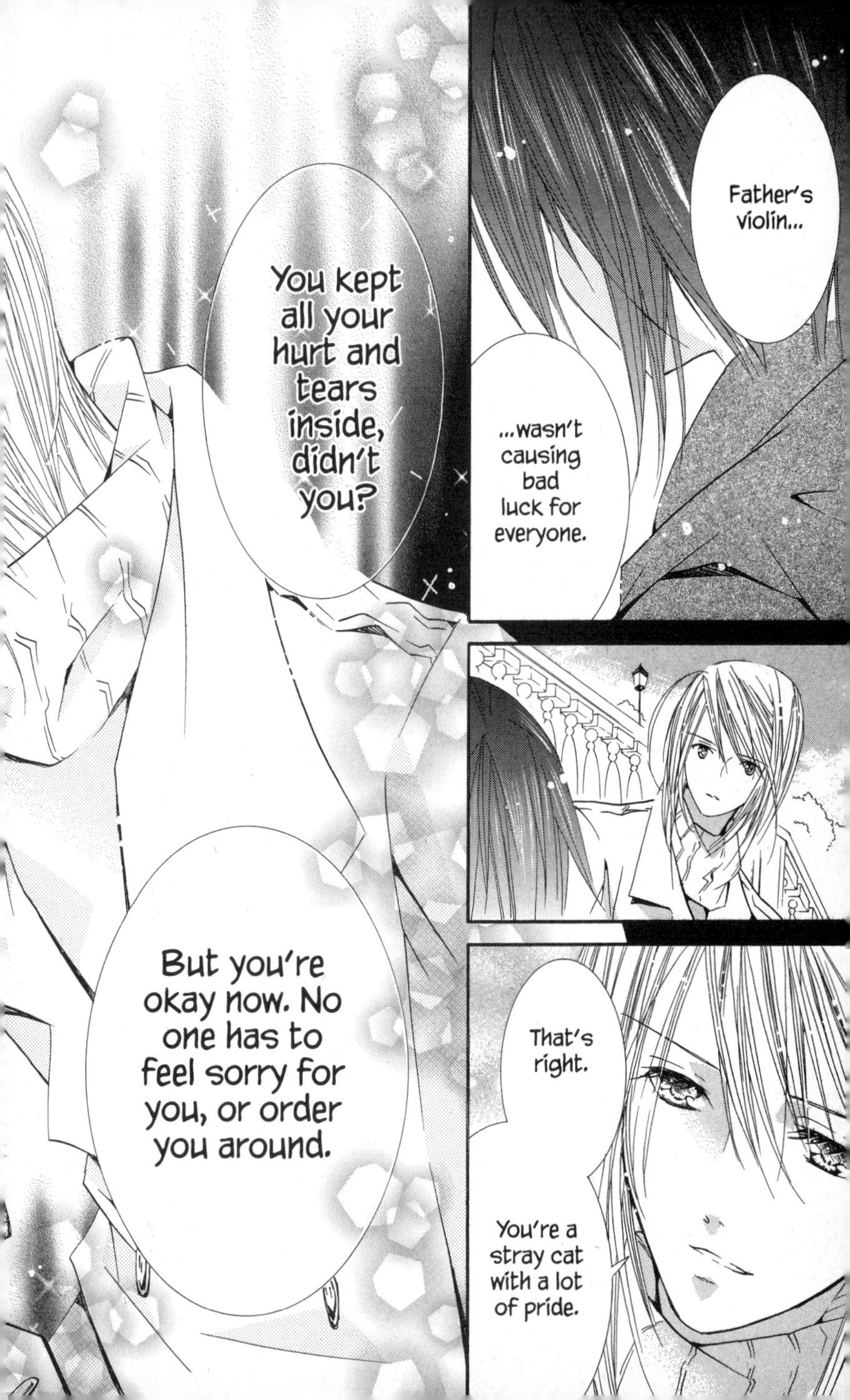
Father's violin...
...wasn't causing bad luck for everyone.
That's right.
You're a stray cat with a lot of pride.
You kept all your hurt and tears inside, didn't you?
But you're okay now. No one has to feel sorry for you, or order you around.

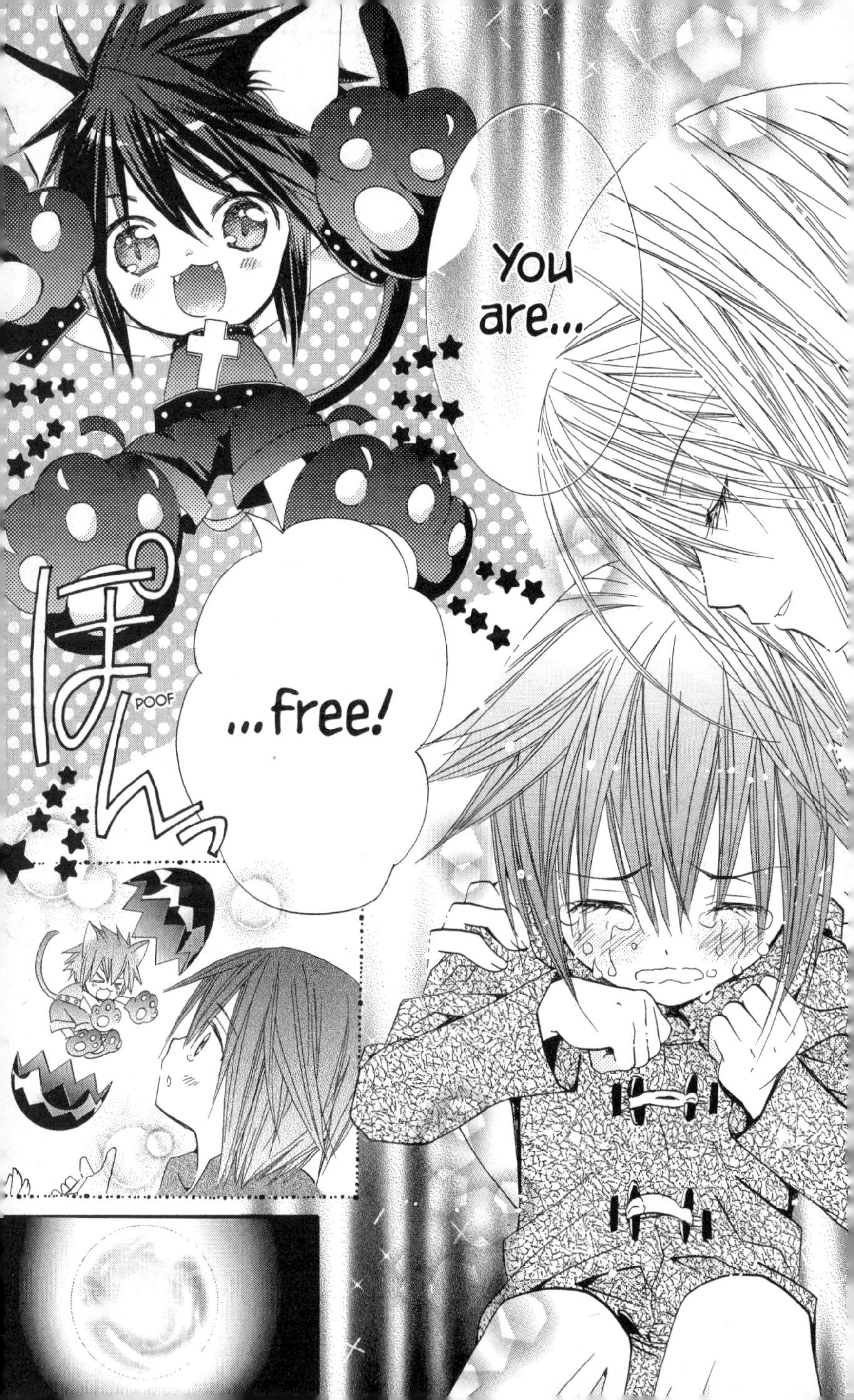
You are...
...free!
ぽん
POOF

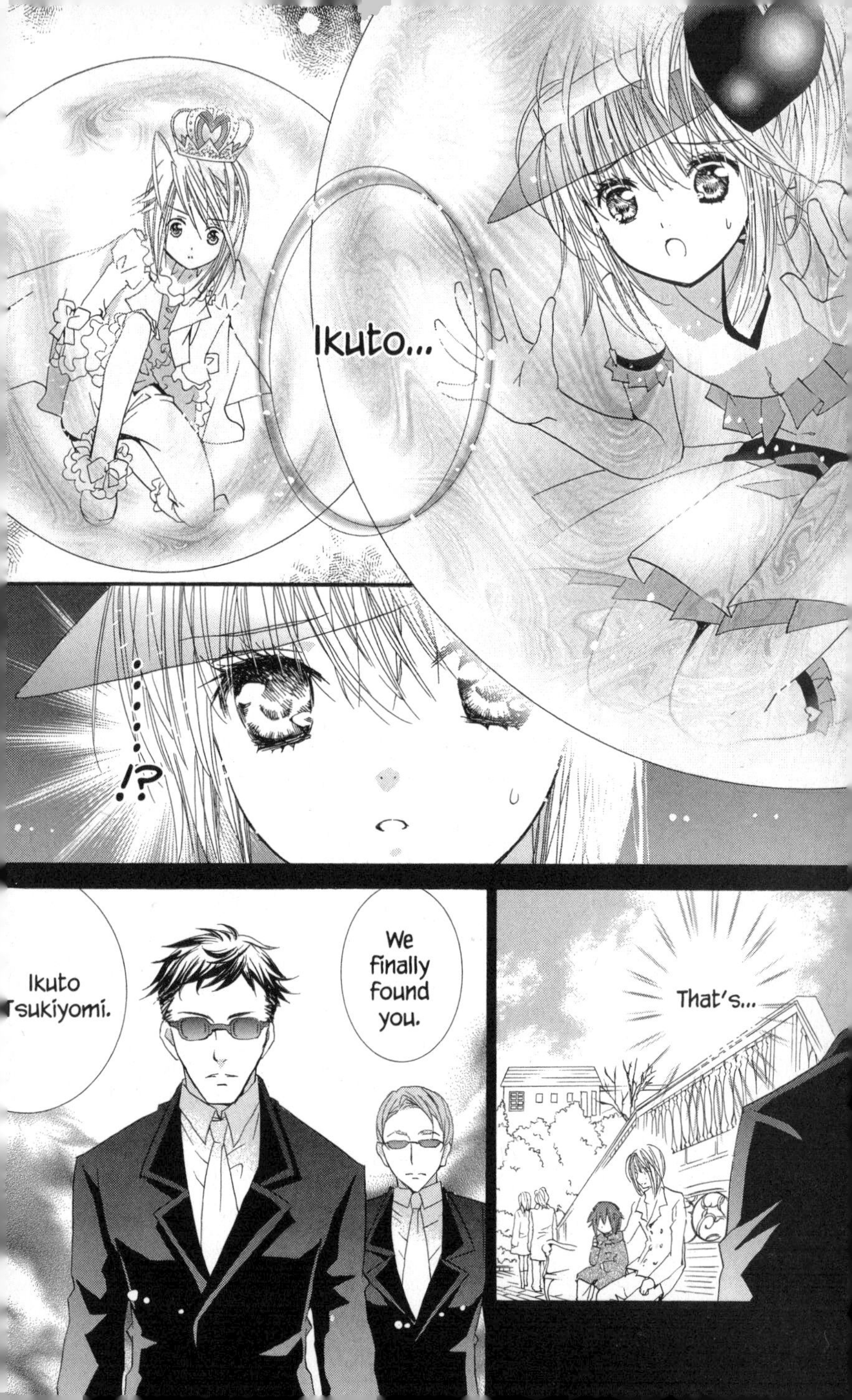
Ikuto...
......!?
That's...
We finally found you.
Ikuto Tsukiyomi.

Shugo
Chara!

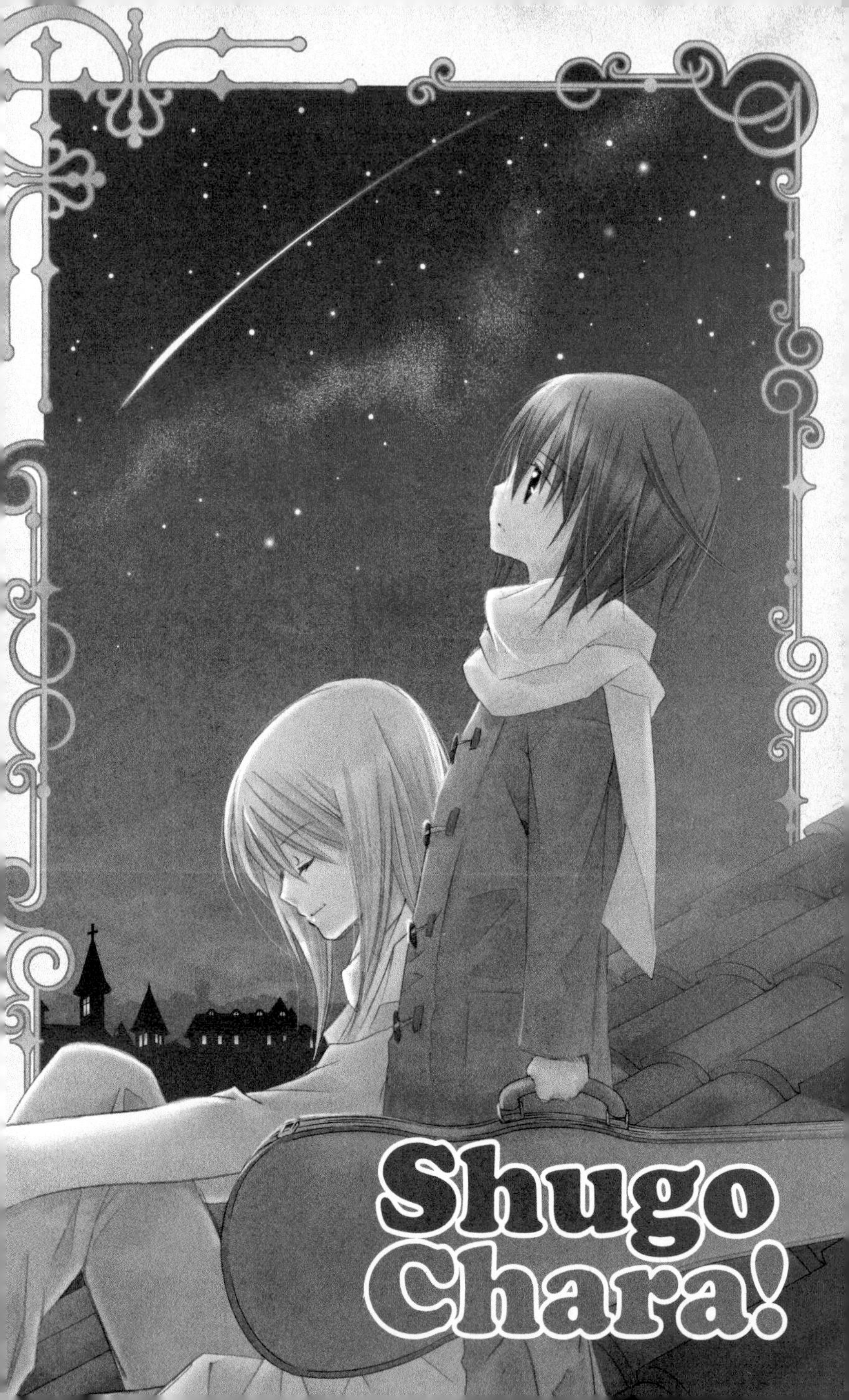
Shugo
Chara!

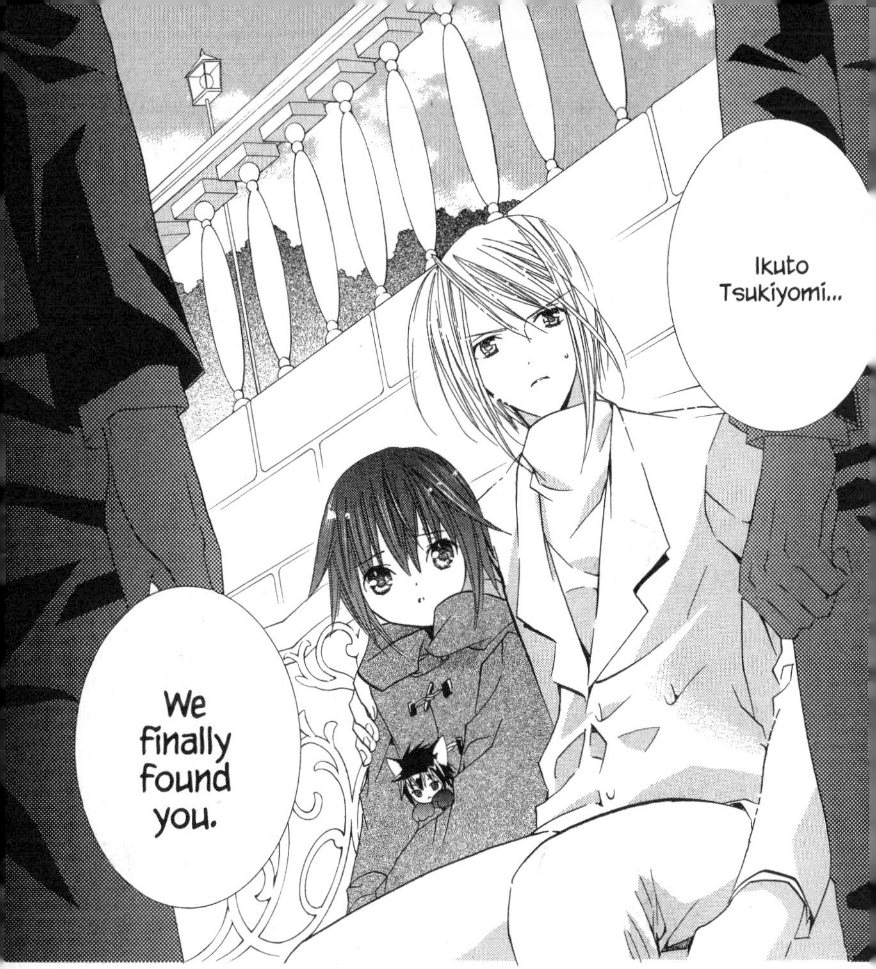
Ikuto Tsukiyomi...
We finally found you.

Q5: Are your personalities like any of the "Shugo Chara!" characters?
A5: It's hard to be objective about ourselves, so we'll each let the other one answer! Banri is similar to Kairi, Nagihiko, and Utau. Shibuko is similar to Amu, Kukai, and Yaya. I guess neither of us are exactly the same as any one character. It might be fun if all our readers tried analyzing which character they're closest to!

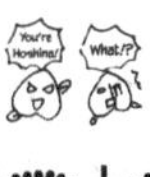
You're Hoshina!
What!?

We'll see you in volume 10!

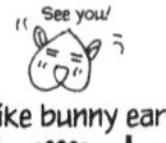
See you!

The leaves look like bunny ears?

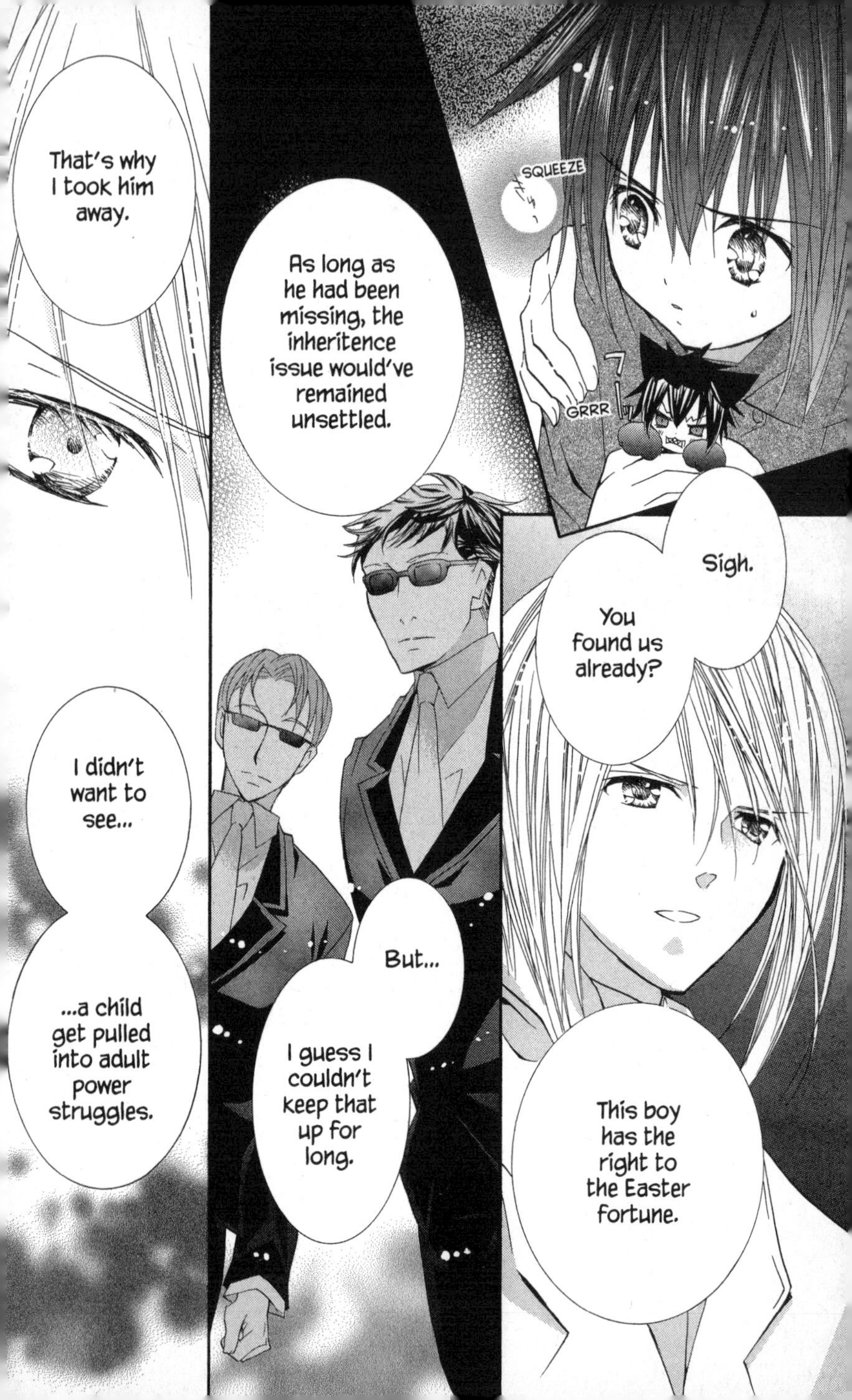
SQUEEZE
GRRR
Sigh.
You found us already?
This boy has the right to the Easter fortune.
As long as he had been missing, the inheritence issue would've remained unsettled.
But...
I guess I couldn't keep that up for long.
That's why I took him away.
I didn't want to see...
...a child get pulled into adult power struggles.

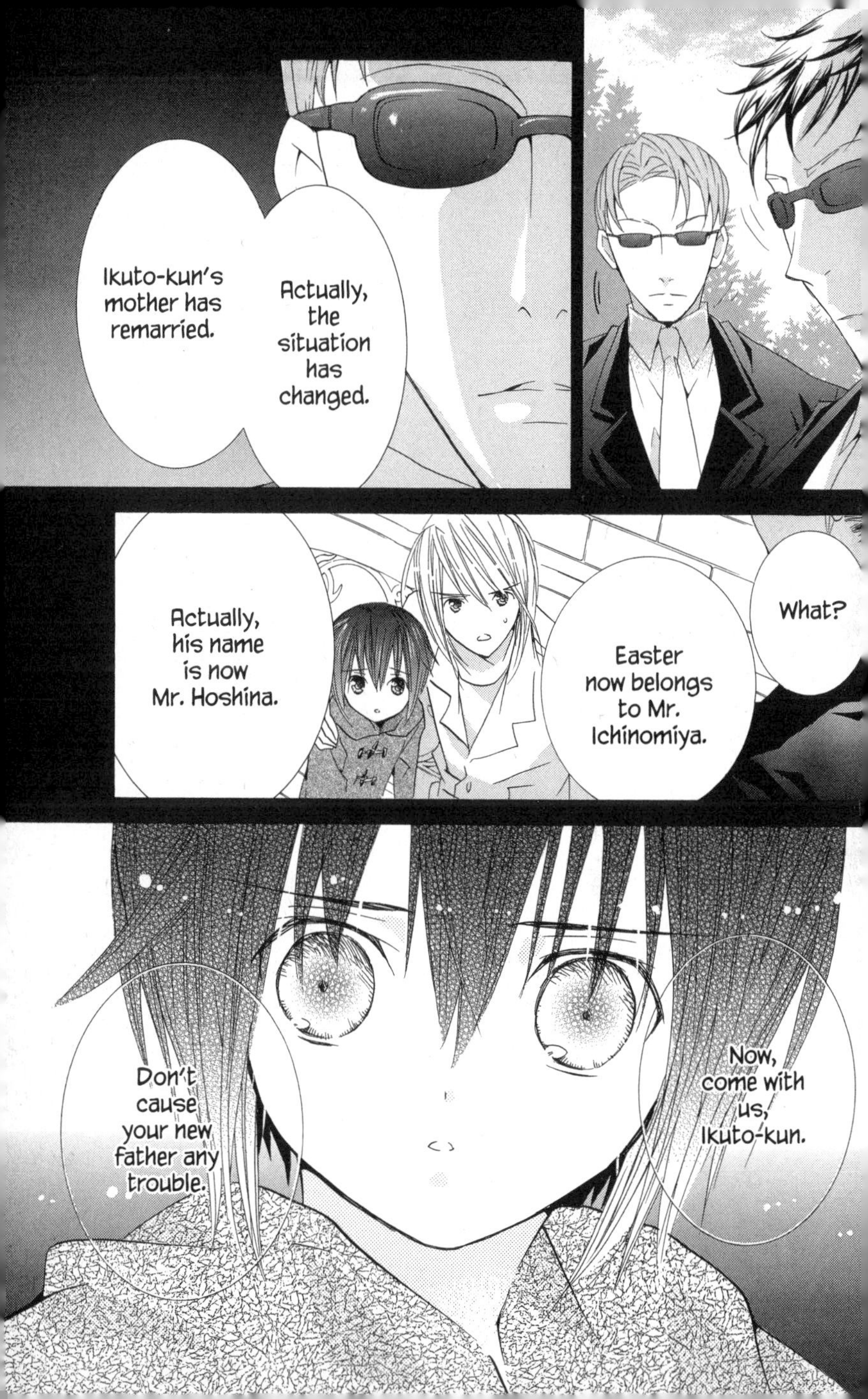
Actually, the situation has changed.
Ikuto-kun's mother has remarried.
What?
Easter now belongs to Mr. Ichinomiya.
Actually, his name is now Mr. Hoshina.
Now, come with us, Ikuto-kun.
Don't cause your new father any trouble.

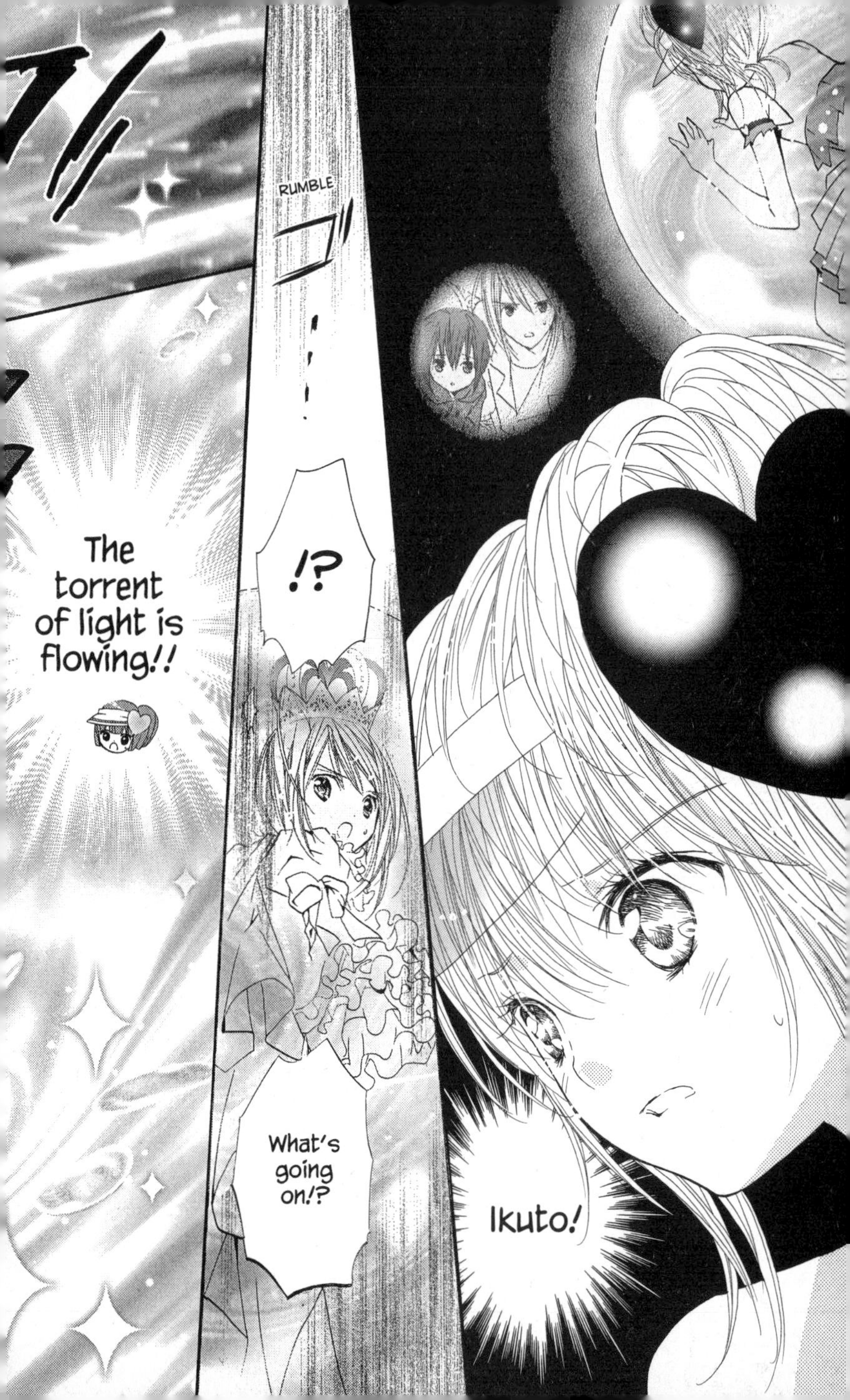
Ikuto!
RUMBLE
!?
What's going on!?
The torrent of light is flowing!!

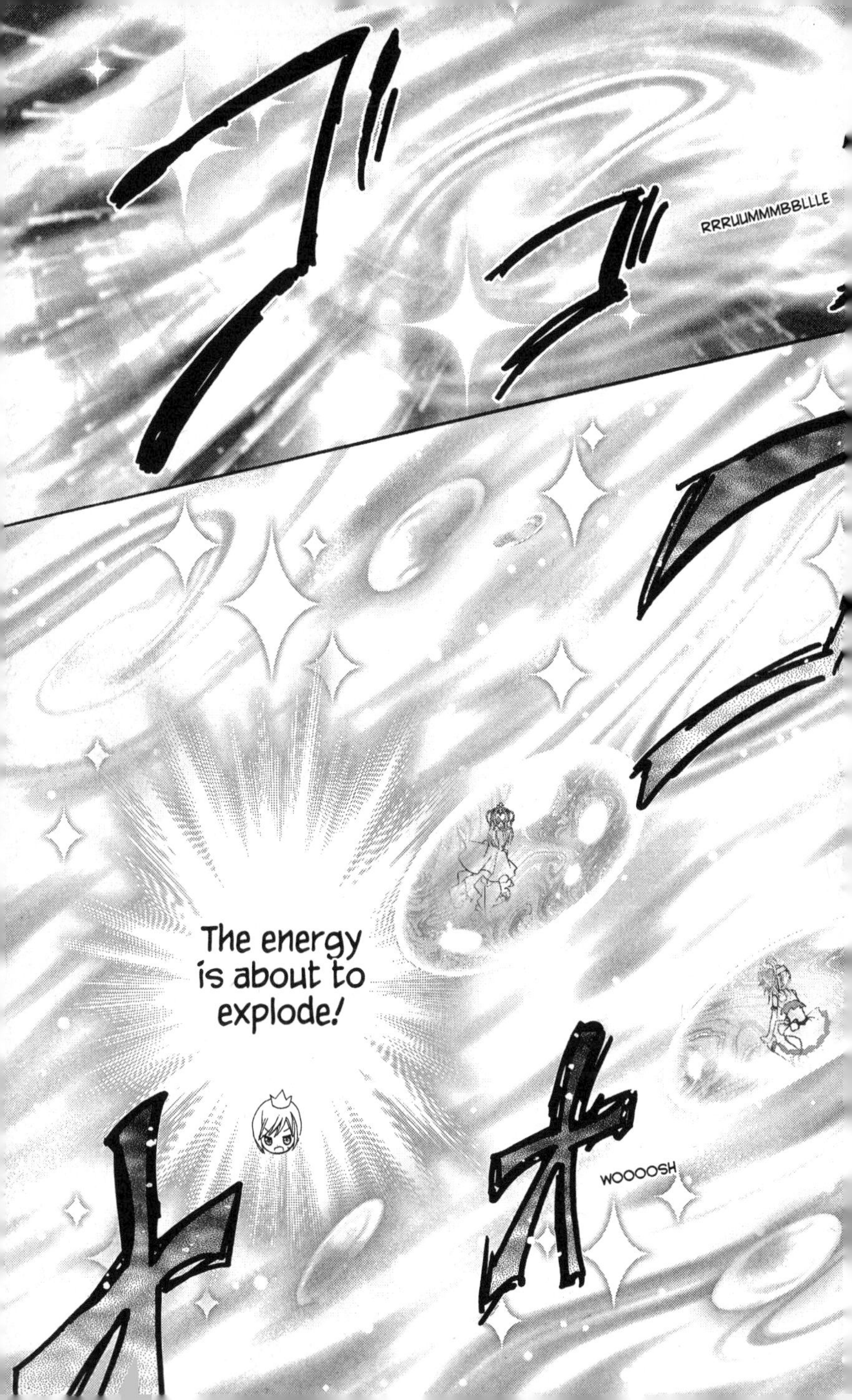
RRRUUMMMBBLLLE
The energy is about to explode!
WOOOOSH

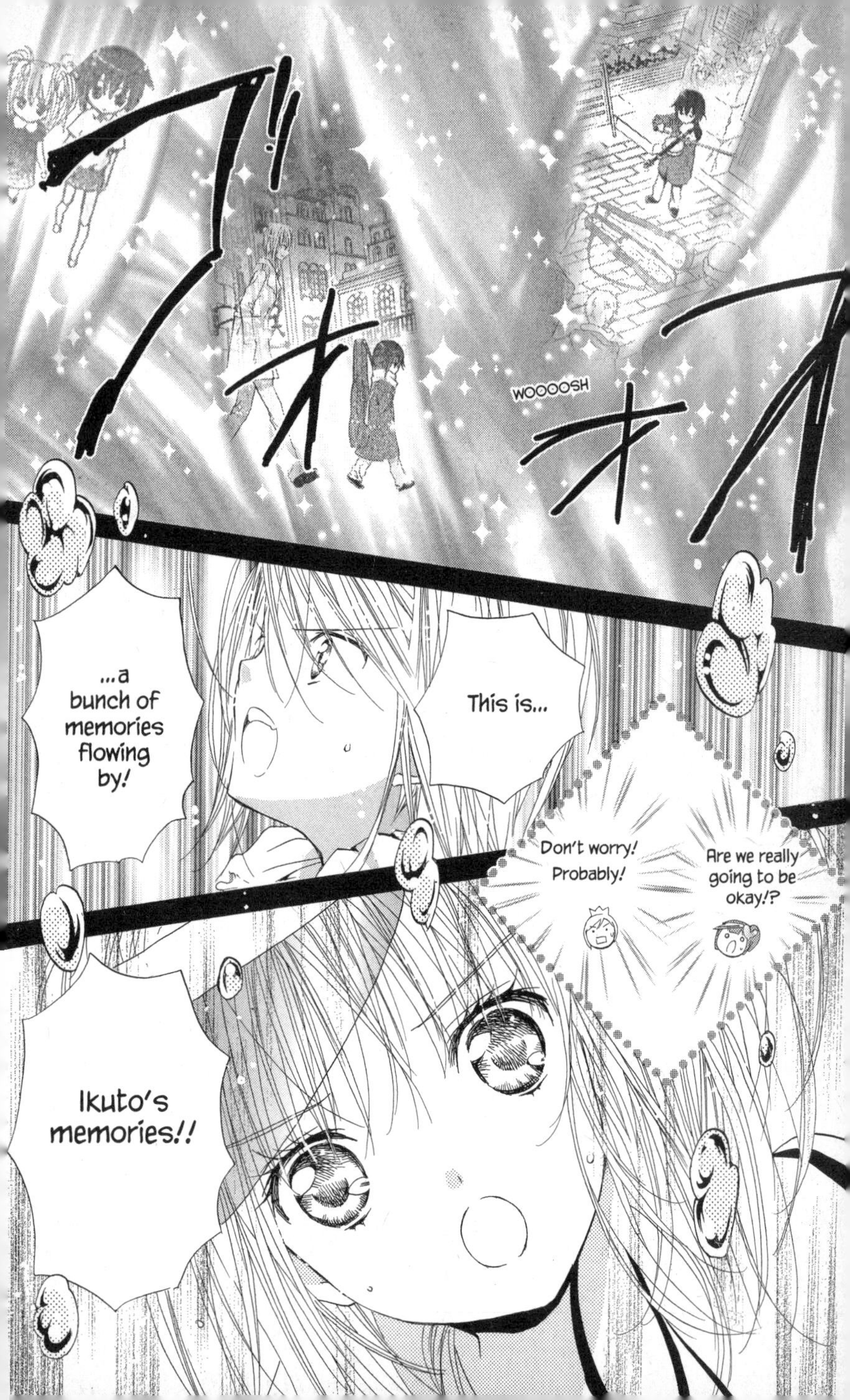
WOOOOSH
This is...
...a bunch of memories flowing by!
Are we really going to be okay!?
Don't worry! Probably!
Ikuto's memories!!

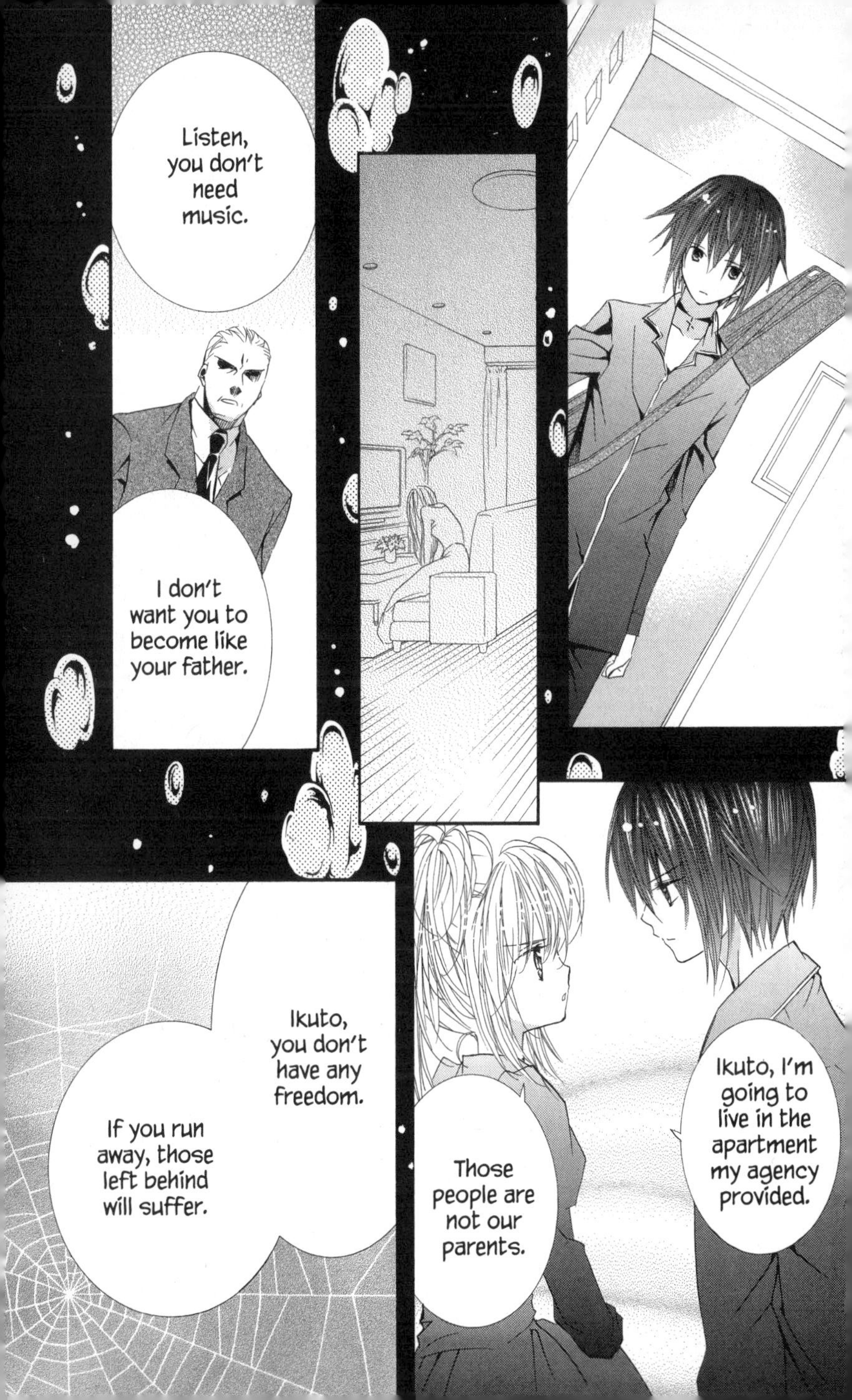
Listen, you don't need music.
I don't want you to become like your father.
Ikuto, I'm going to live in the apartment my agency provided.
Those people are not our parents.
Ikuto, you don't have any freedom.
If you run away, those left behind will suffer.

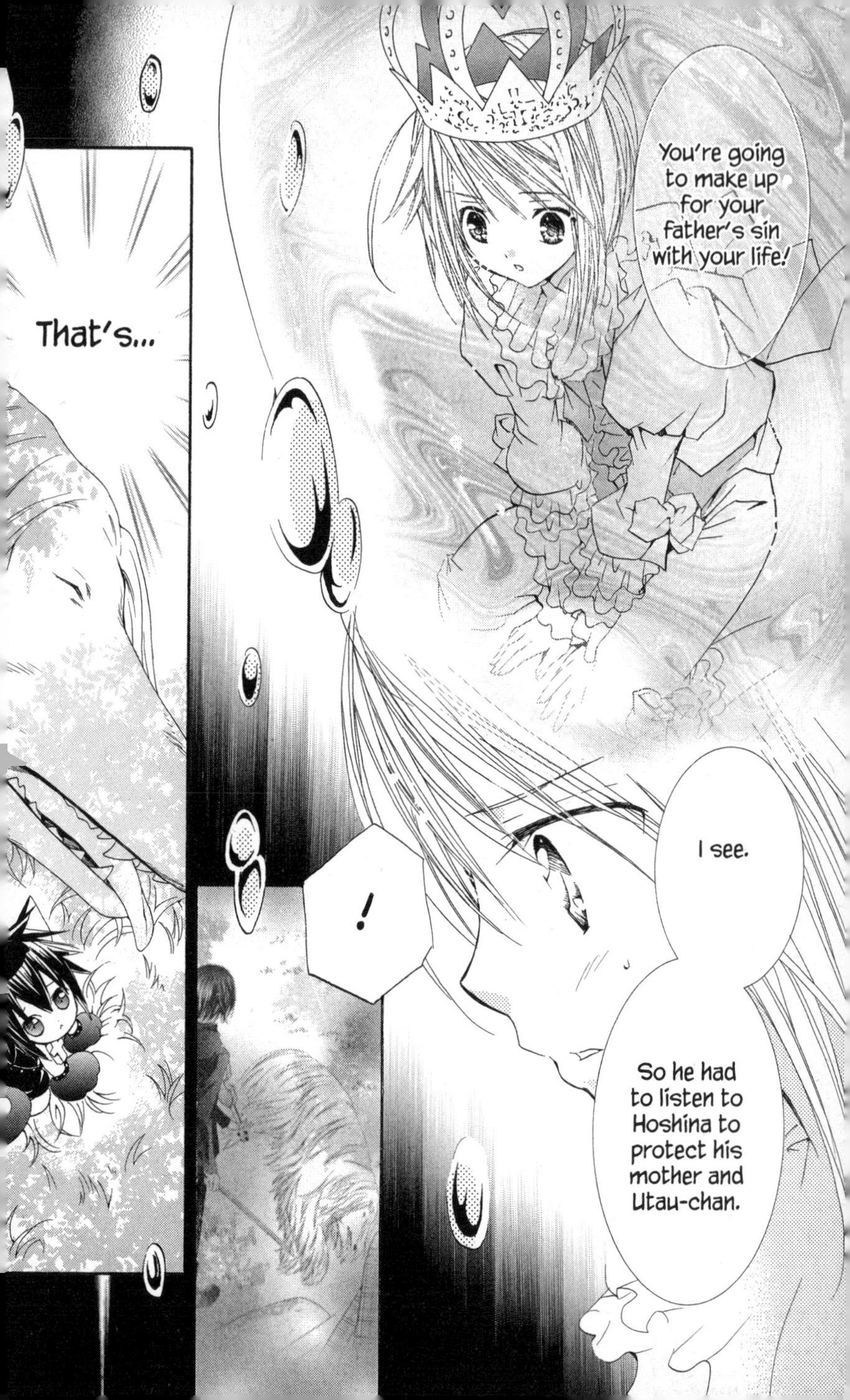
You're going to make up for your father's sin with your life!
I see.
!
So he had to listen to Hoshina to protect his mother and Utau-chan.
That's...

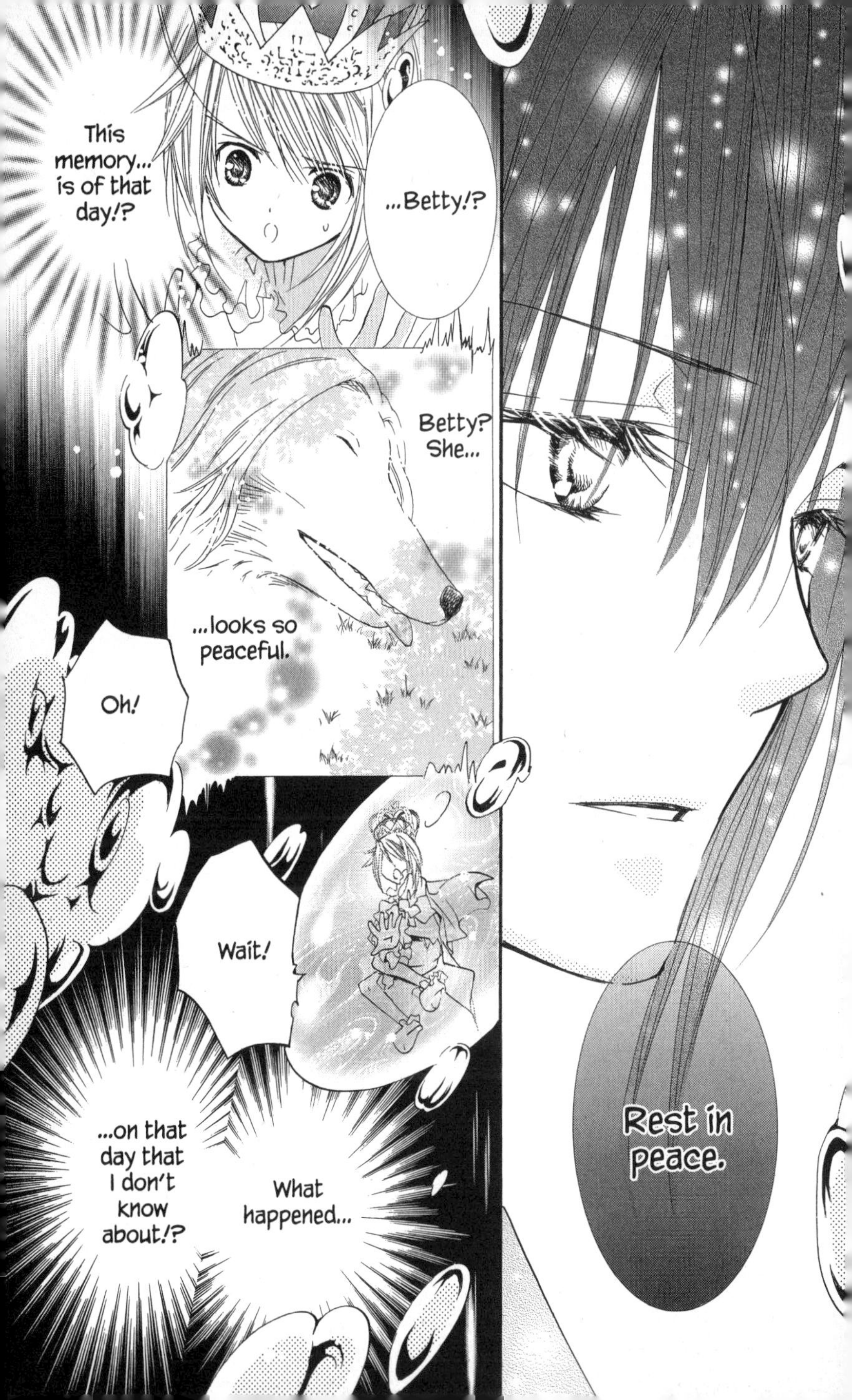
Rest in peace.
...Betty!?
This memory... is of that day!?
Betty? She...
...looks so peaceful.
Oh!
Wait!
What happened...
...on that day that I don't know about!?

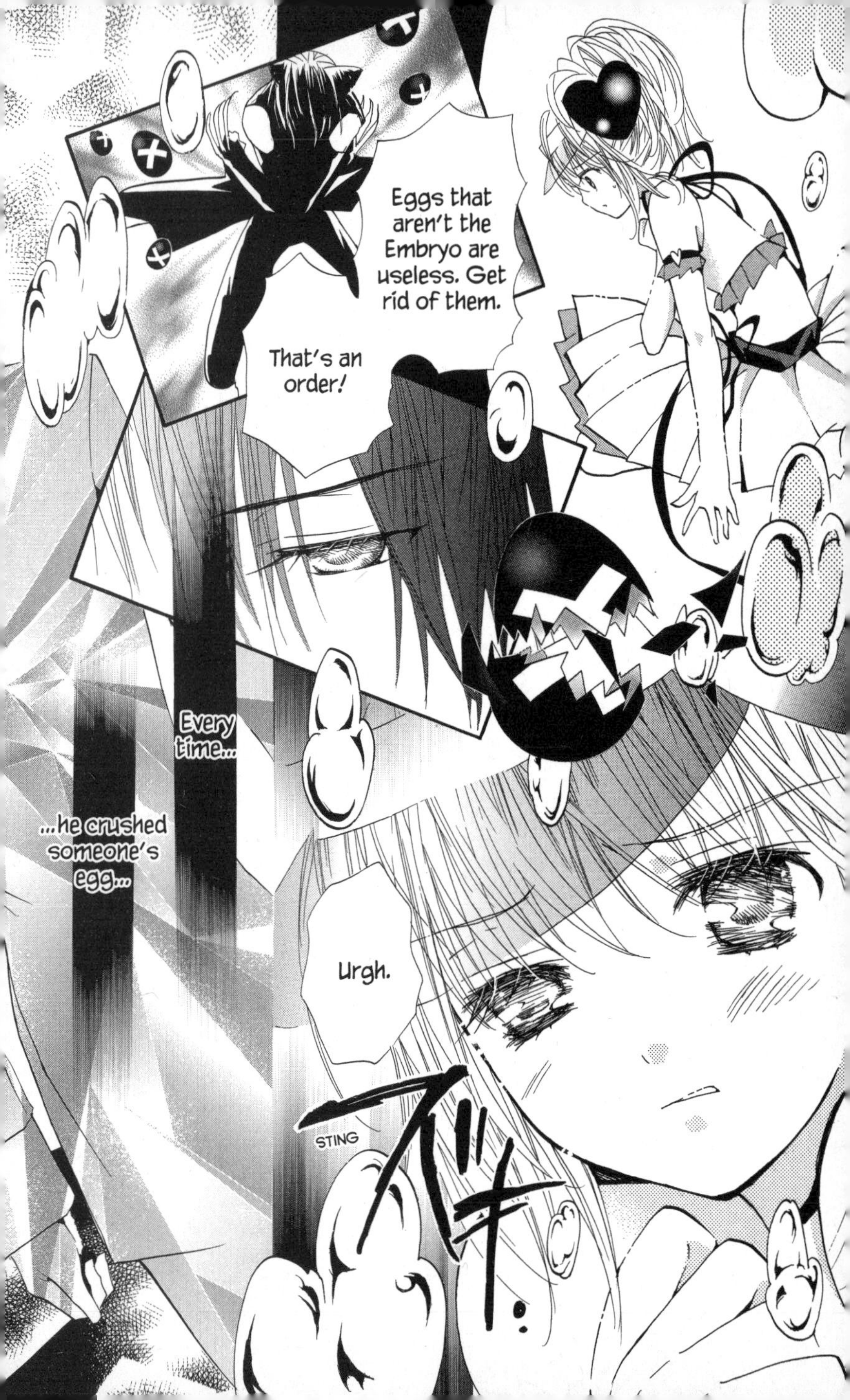
Eggs that aren't the Embryo are useless. Get rid of them.
That's an order!
Every time...
...he crushed someone's egg...
Urgh.
STING

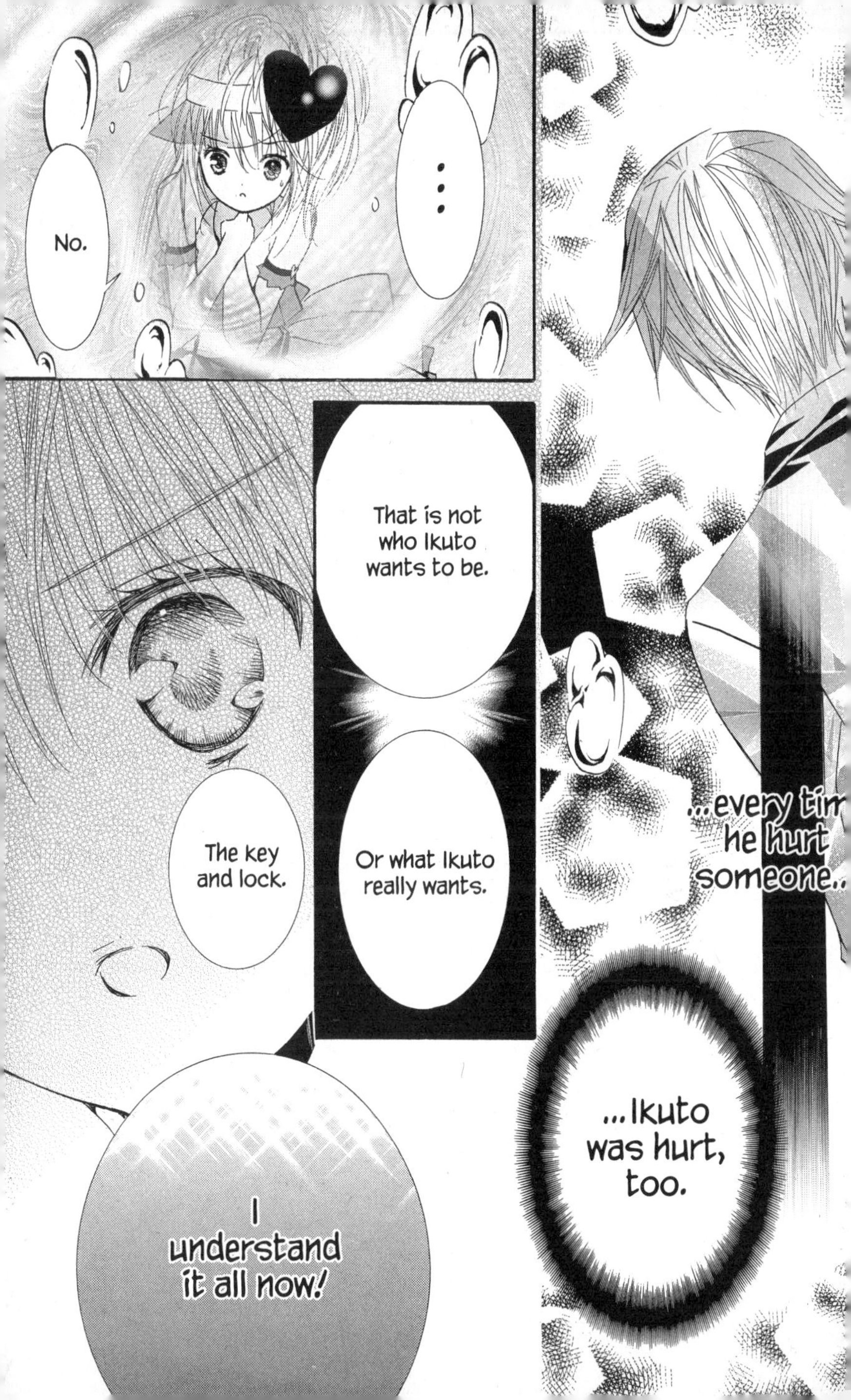
...every tim he hurt someone...
...Ikuto was hurt, too.
...
No.
That is not who Ikuto wants to be.
Or what Ikuto really wants.
The key and lock.
I understand it all now!

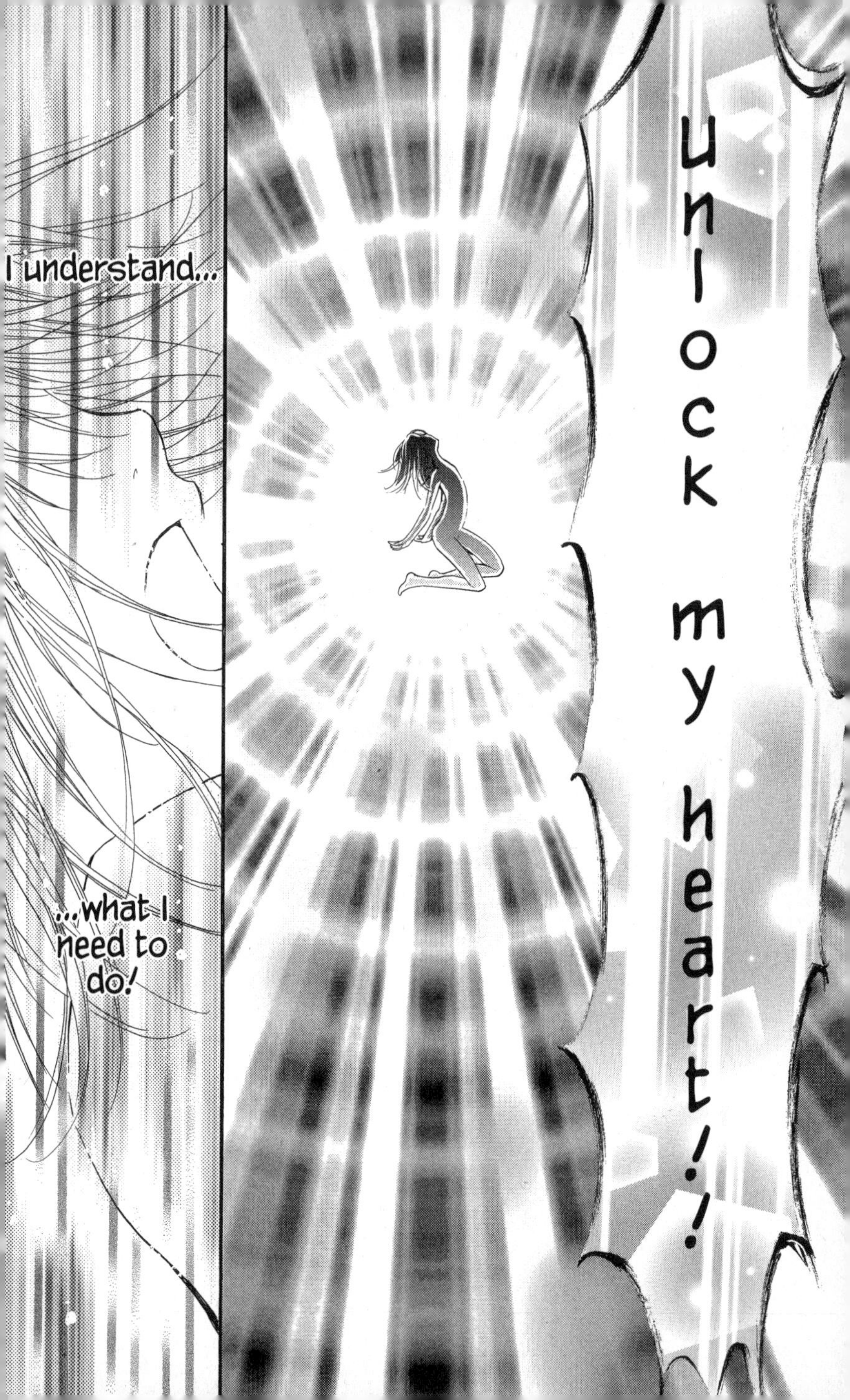
Unlock my heart!!
I understand...
...what I need to do!

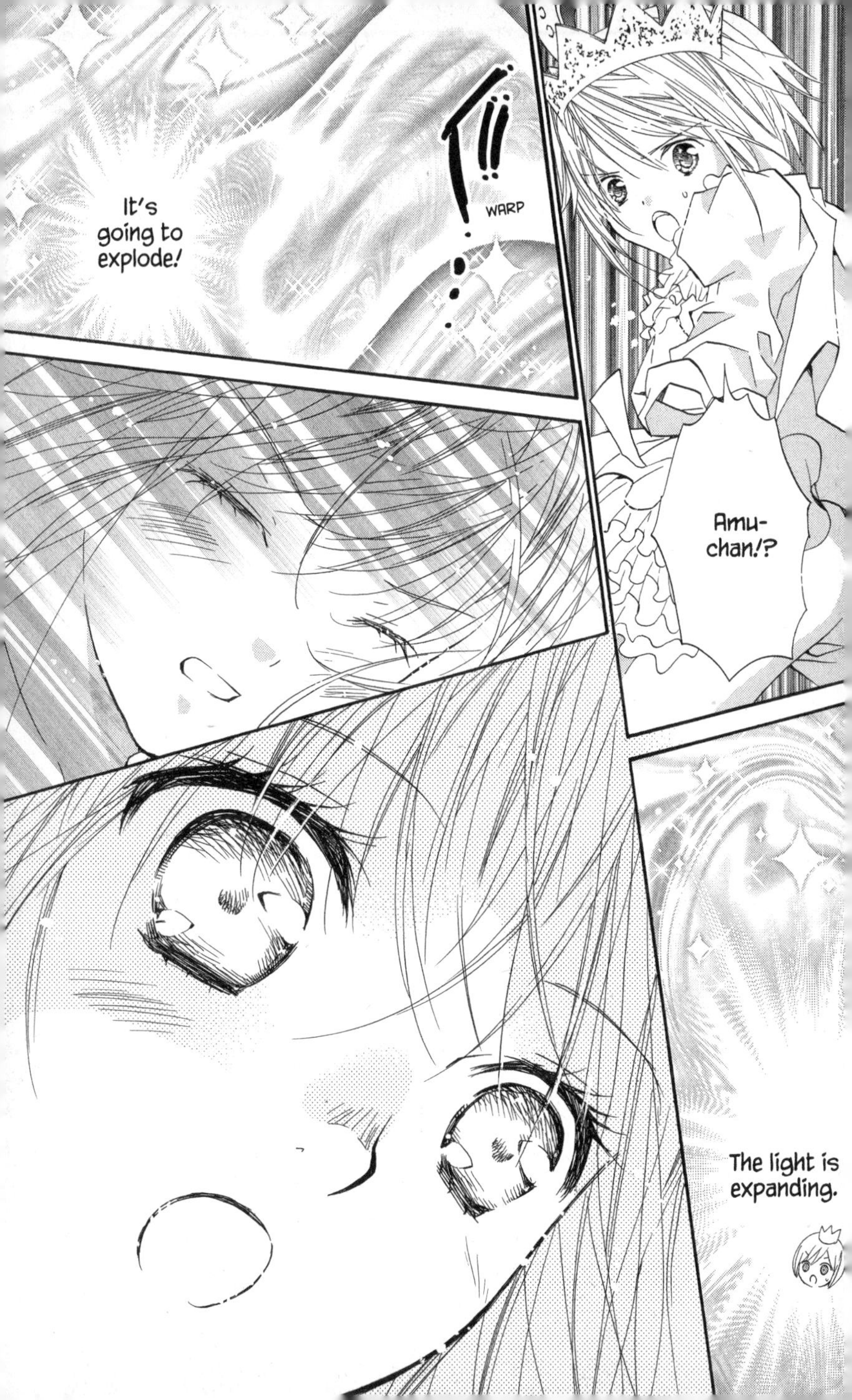
Amu-
chan!?
!!
WARP
It's
going to
explode!
The light is
expanding.

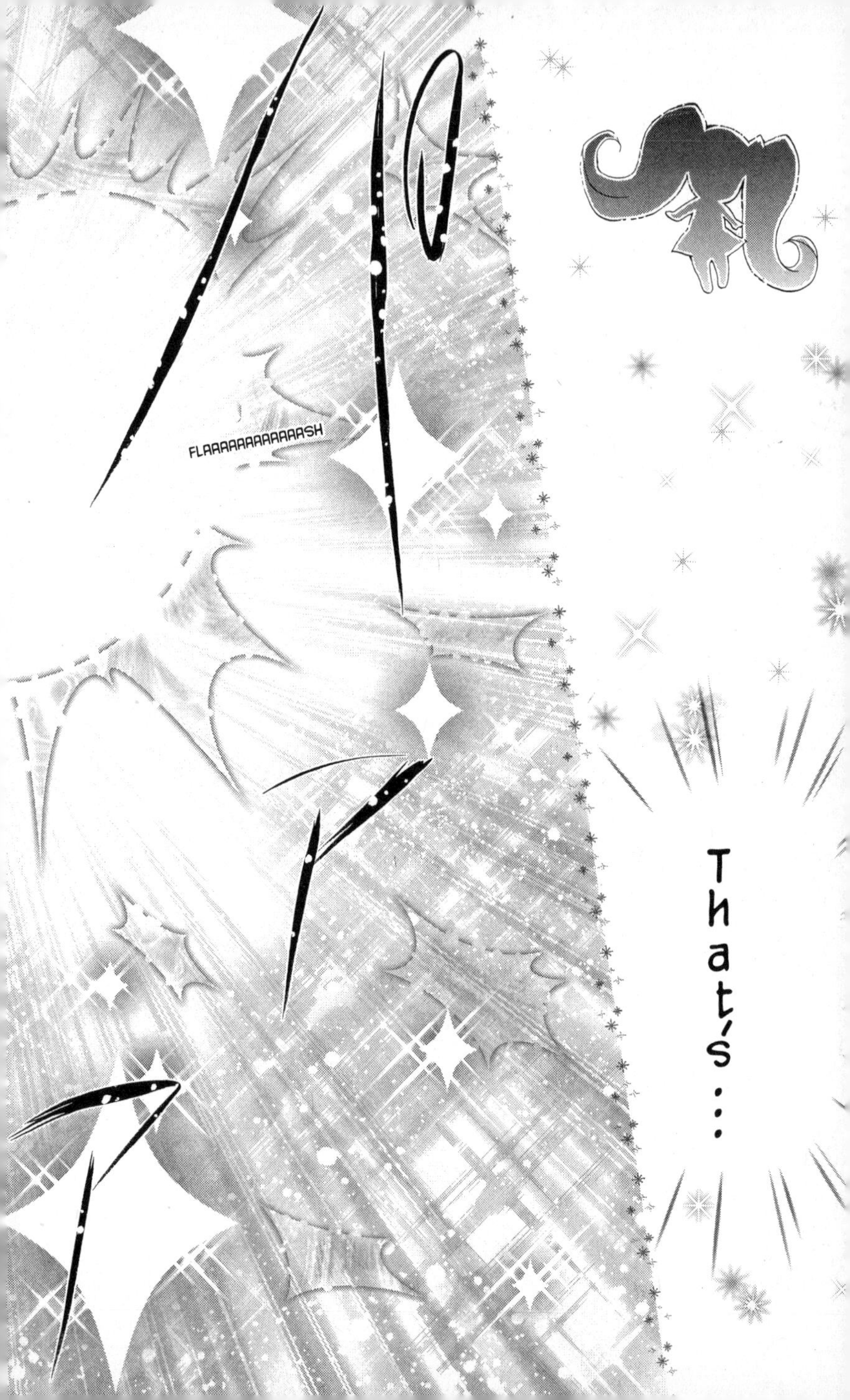
That's...
FLAAAAAAAAAAAAASH

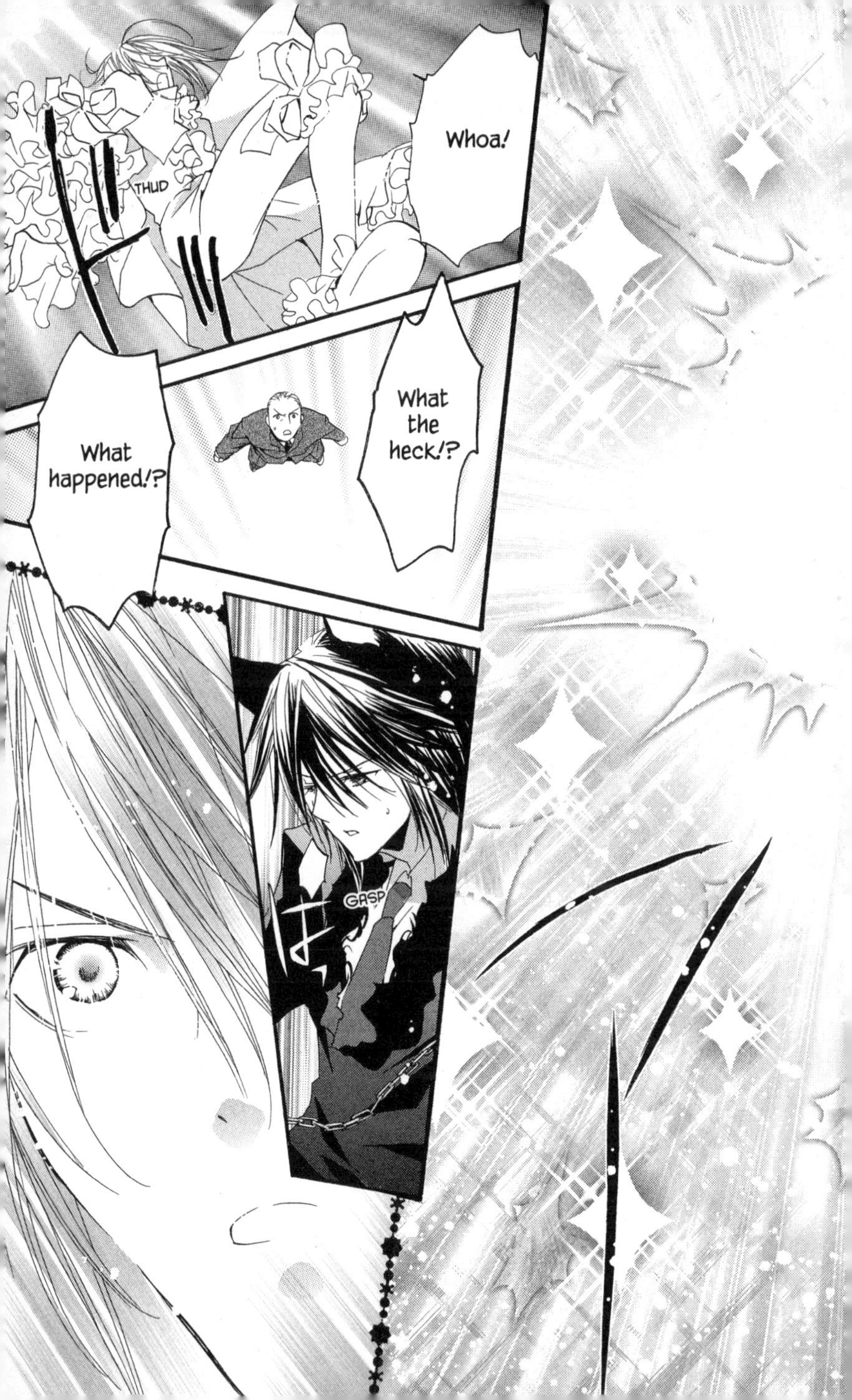
Whoa!
THUD
What the heck!?
What happened!?
GASP

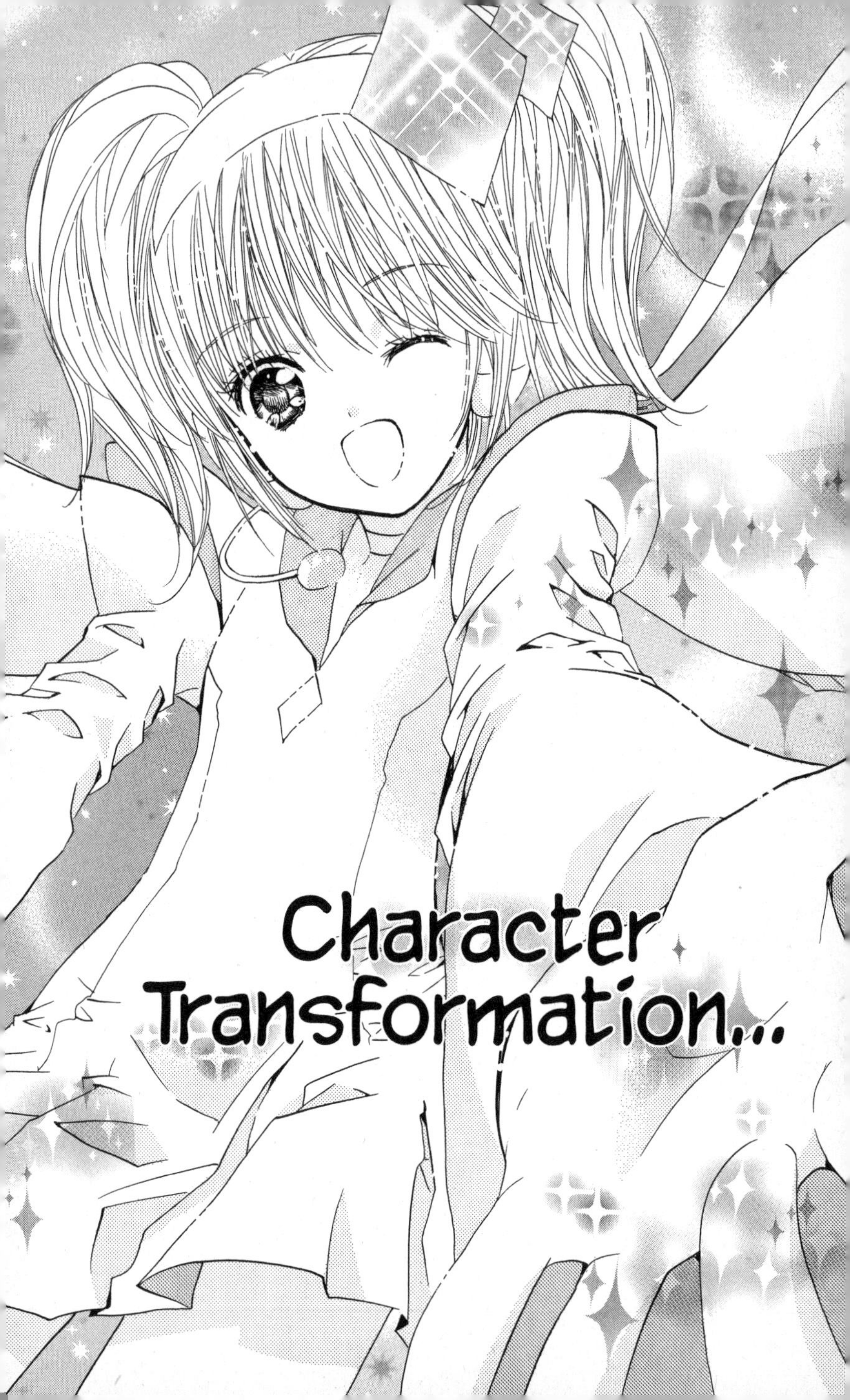
Character Transformation...

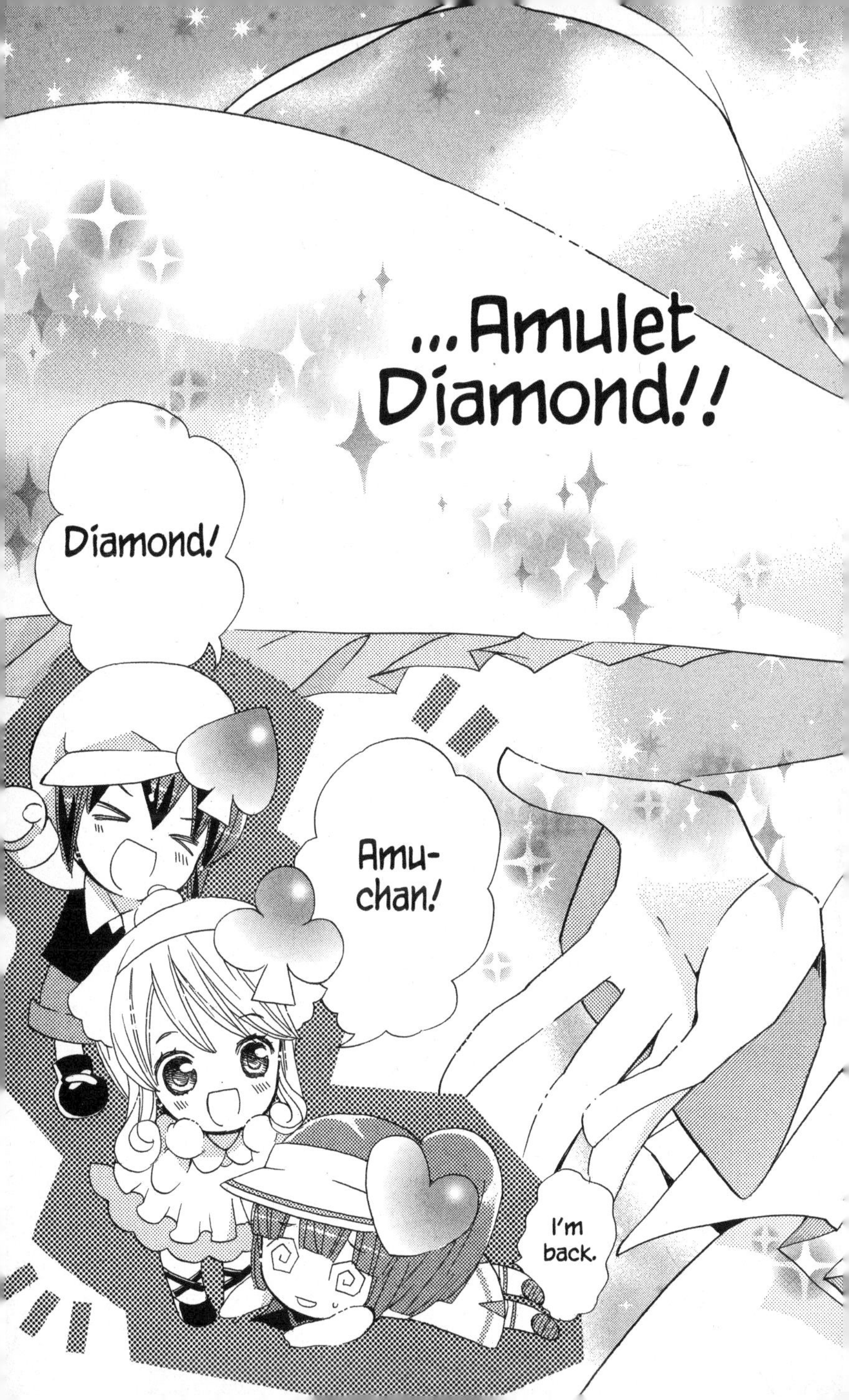
...Amulet Diamond!!
Diamond!
Amu-chan!
I'm back.

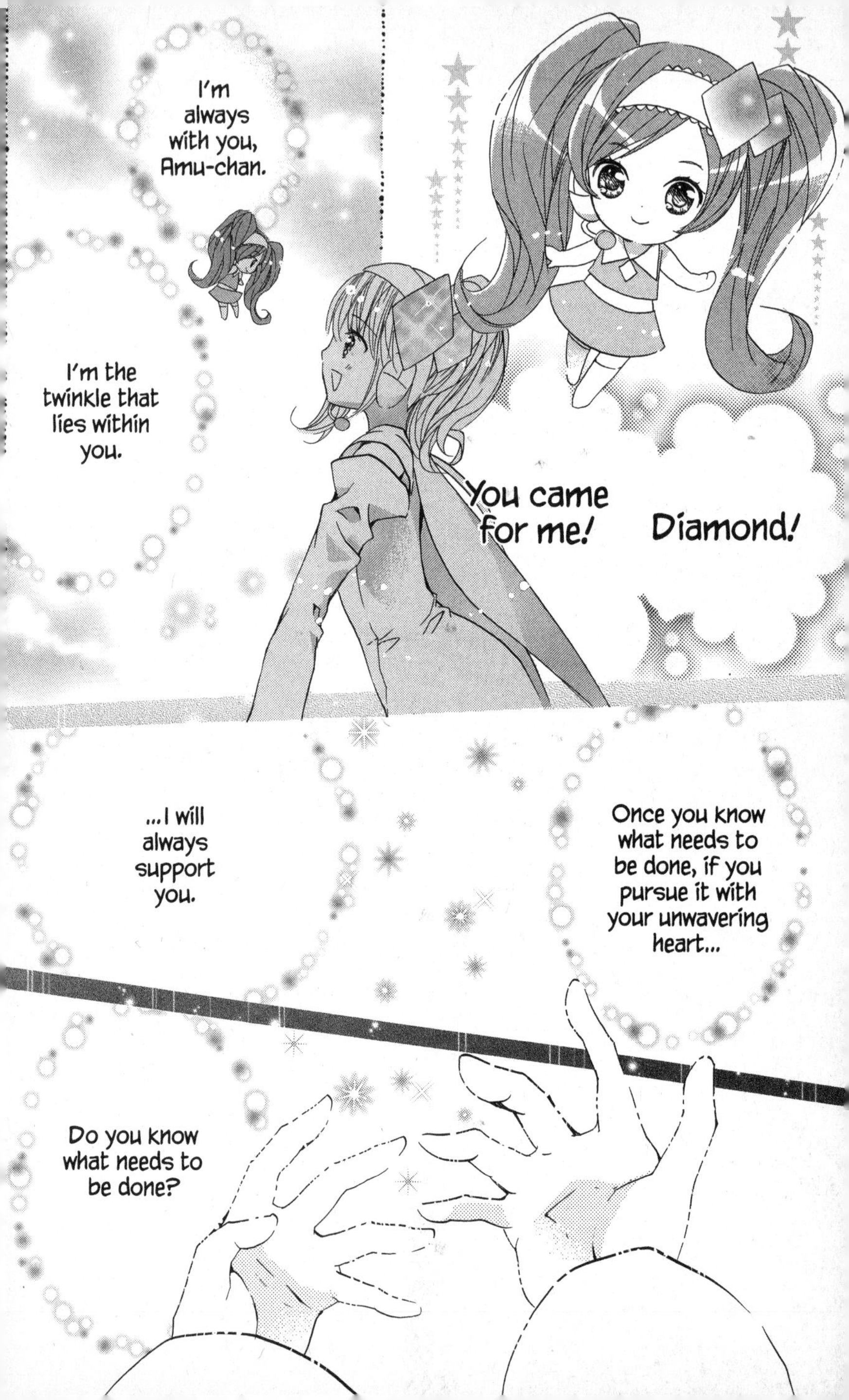
Diamond!
You came for me!
I'm always with you, Amu-chan.
I'm the twinkle that lies within you.
Once you know what needs to be done, if you pursue it with your unwavering heart...
...I will always support you.
Do you know what needs to be done?

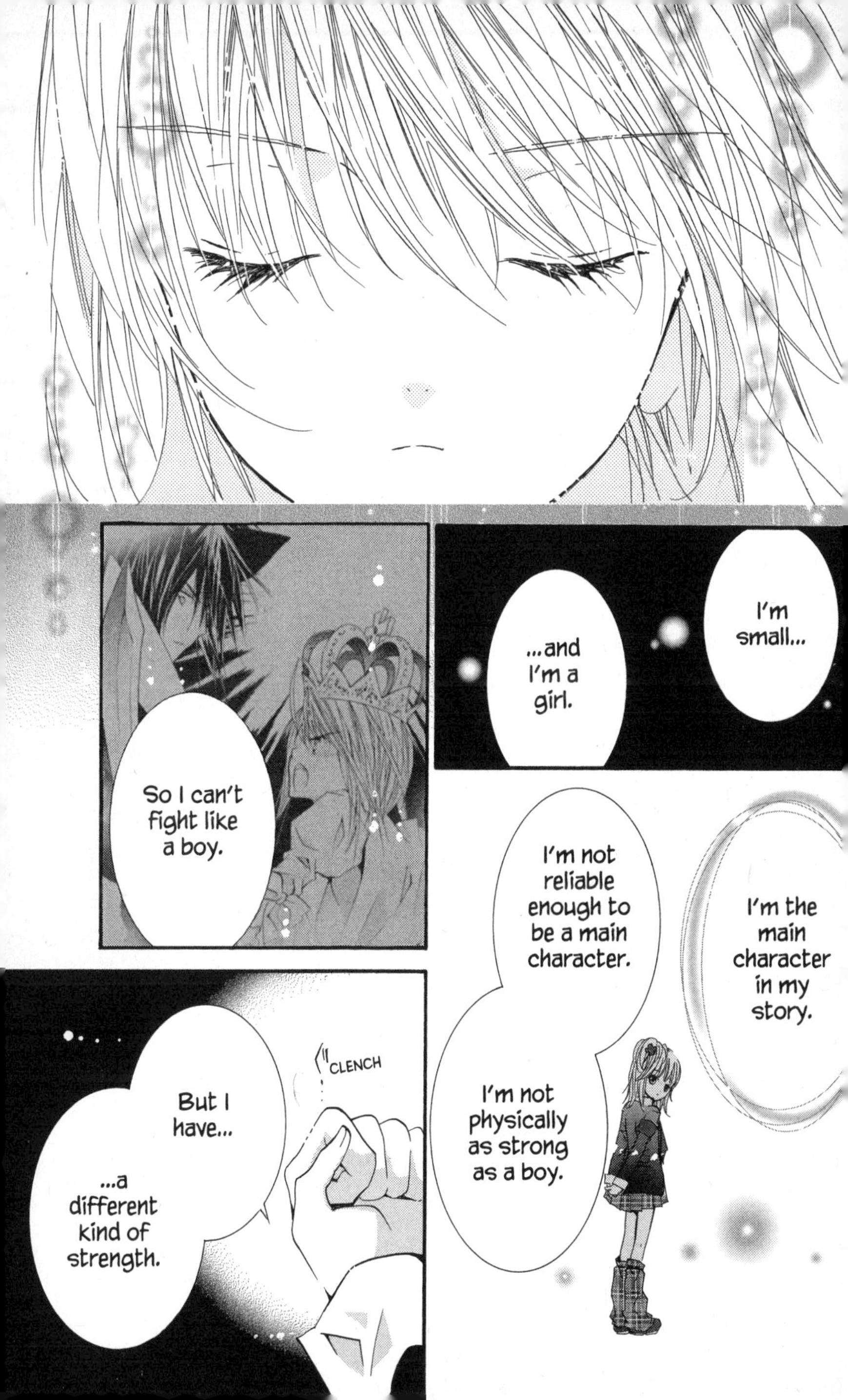
I'm small...
...and I'm a girl.
So I can't fight like a boy.
I'm the main character in my story.
I'm not reliable enough to be a main character.
I'm not physically as strong as a boy.
CLENCH
But I have...
...a different kind of strength.

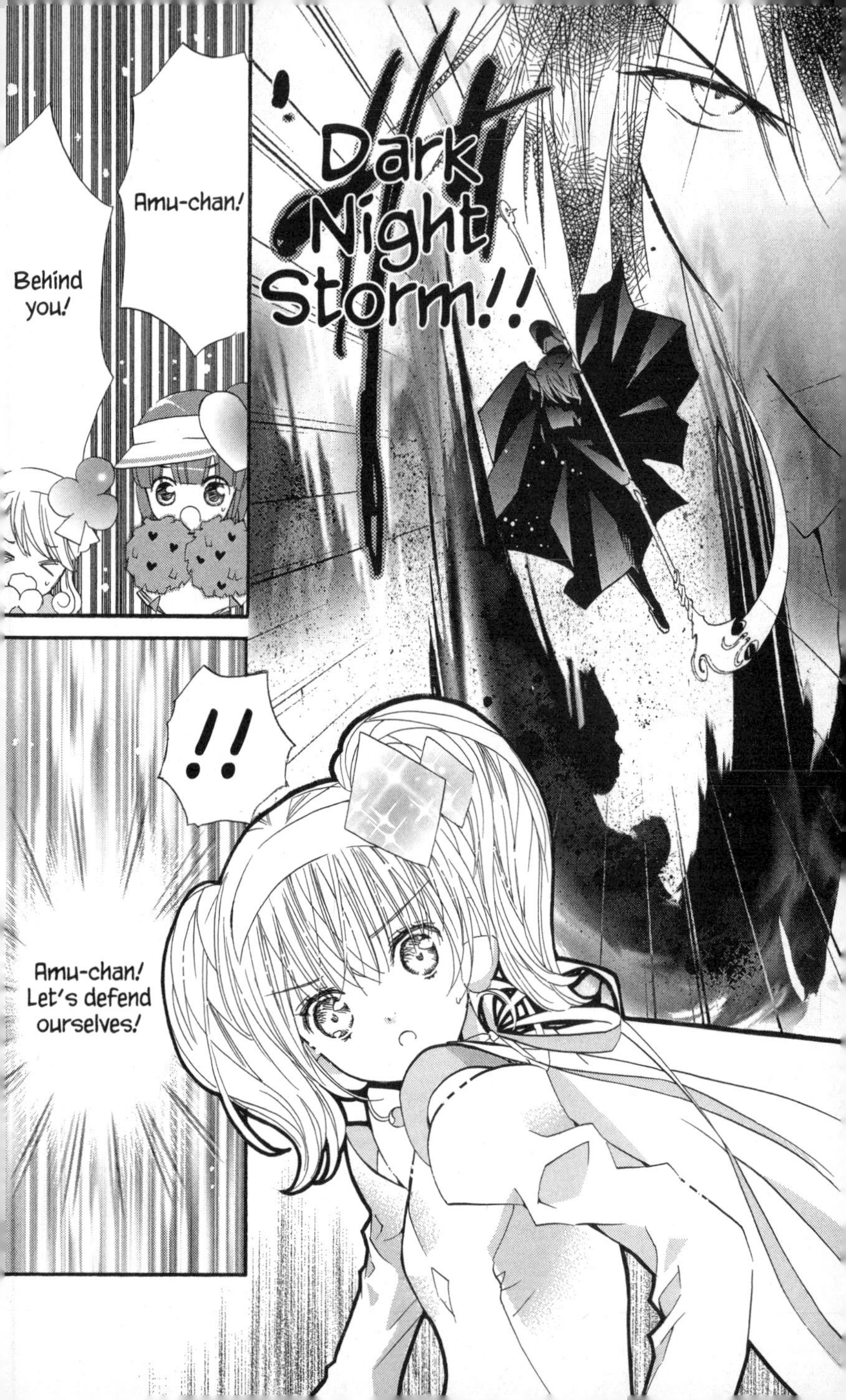
Dark Night Storm!!
!!
Amu-chan!
Behind you!
Amu-chan! Let's defend ourselves!

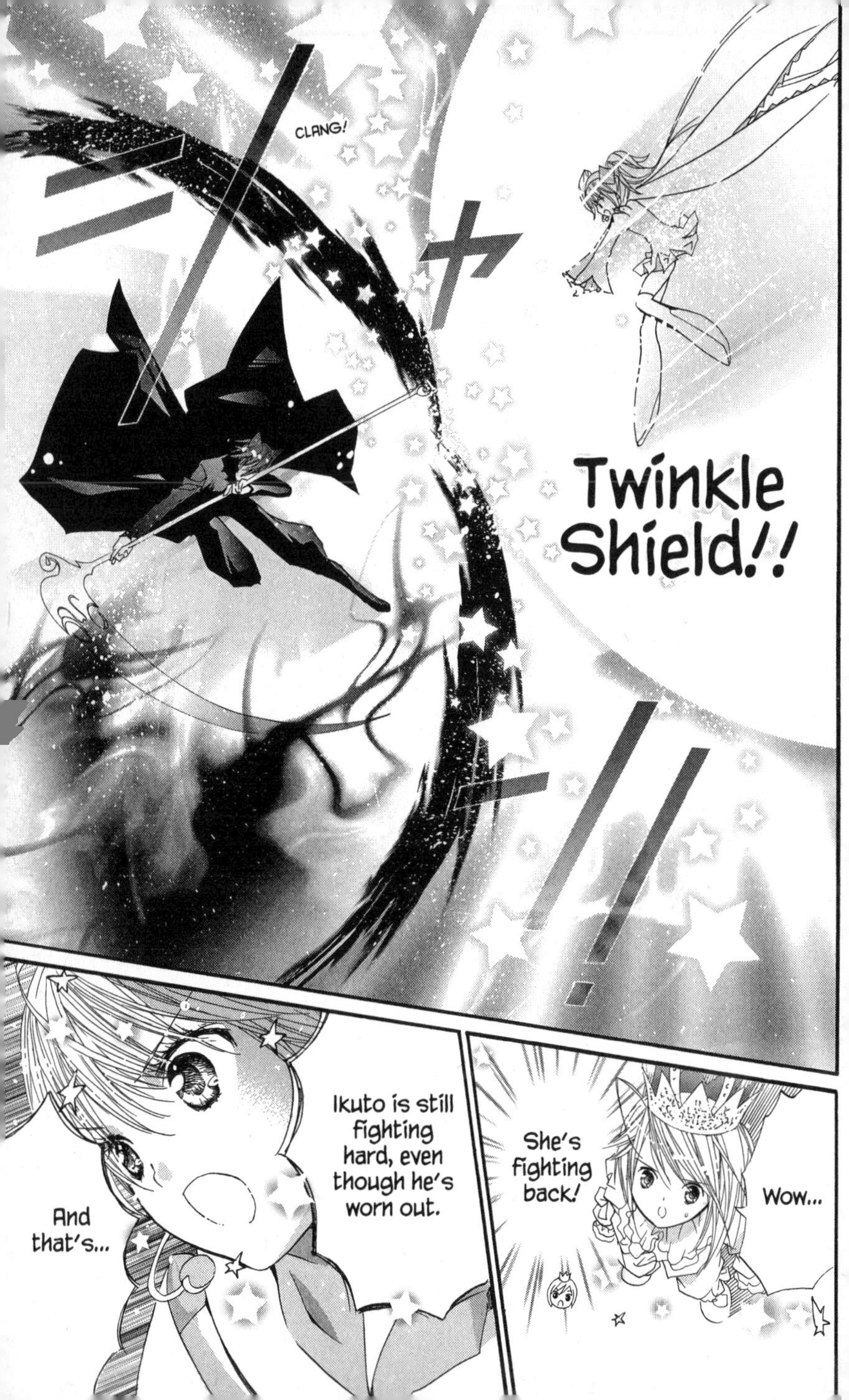
CLANG!
Twinkle Shield!!
Wow...
She's fighting back!
Ikuto is still fighting hard, even though he's worn out.
And that's...

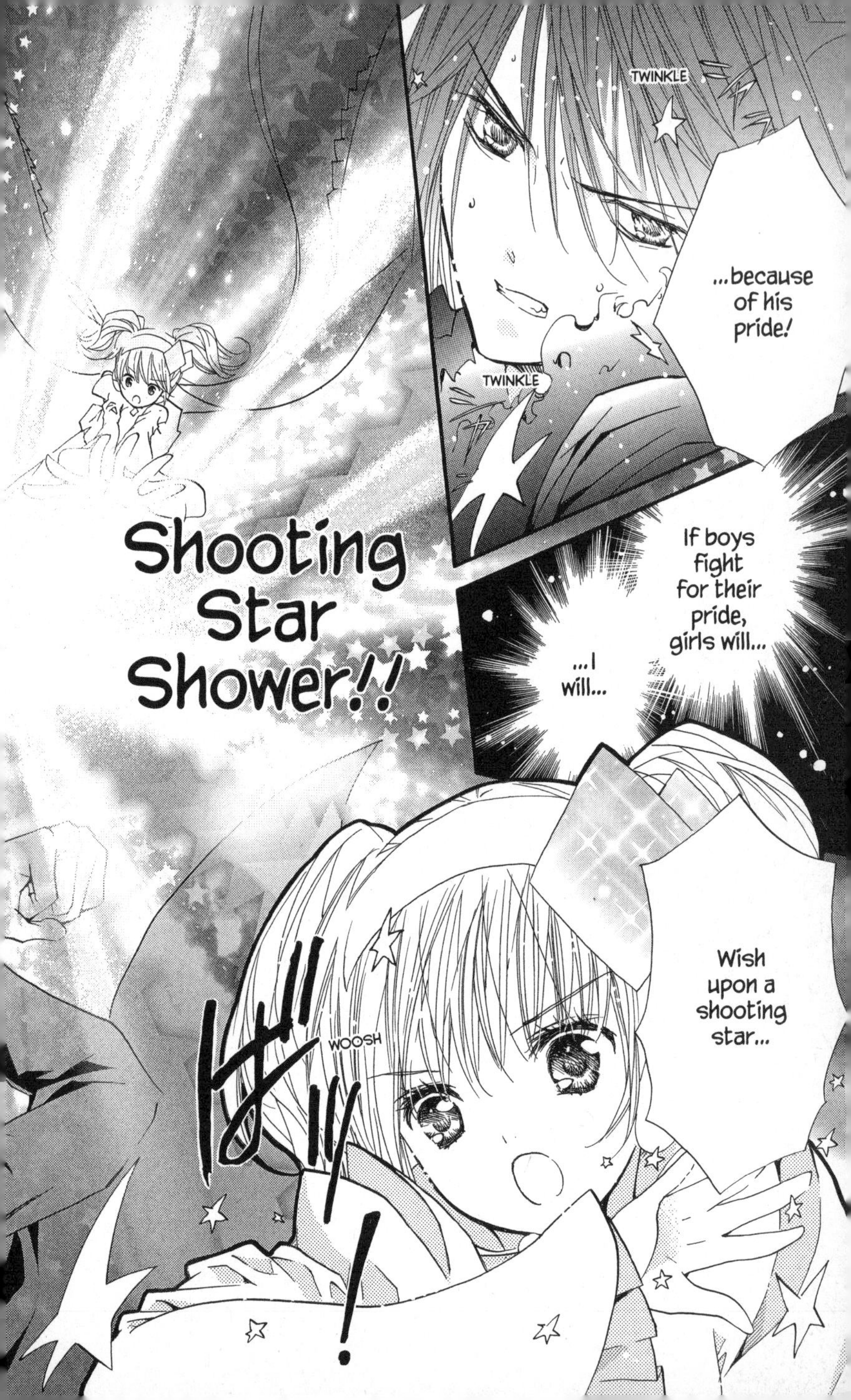
TWINKLE
...because of his pride!
TWINKLE
If boys fight for their pride, girls will...
...I will...
Wish upon a shooting star...
WOOSH
Shooting Star Shower!!

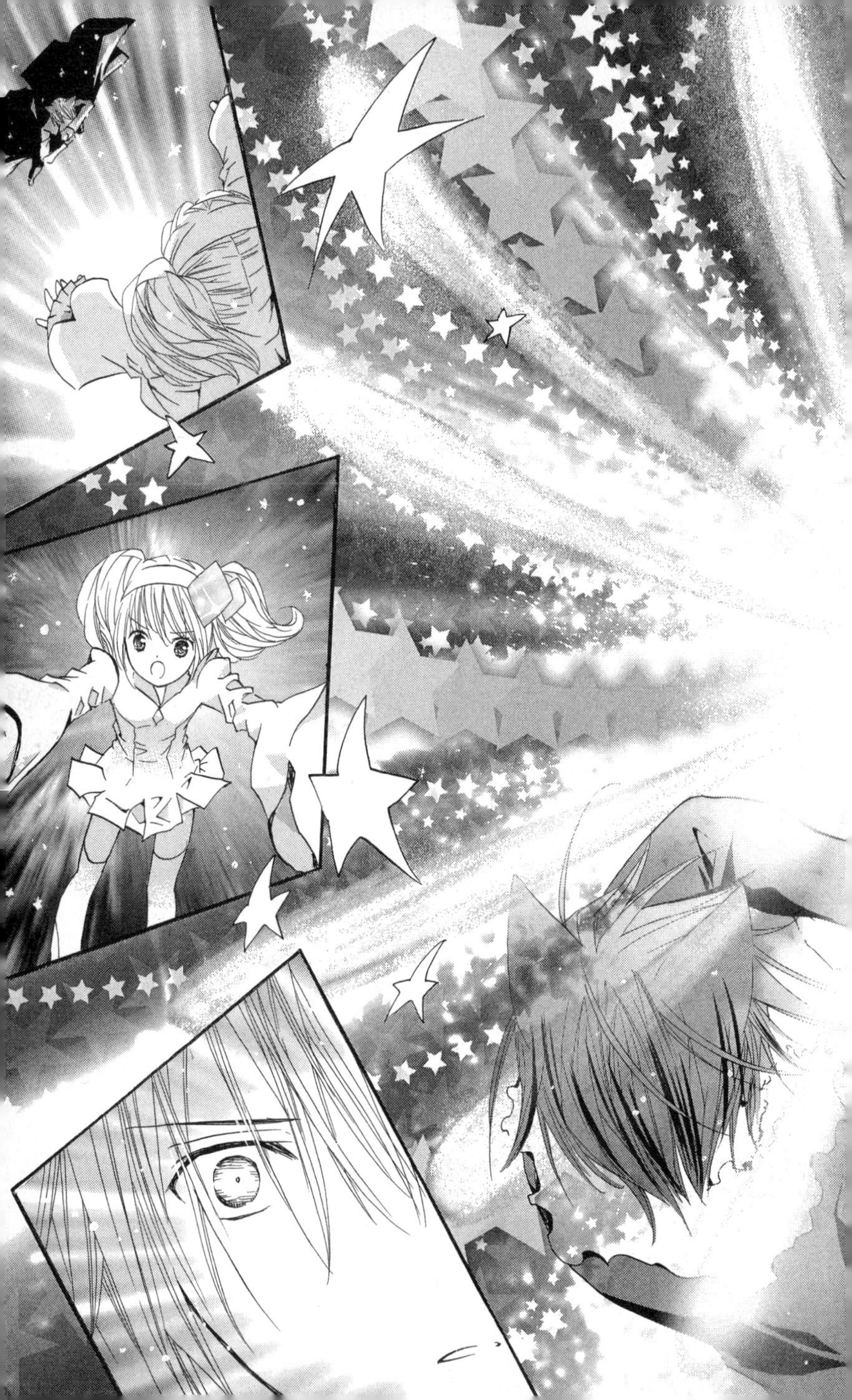

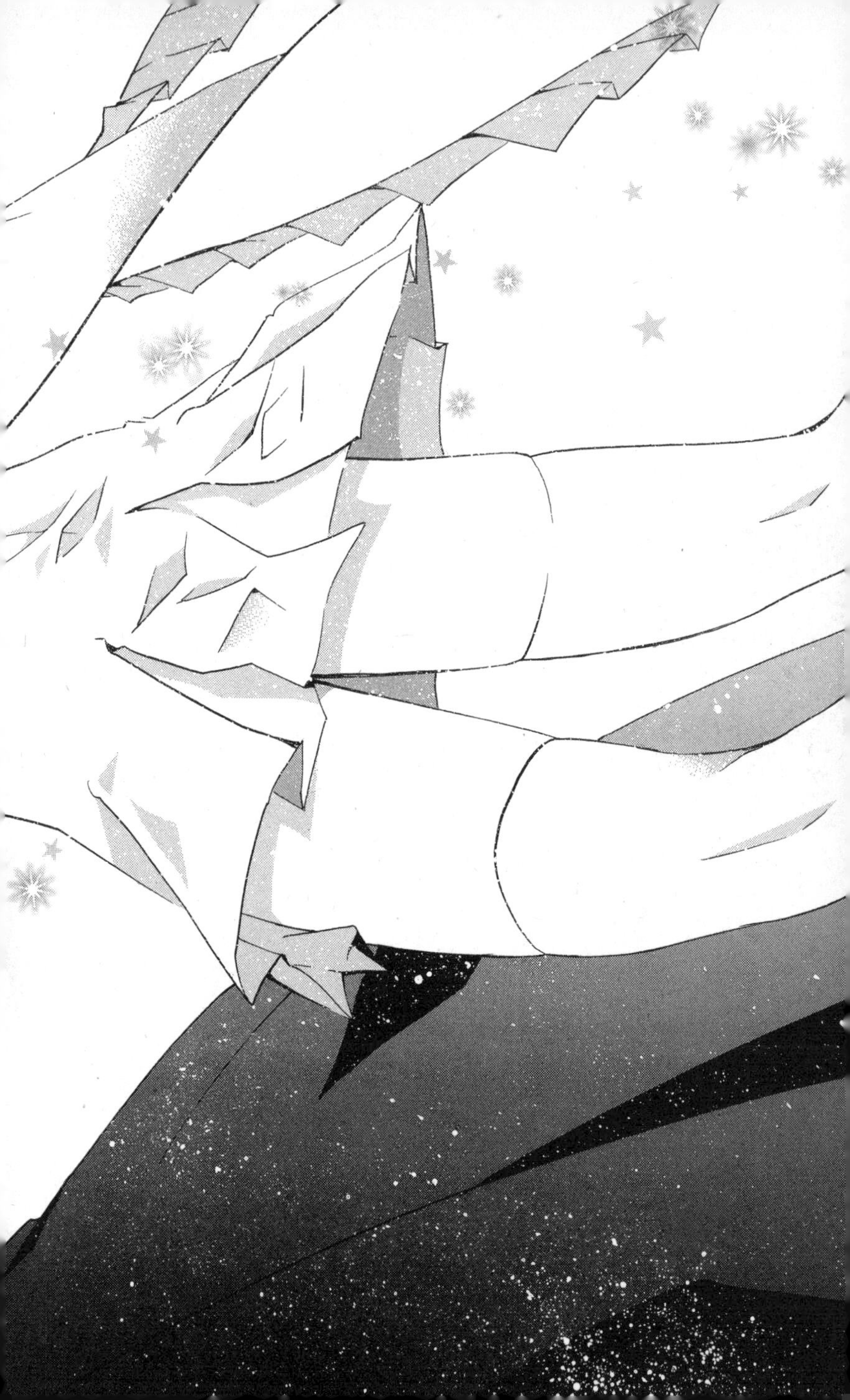

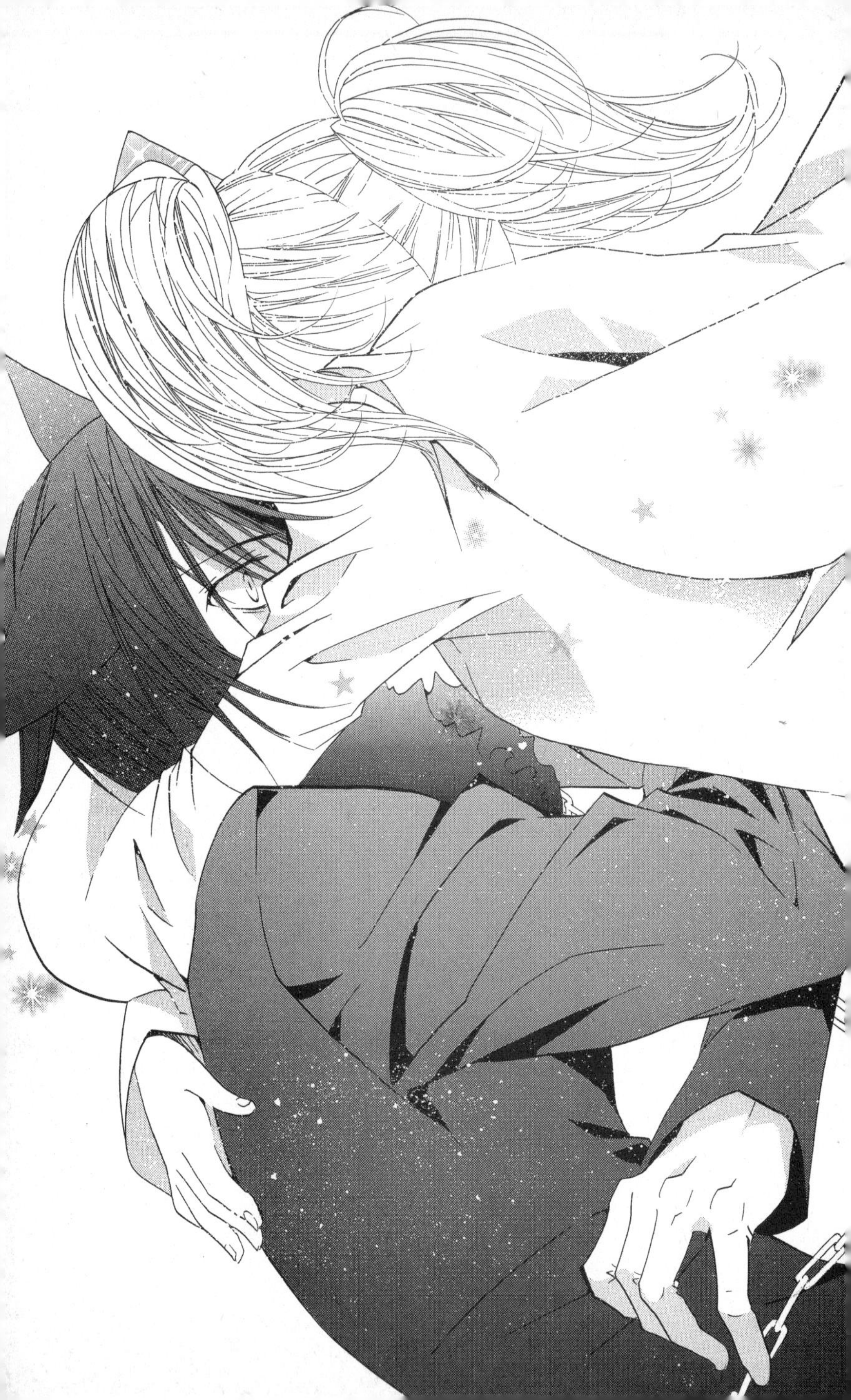

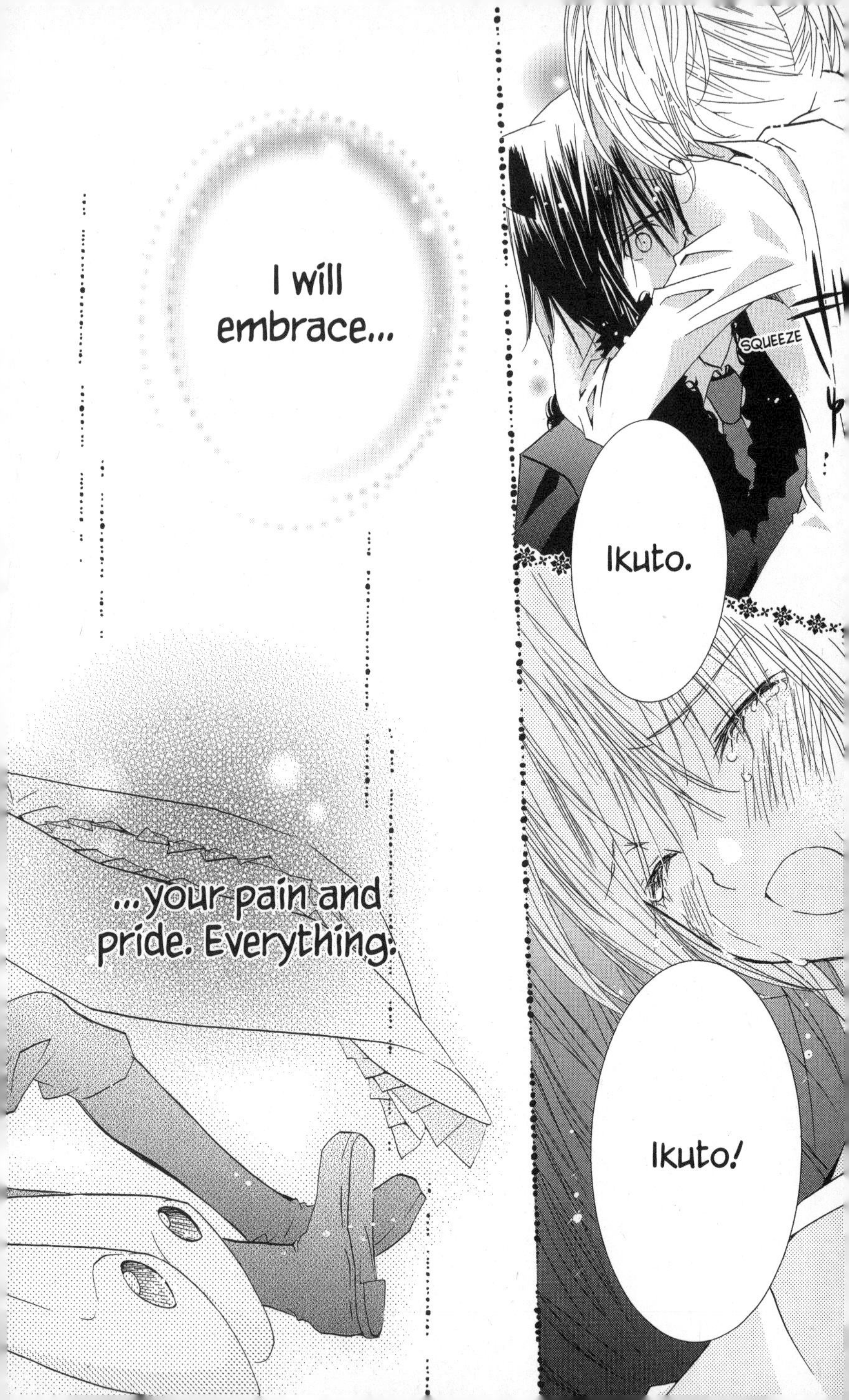
SQUEEZE
Ikuto.
Ikuto!
I will embrace...
...your pain and pride. Everything.

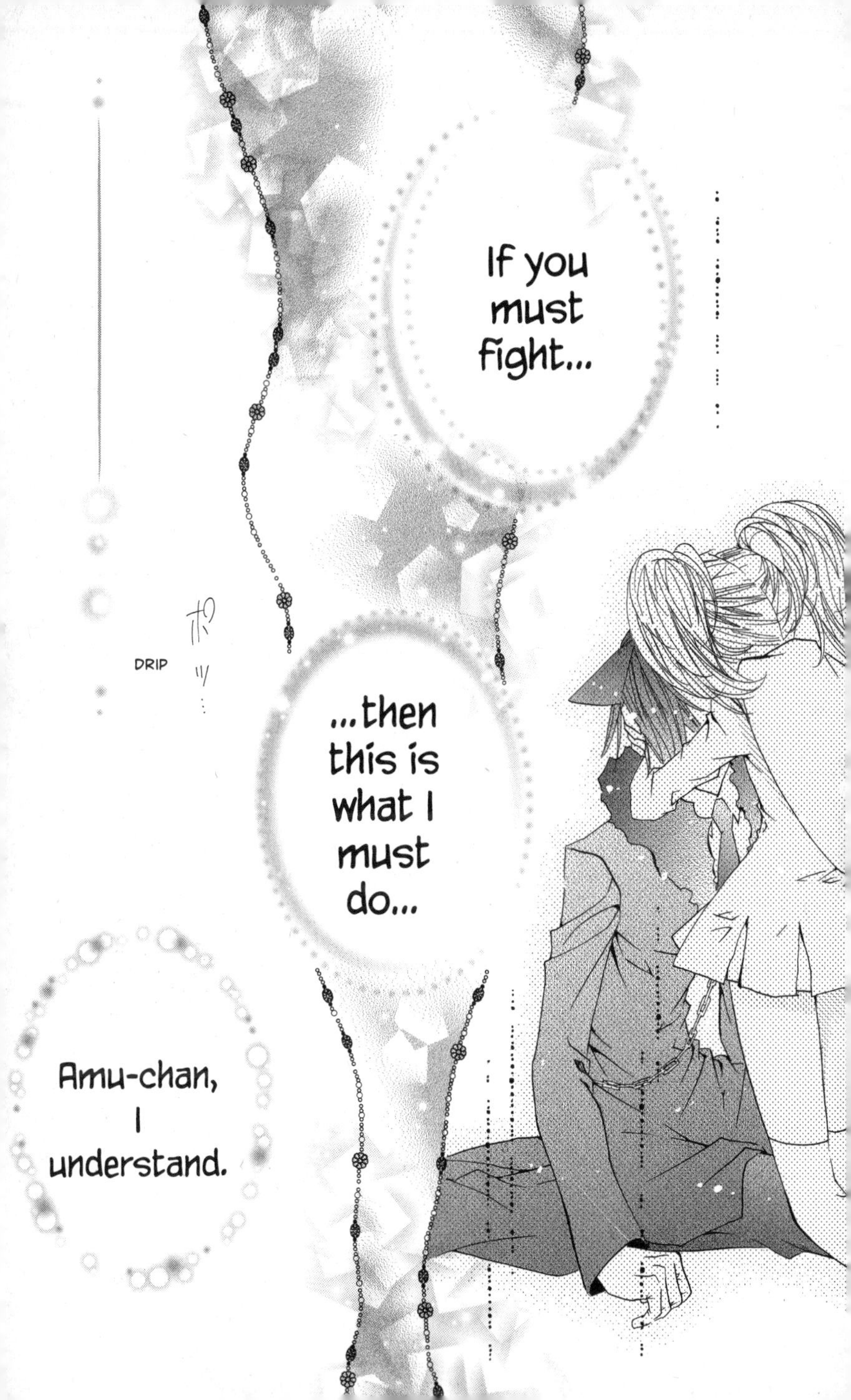
If you must fight...
...then this is what I must do...
ポツ
DRIP
Amu-chan, I understand.

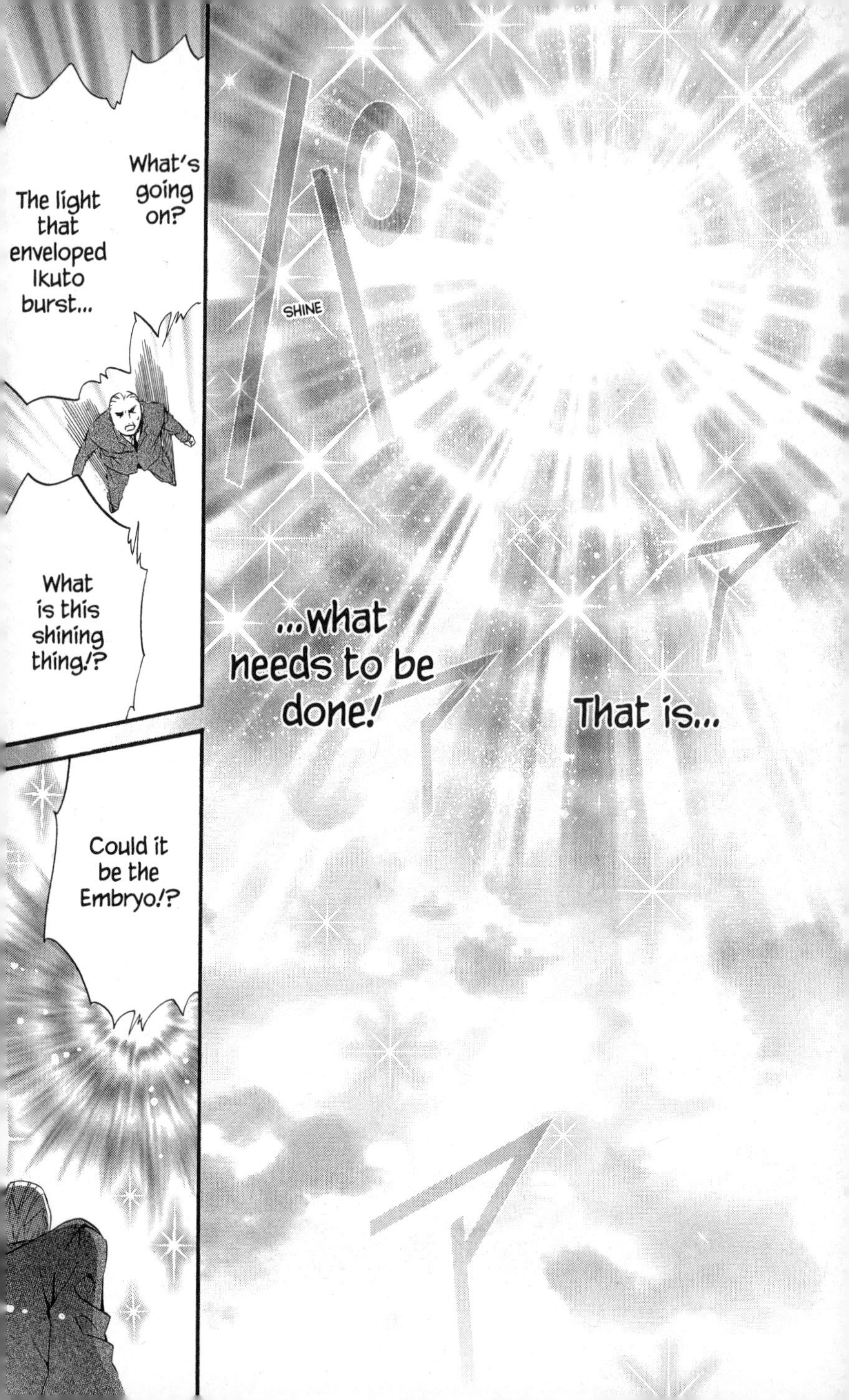
That is...
...what needs to be done!
SHINE
What's going on?
The light that enveloped Ikuto burst...
What is this shining thing!?
Could it be the Embryo!?

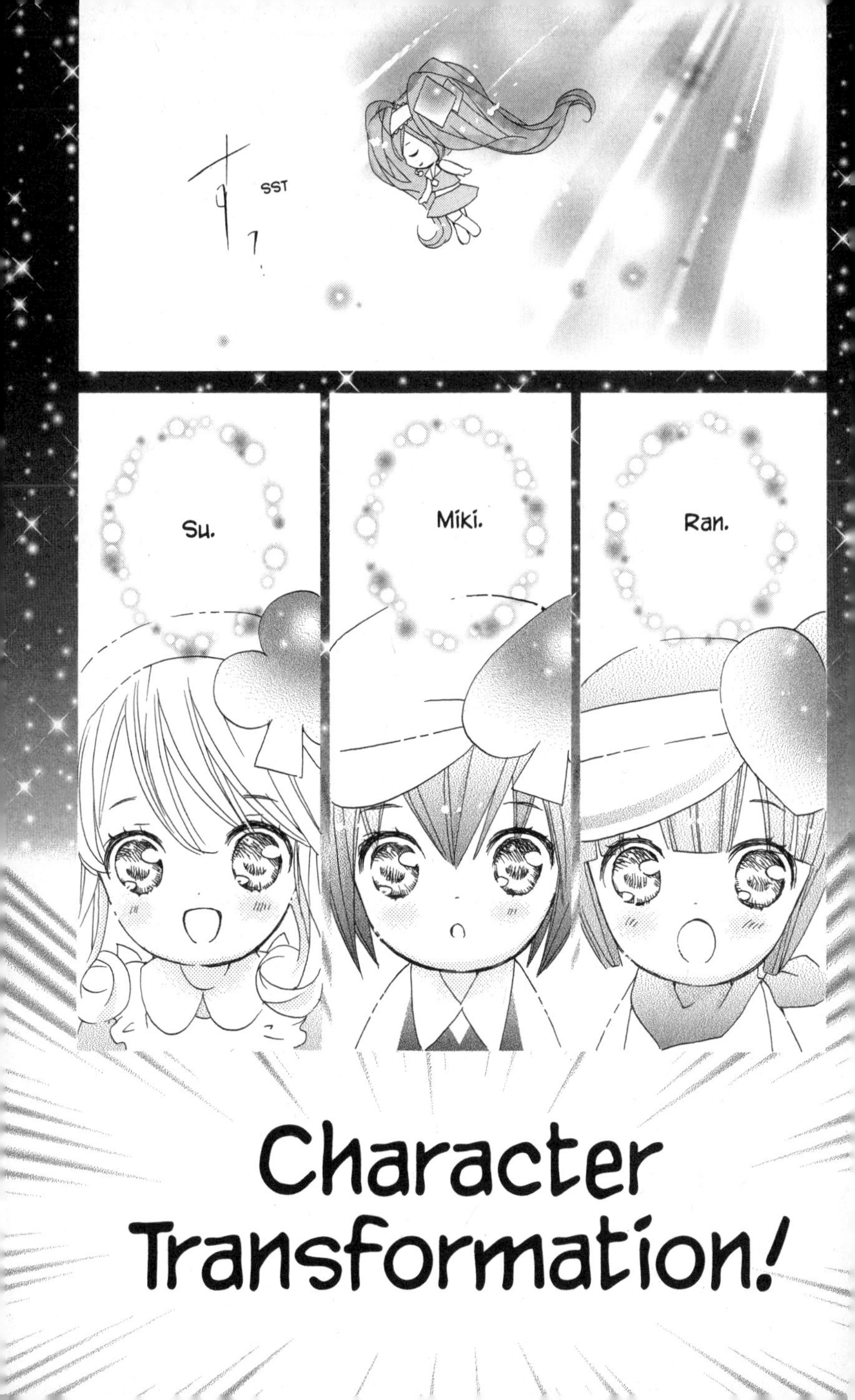
SST
Ran.
Miki.
Su.
Character Transformation!

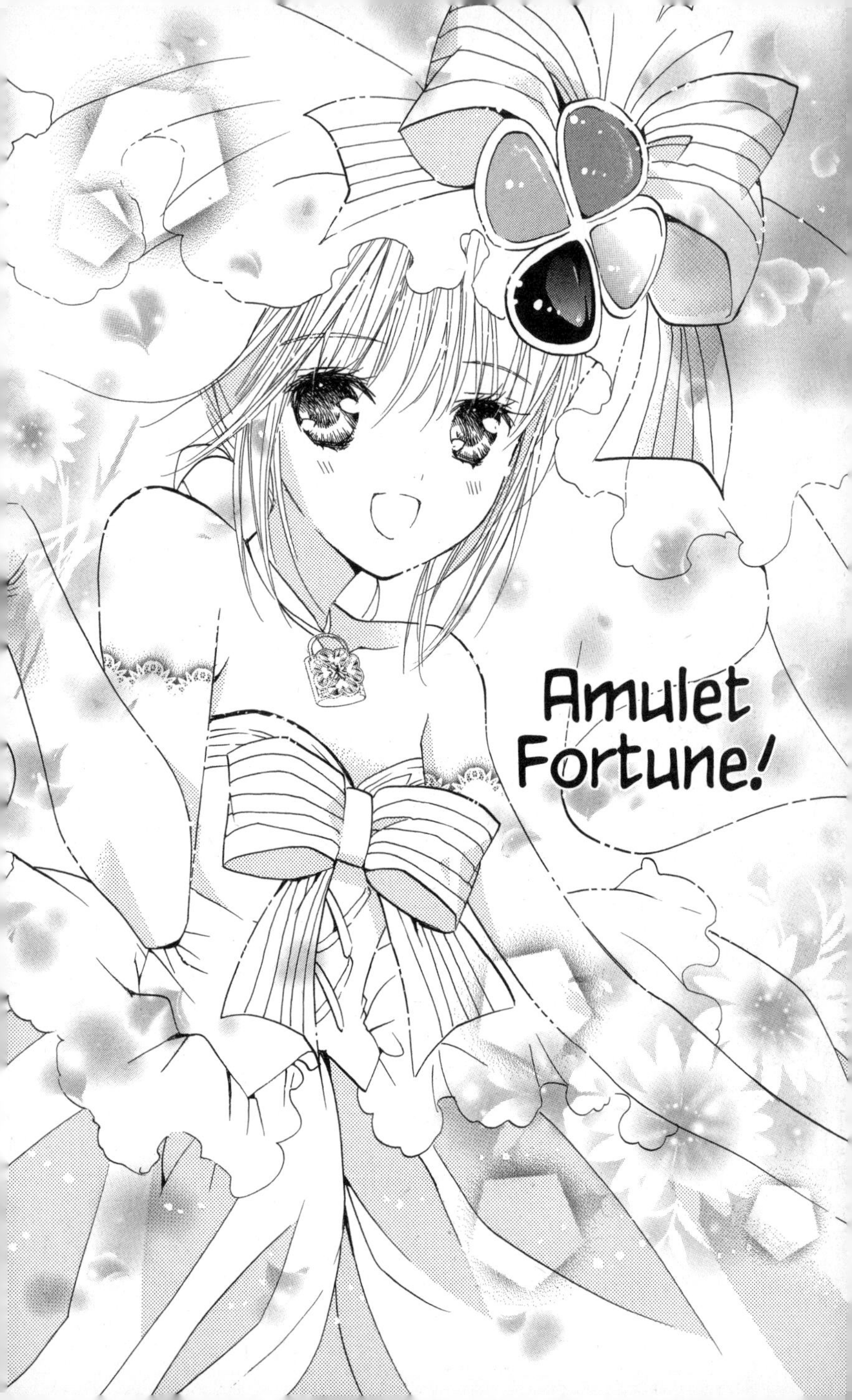
Amulet Fortune!

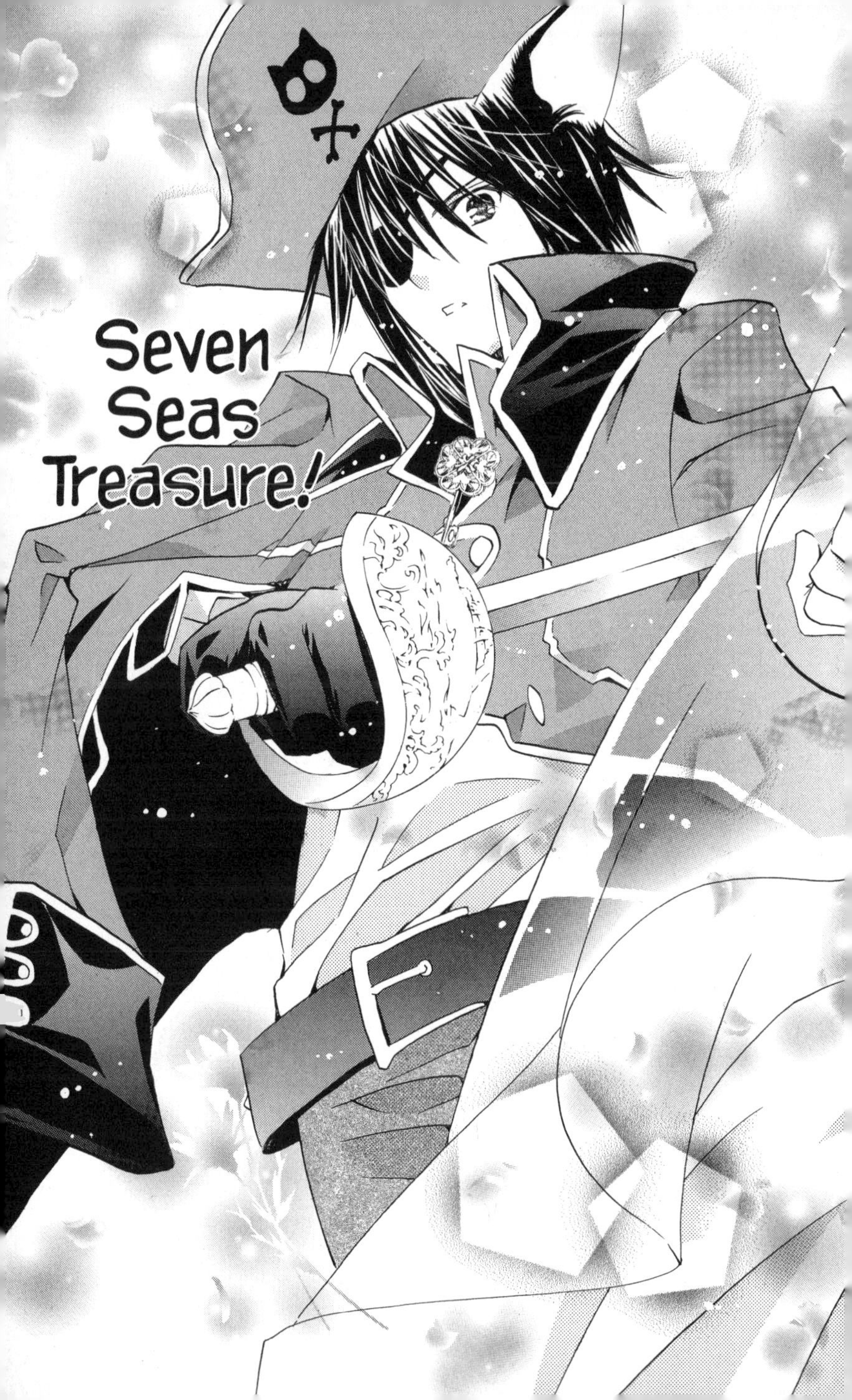
Seven Seas Treasure!

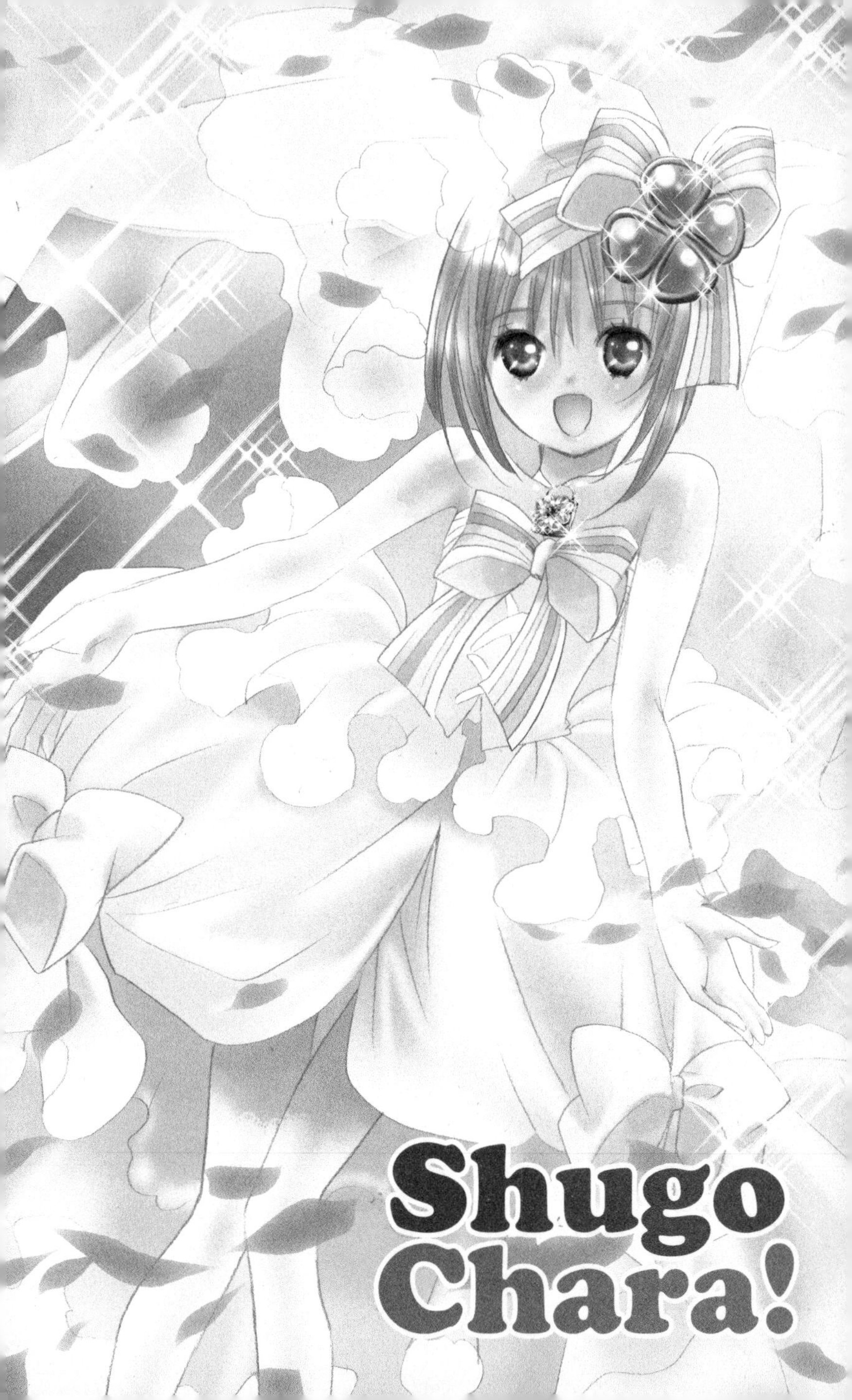
Shugo
Chara!

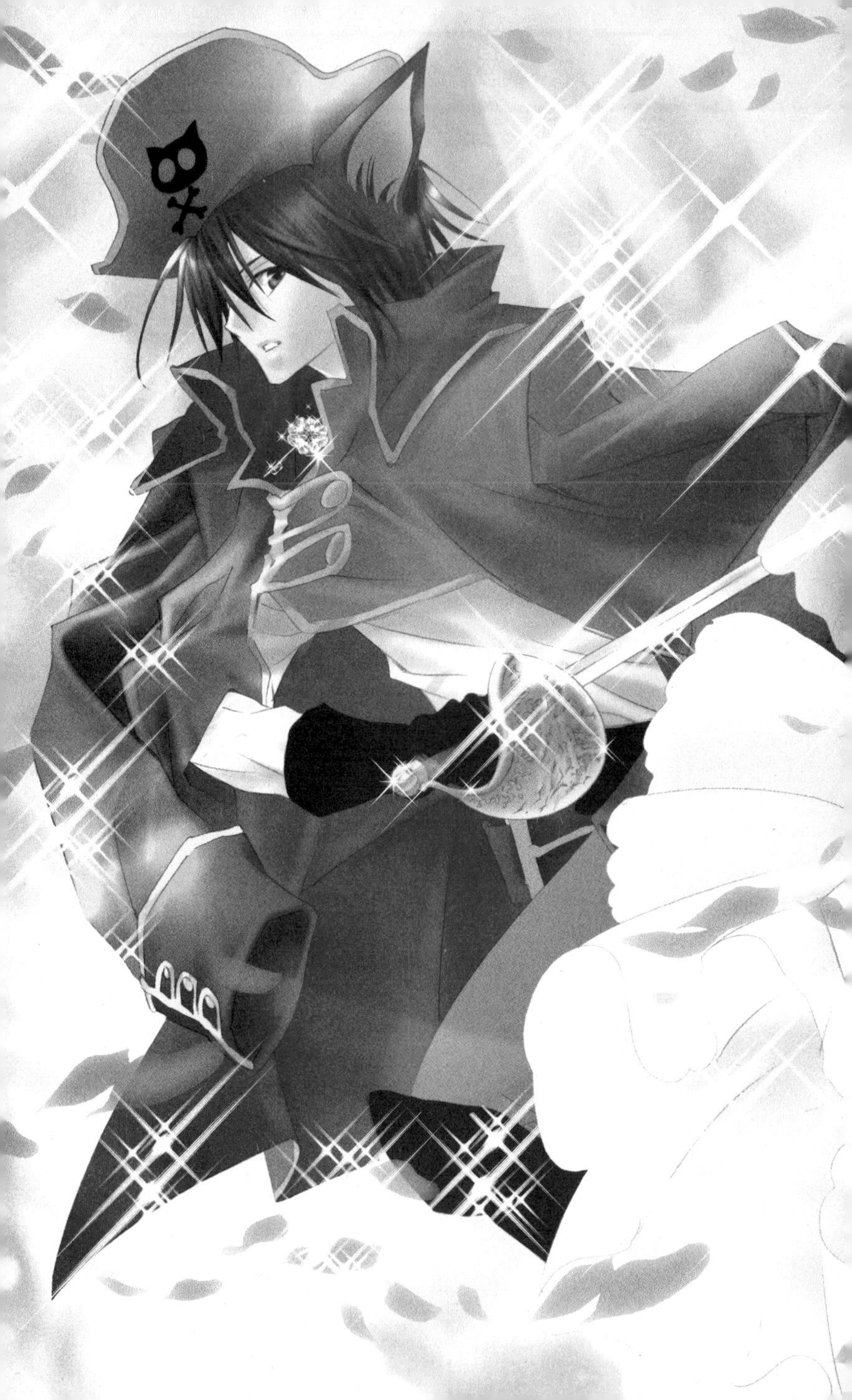

Shugo
Chara!

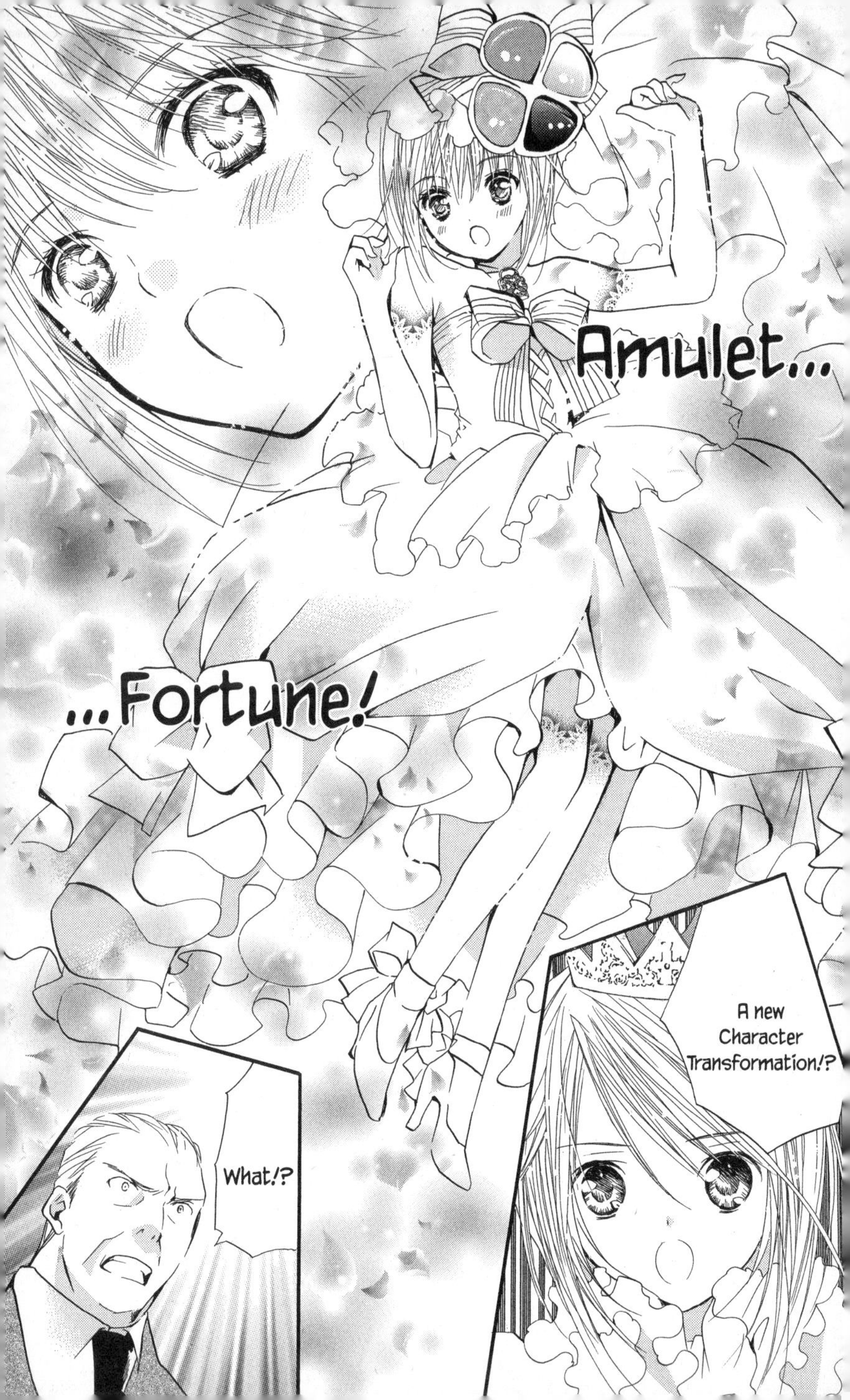
Amulet...
...Fortune!
A new Character Transformation!?
What!?

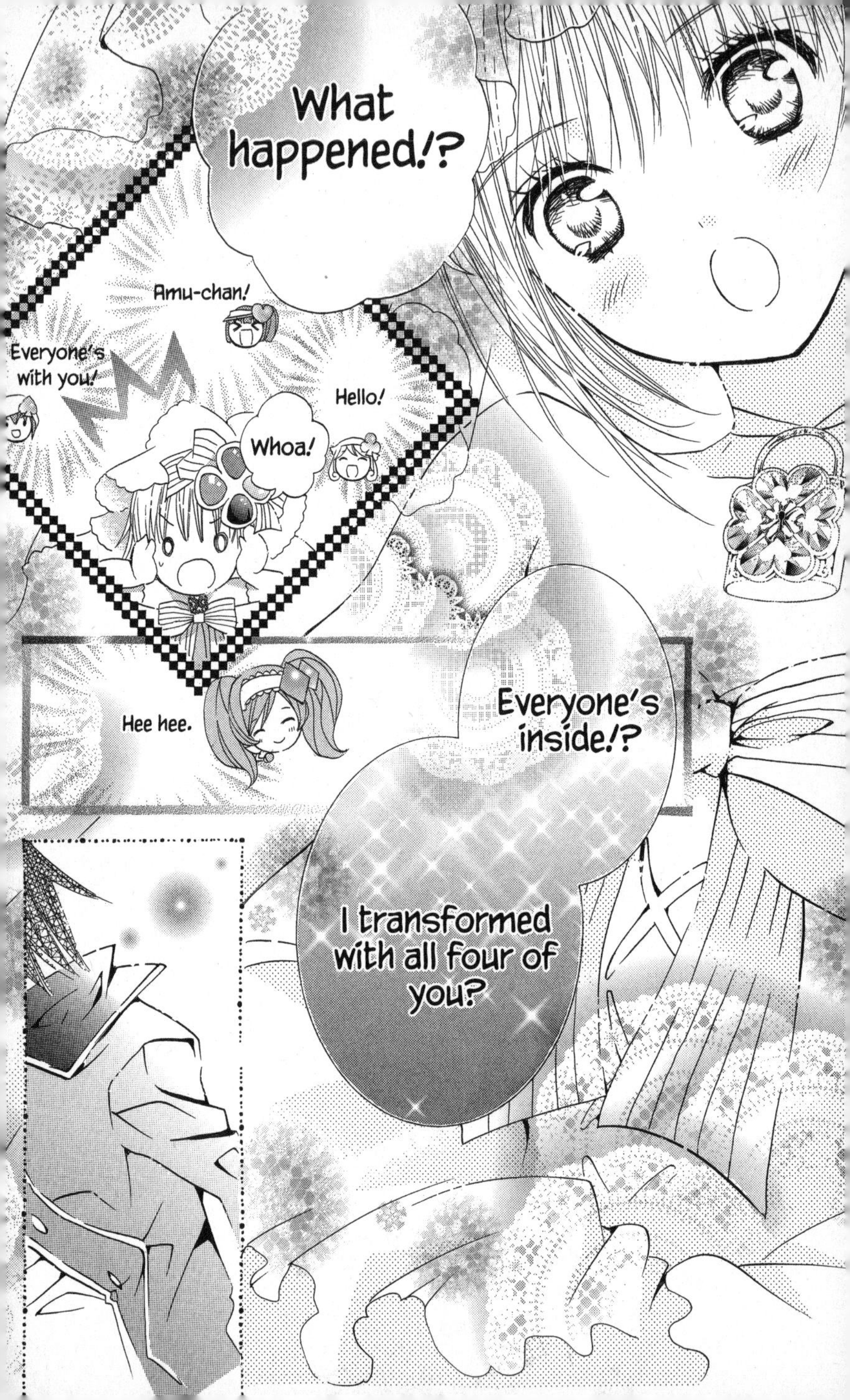
What happened!?
Amu-chan!
Hello!
Whoa!
Everyone's with you!
Hee hee.
Everyone's inside!?
I transformed with all four of you?

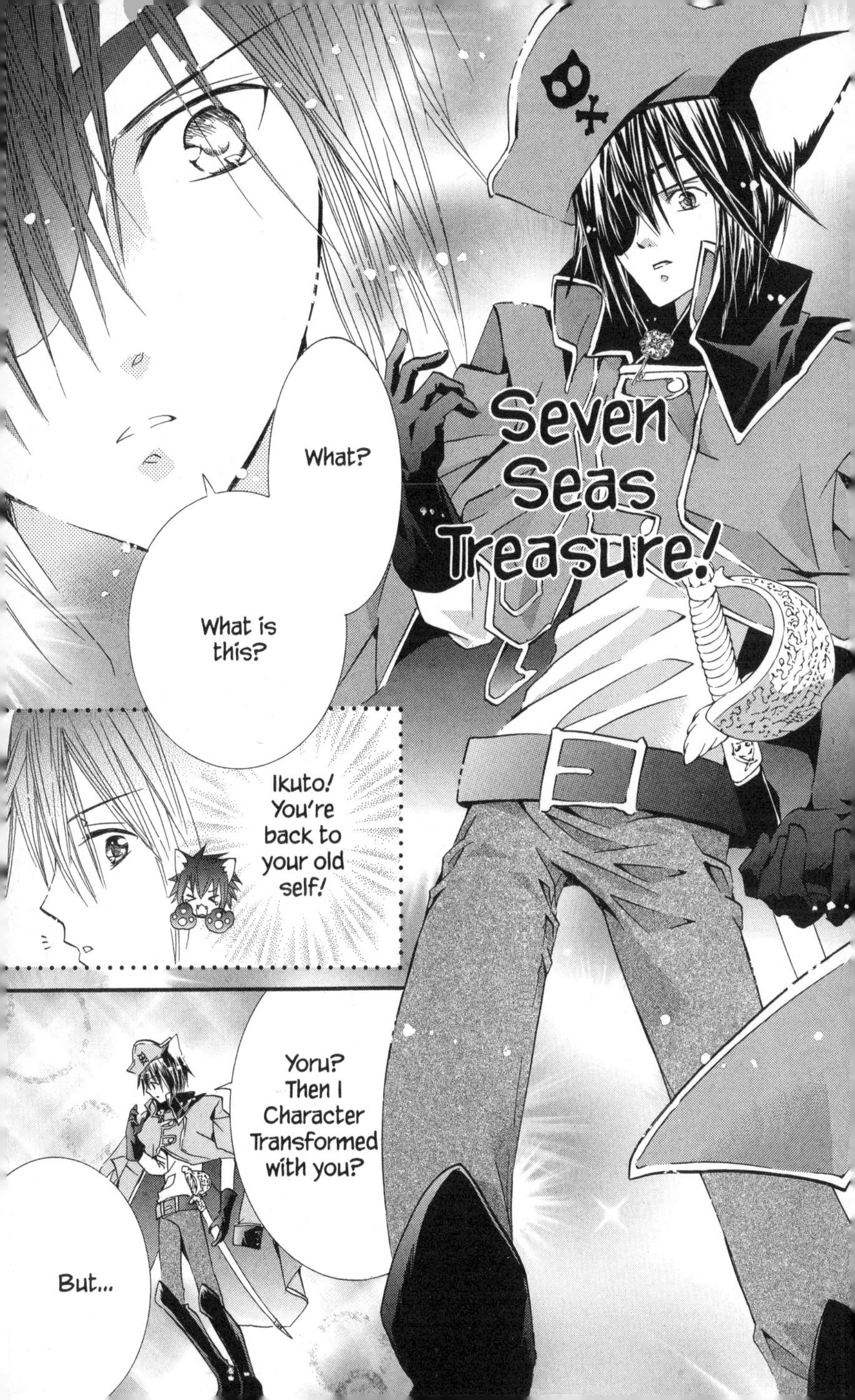
Seven Seas Treasure!
What?
What is this?
Ikuto! You're back to your old self!
Yoru? Then I Character Transformed with you?
But...

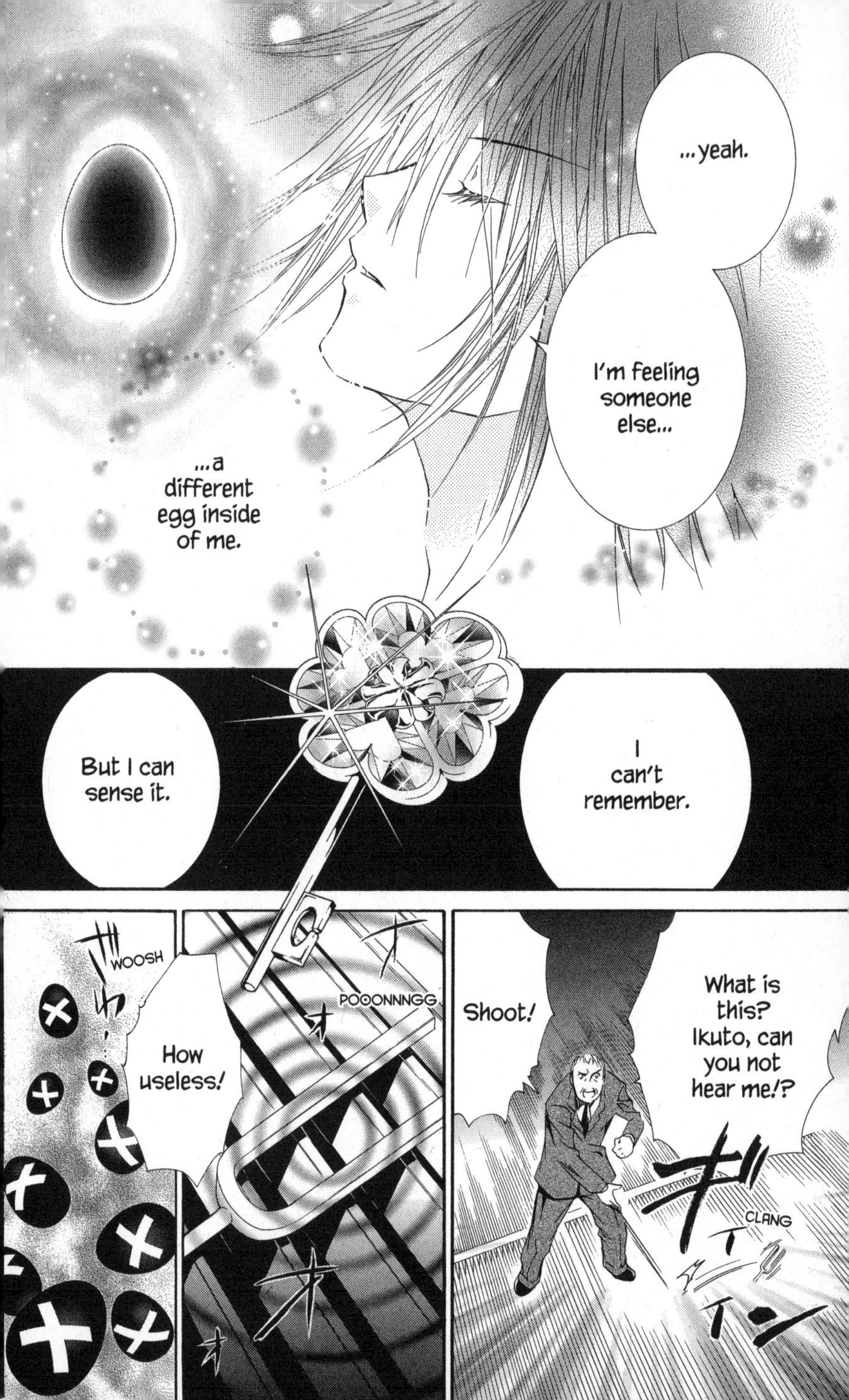
...yeah.
I'm feeling someone else...
...a different egg inside of me.
I can't remember.
But I can sense it.
What is this? Ikuto, can you not hear me!?
Shoot!
CLANG
POOONNNGG
WOOSH
How useless!

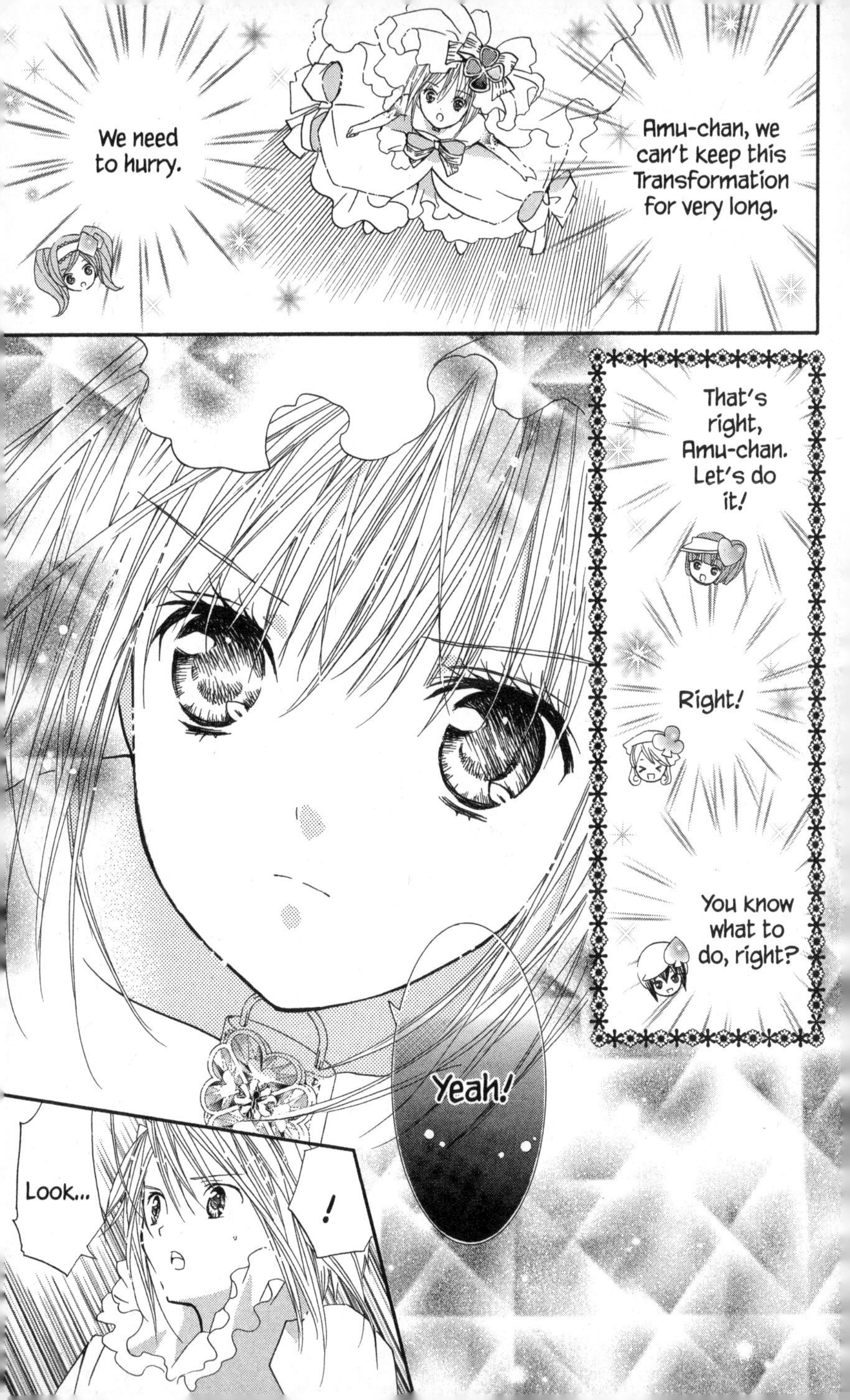
Amu-chan, we can't keep this Transformation for very long.
We need to hurry.
That's right, Amu-chan. Let's do it!
Right!
You know what to do, right?
Yeah!
!
Look...

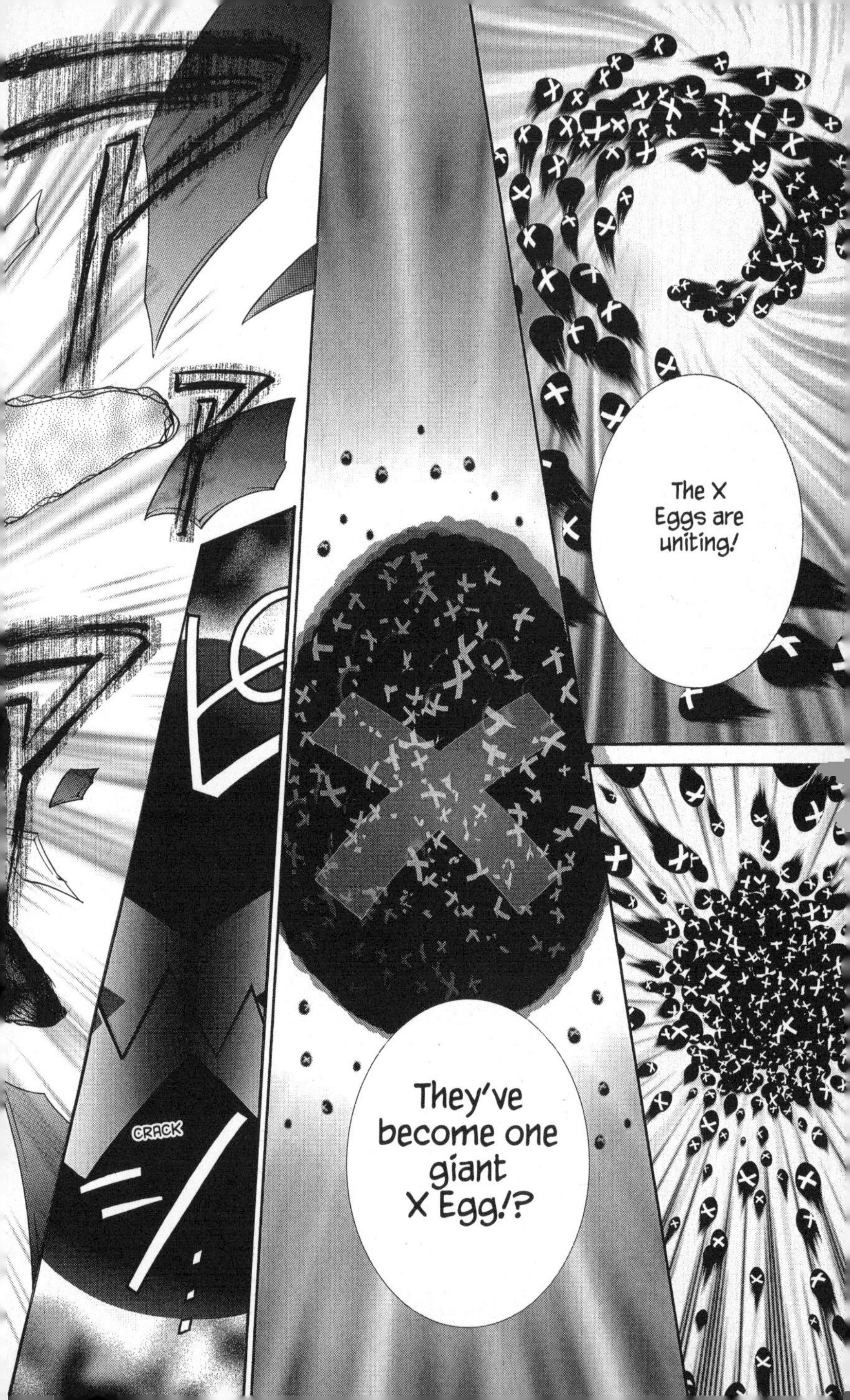
The X Eggs are uniting!
They've become one giant X Egg!?
CRACK

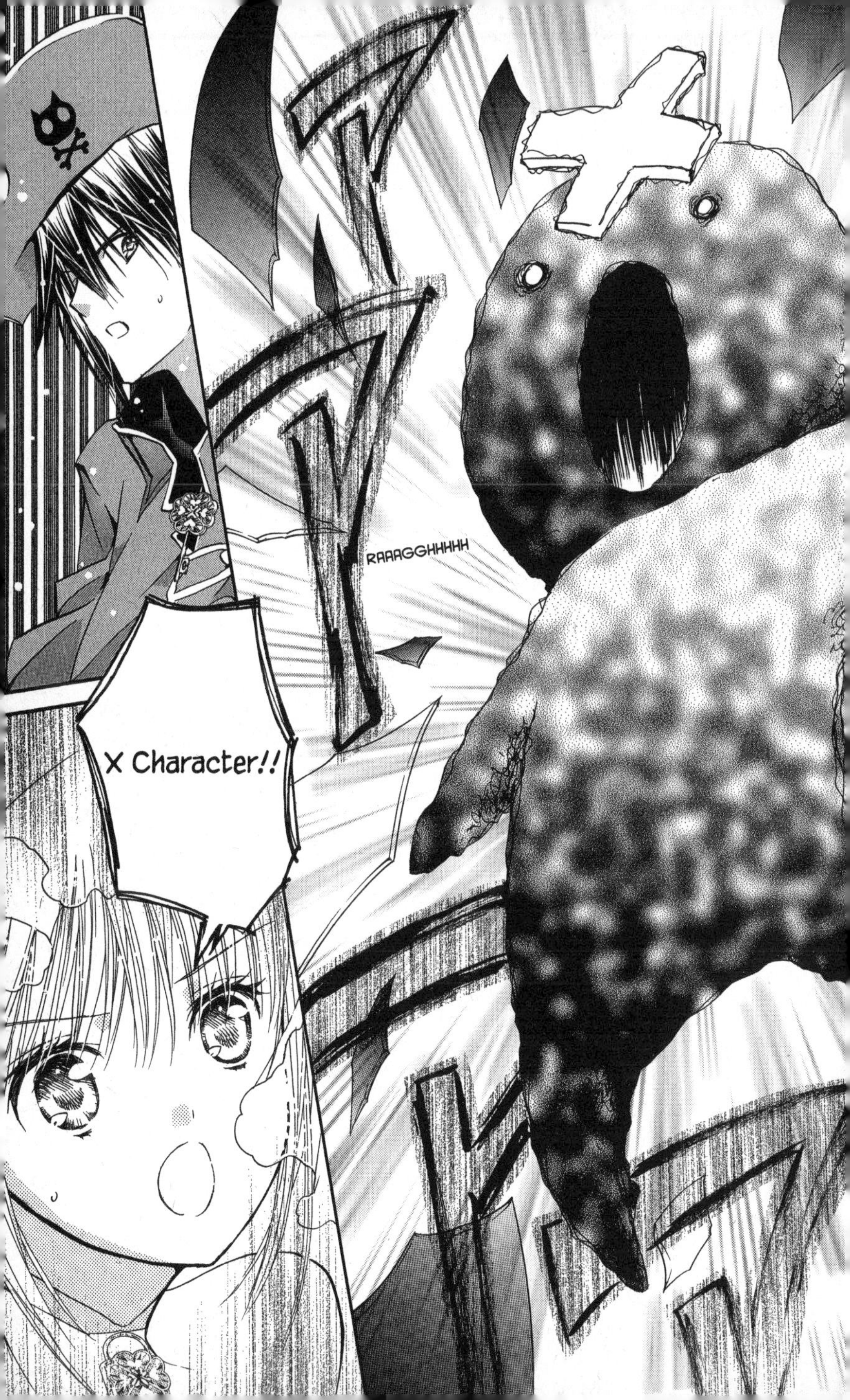
RAAAGGHHHHH
X Character!!

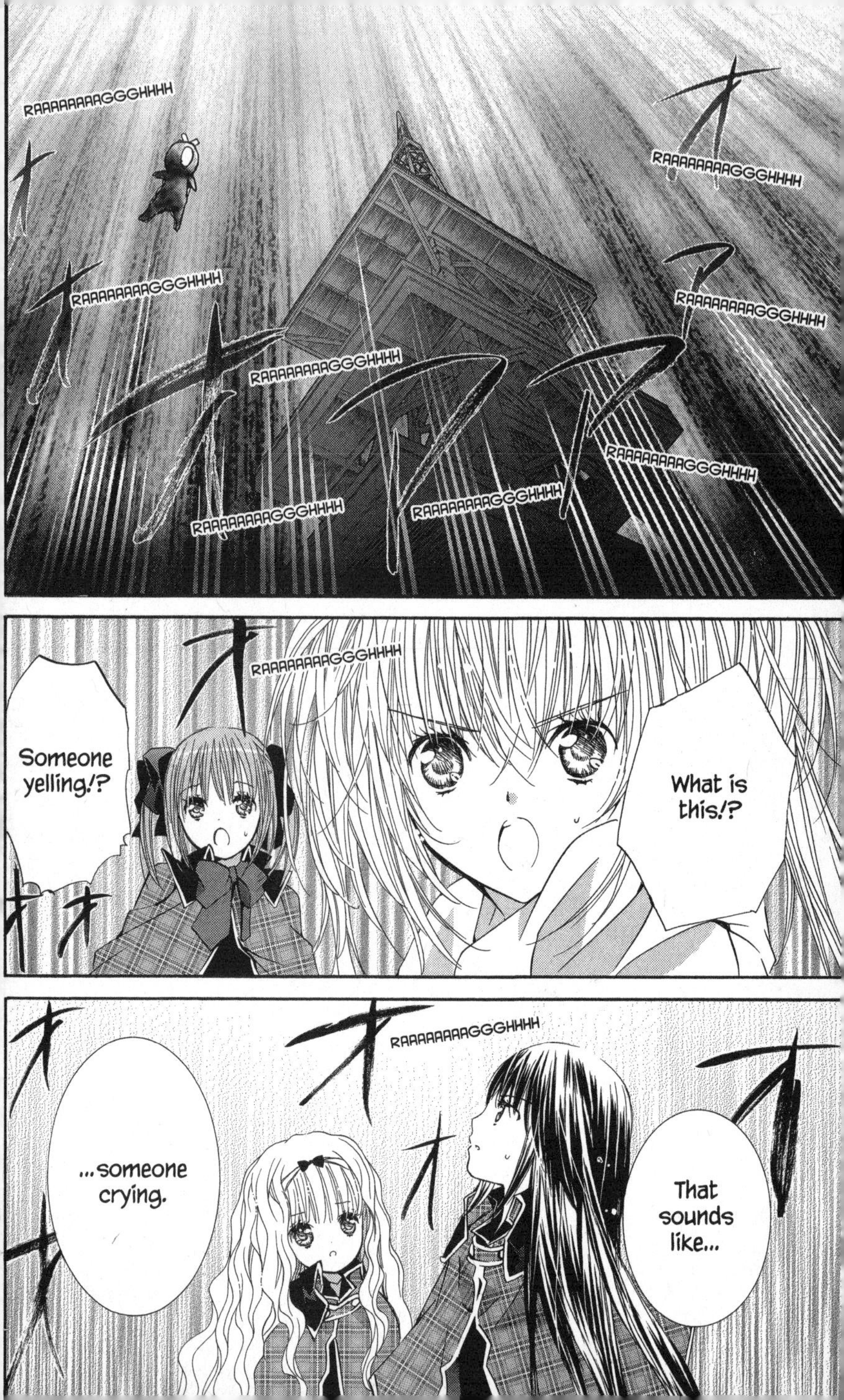
RAAAAAAAAGGGHHHH
RAAAAAAAAGGGHHHH
RAAAAAAAAGGGHHHH
RAAAAAAAAGGGHHHH
RAAAAAAAAGGGHHHH
RAAAAAAAAGGGHHHH
RAAAAAAAAGGGHHHH
RAAAAAAAAGGGHHHH
What is this!?
RAAAAAAAAGGGHHHH
Someone yelling!?
That sounds like...
RAAAAAAAAGGGHHHH
...someone crying.

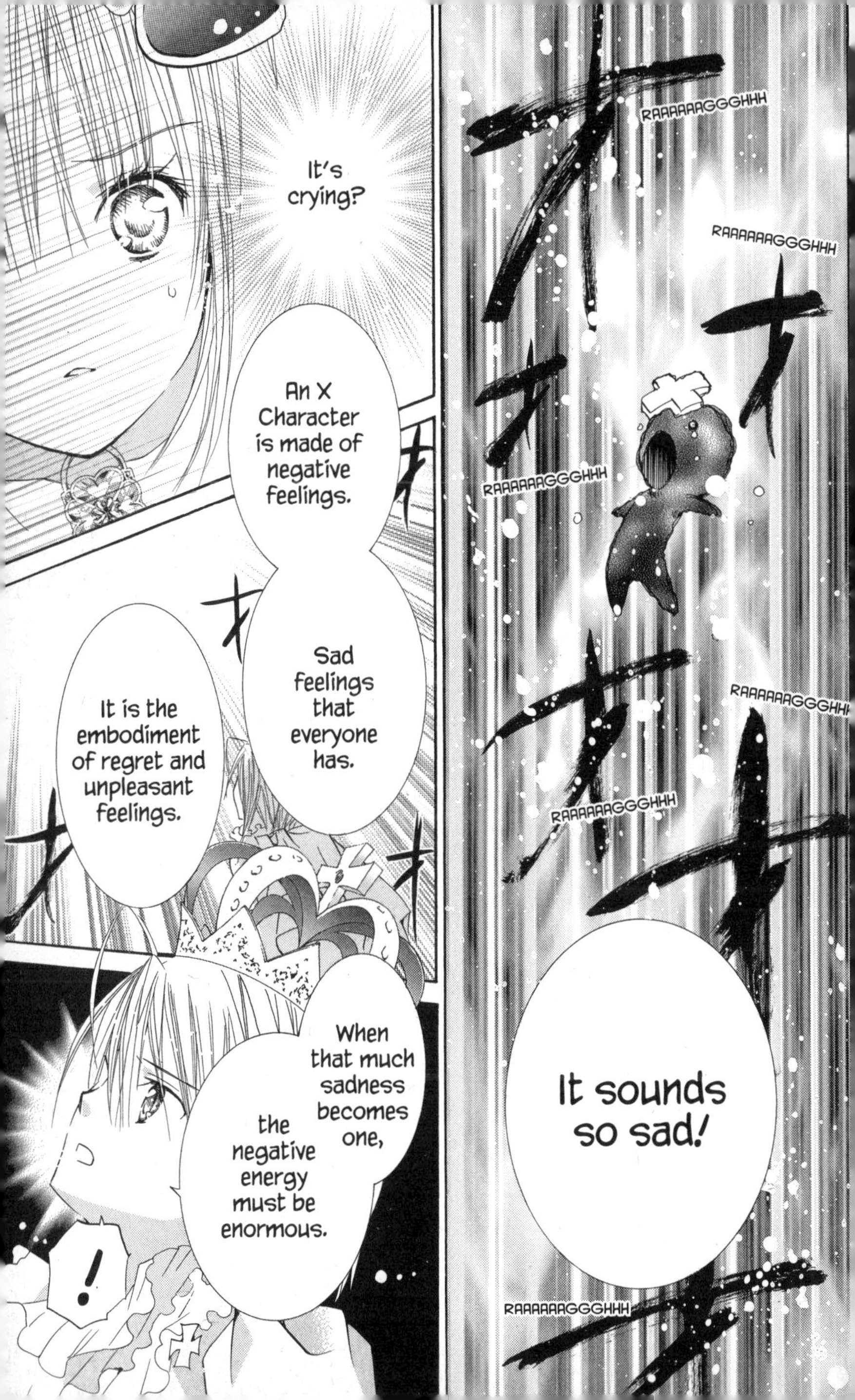
RAAAAAAGGGHHH
RAAAAAAGGGHHH
RAAAAAAGGGHHH
RAAAAAAGGGHHH
RAAAAAAGGGHHH
It sounds so sad!
RAAAAAAGGGHHH
It's crying?
An X Character is made of negative feelings.
Sad feelings that everyone has.
It is the embodiment of regret and unpleasant feelings.
When that much sadness becomes one,
the negative energy must be enormous.
!

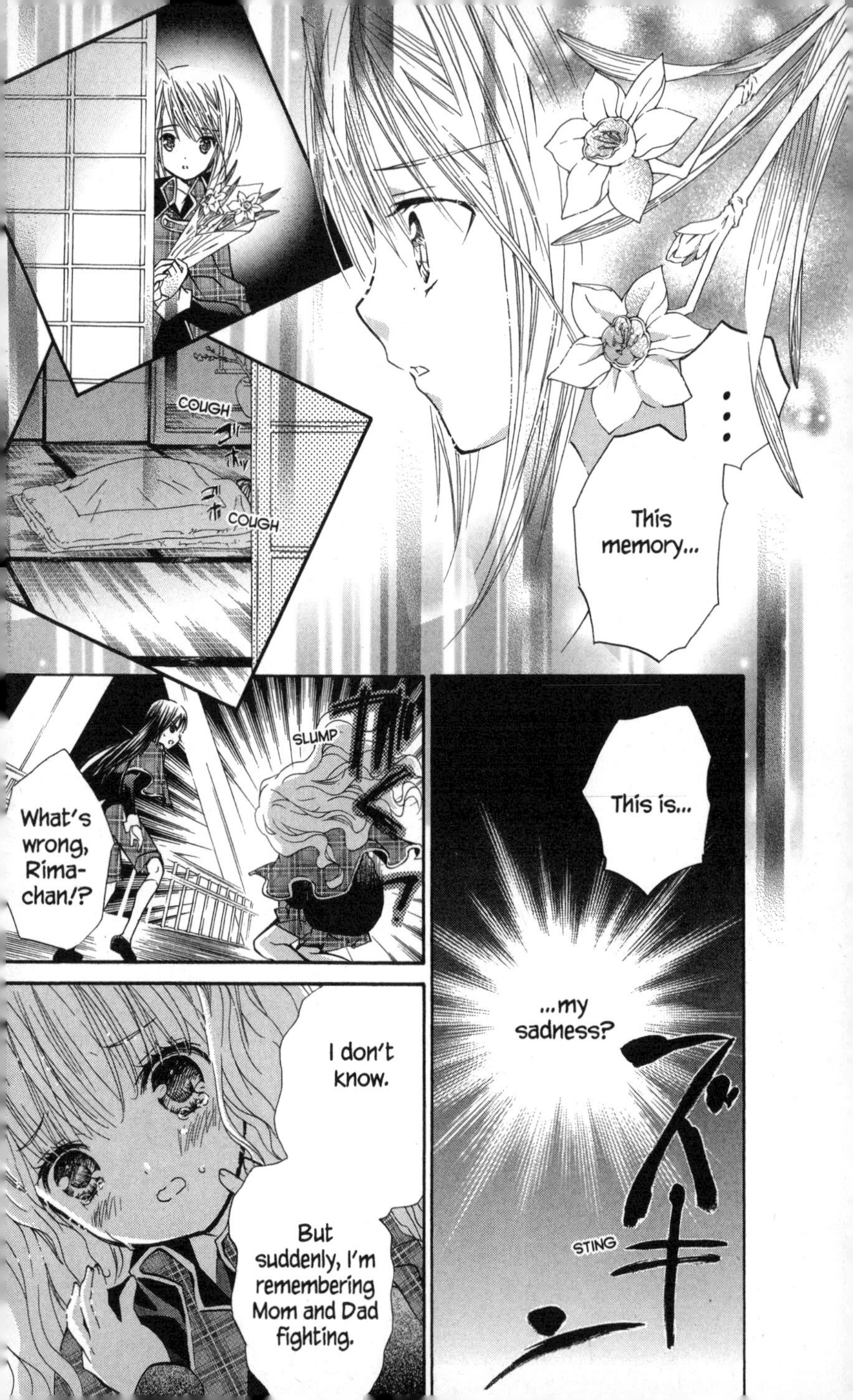
...
This memory...
COUGH
COUGH
This is...
...my sadness?
STING
SLUMP
What's wrong, Rima-chan!?
I don't know.
But suddenly, I'm remembering Mom and Dad fighting.

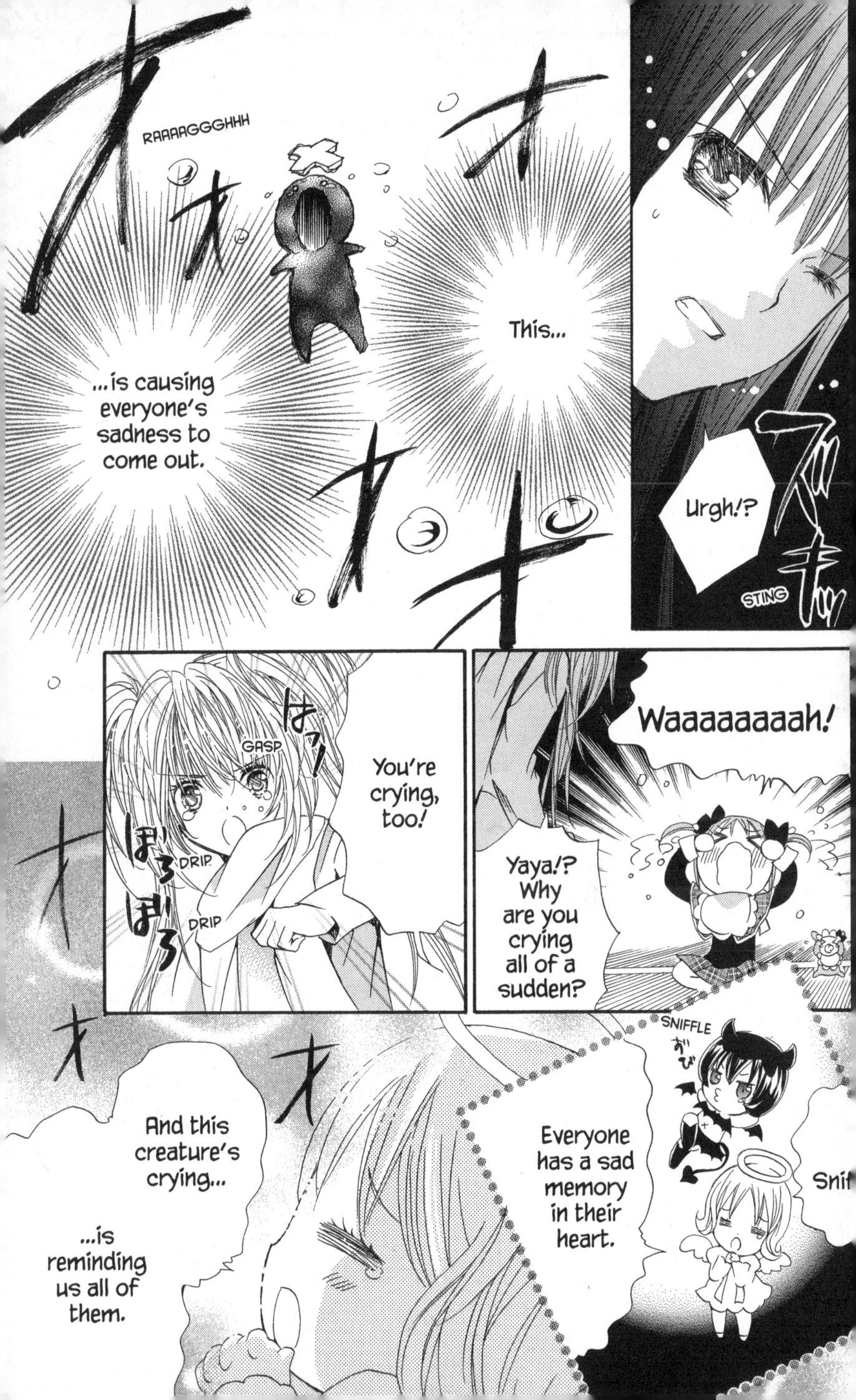
Urgh!?
STING
RAAAAGGGHHH
This...
...is causing everyone's sadness to come out.
Waaaaaaaah!
Yaya!? Why are you crying all of a sudden?
GASP
You're crying, too!
DRIP
DRIP
SNIFFLE
Snif
Everyone has a sad memory in their heart.
And this creature's crying...
...is reminding us all of them.

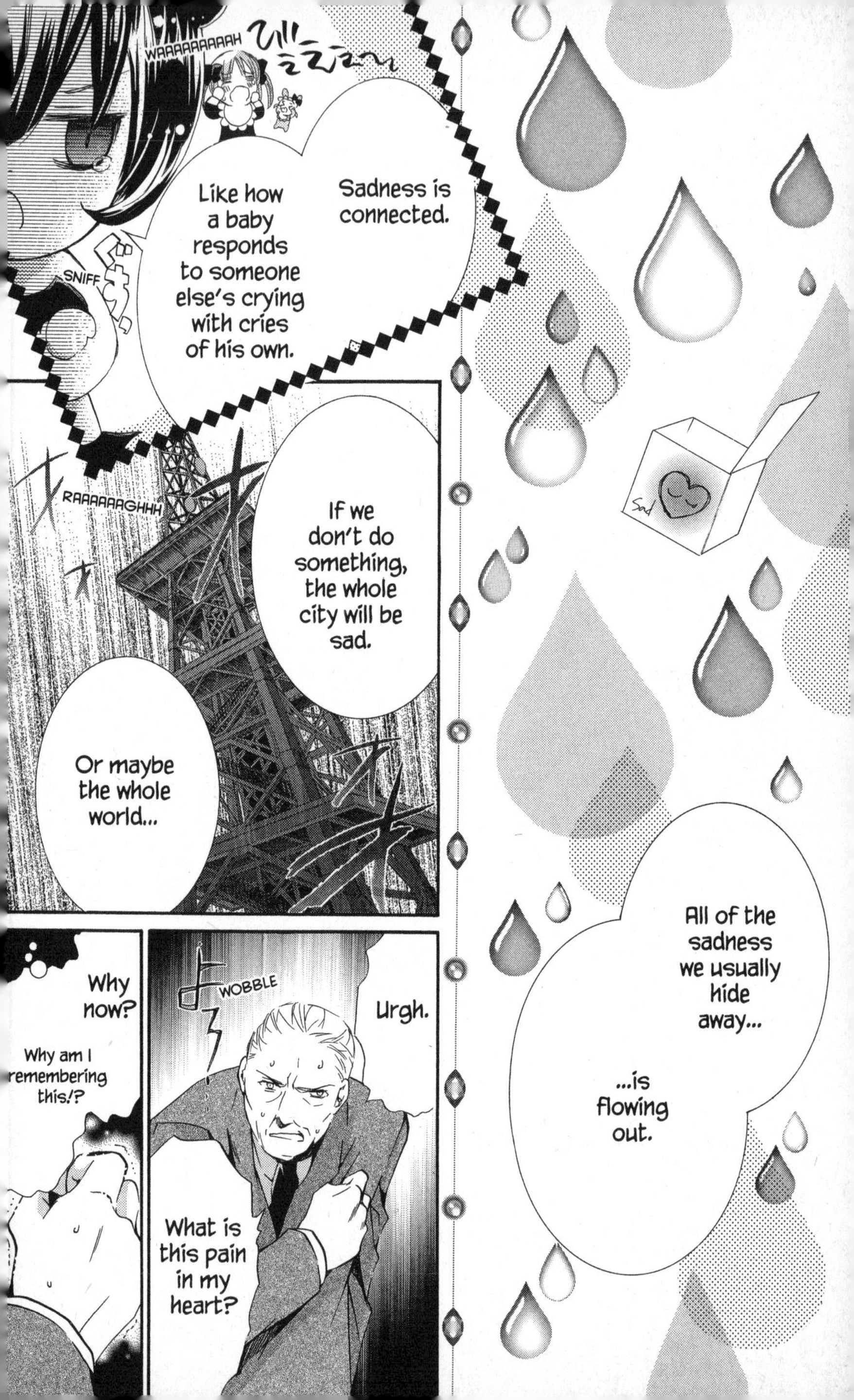
All of the sadness we usually hide away...
...is flowing out.
Sad
WAAAAAAAAAAH
Sadness is connected.
Like how a baby responds to someone else's crying with cries of his own.
SNIFF
If we don't do something, the whole city will be sad.
RAAAAAAGHHH
Or maybe the whole world...
Urgh.
WOBBLE
What is this pain in my heart?
Why now?
Why am I remembering this!?

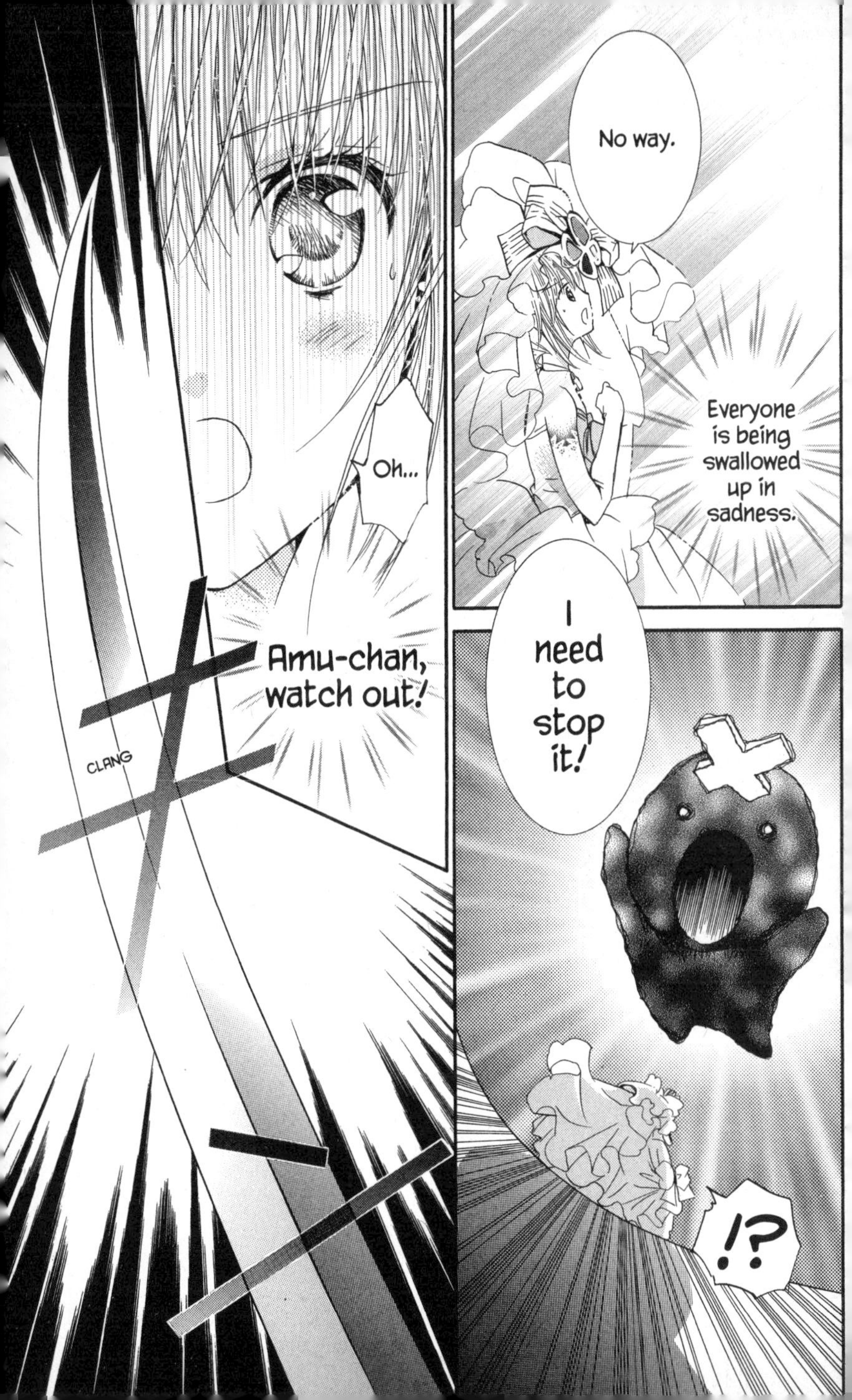
No way.
Everyone is being swallowed up in sadness.
I need to stop it!
!?
Oh...
Amu-chan, watch out!
CLANG

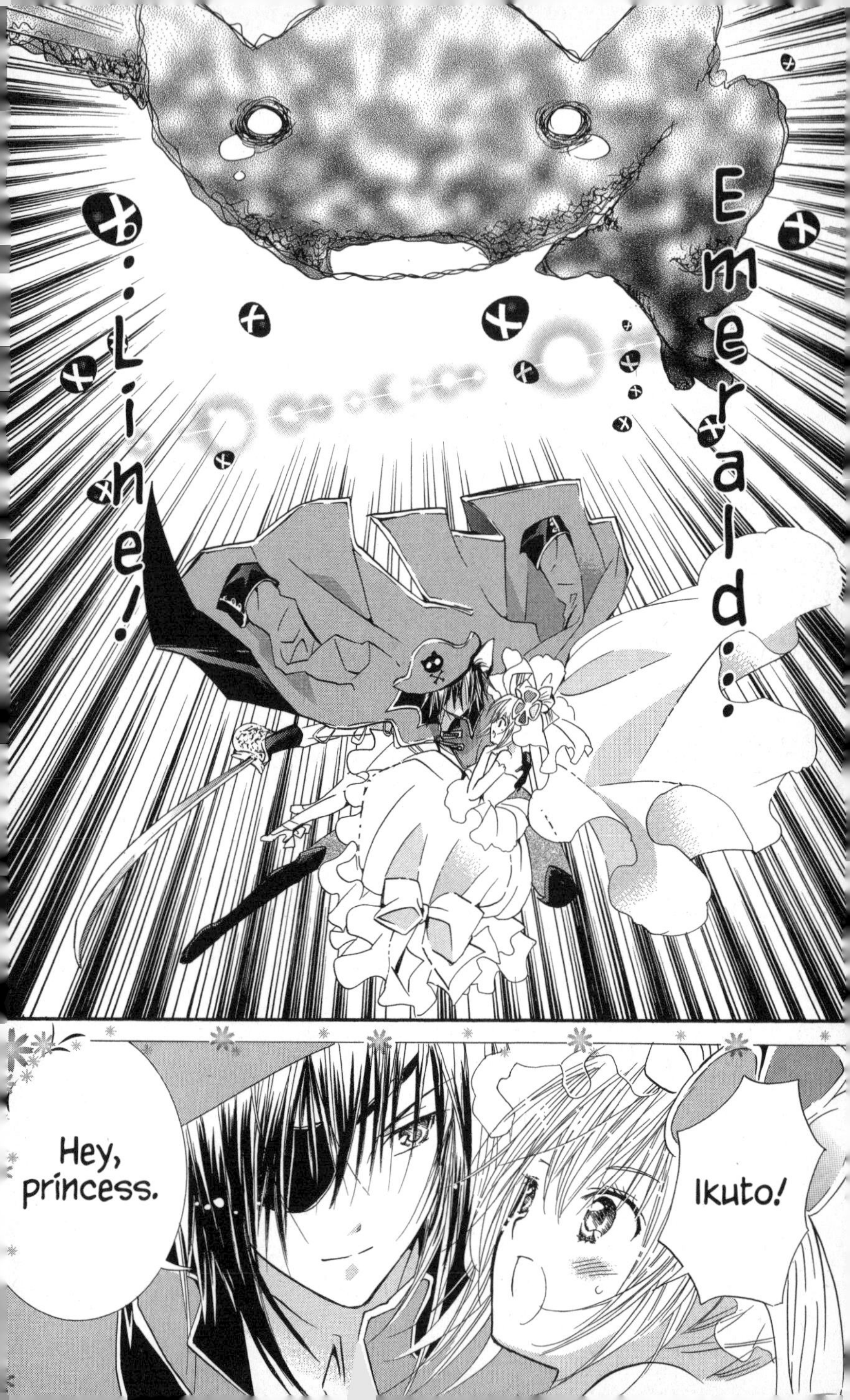

Emerald...
...Line!
Ikuto!
Hey, princess.

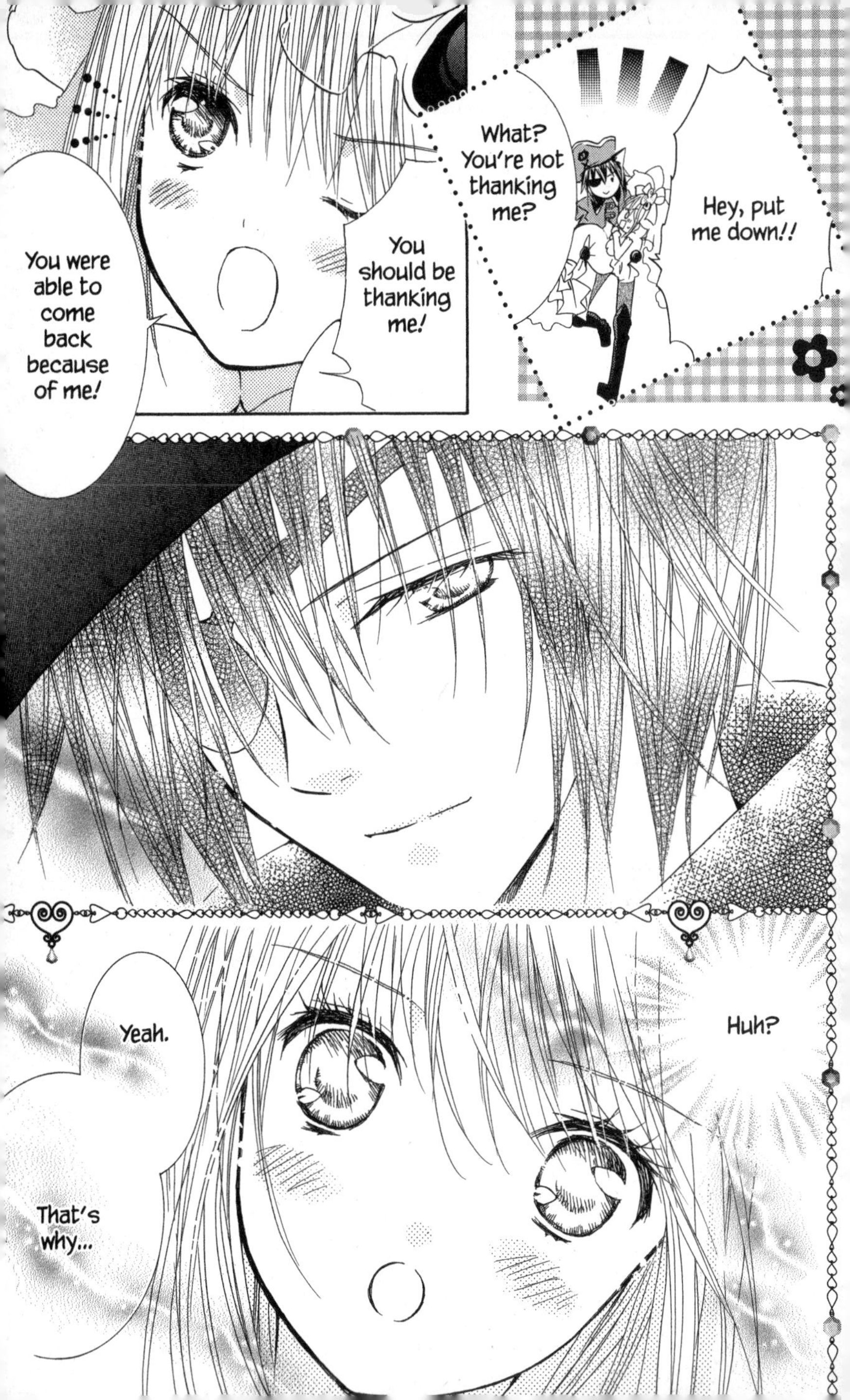
Hey, put me down!!
What? You're not thanking me?
You should be thanking me!
You were able to come back because of me!
Huh?
Yeah.
That's why...

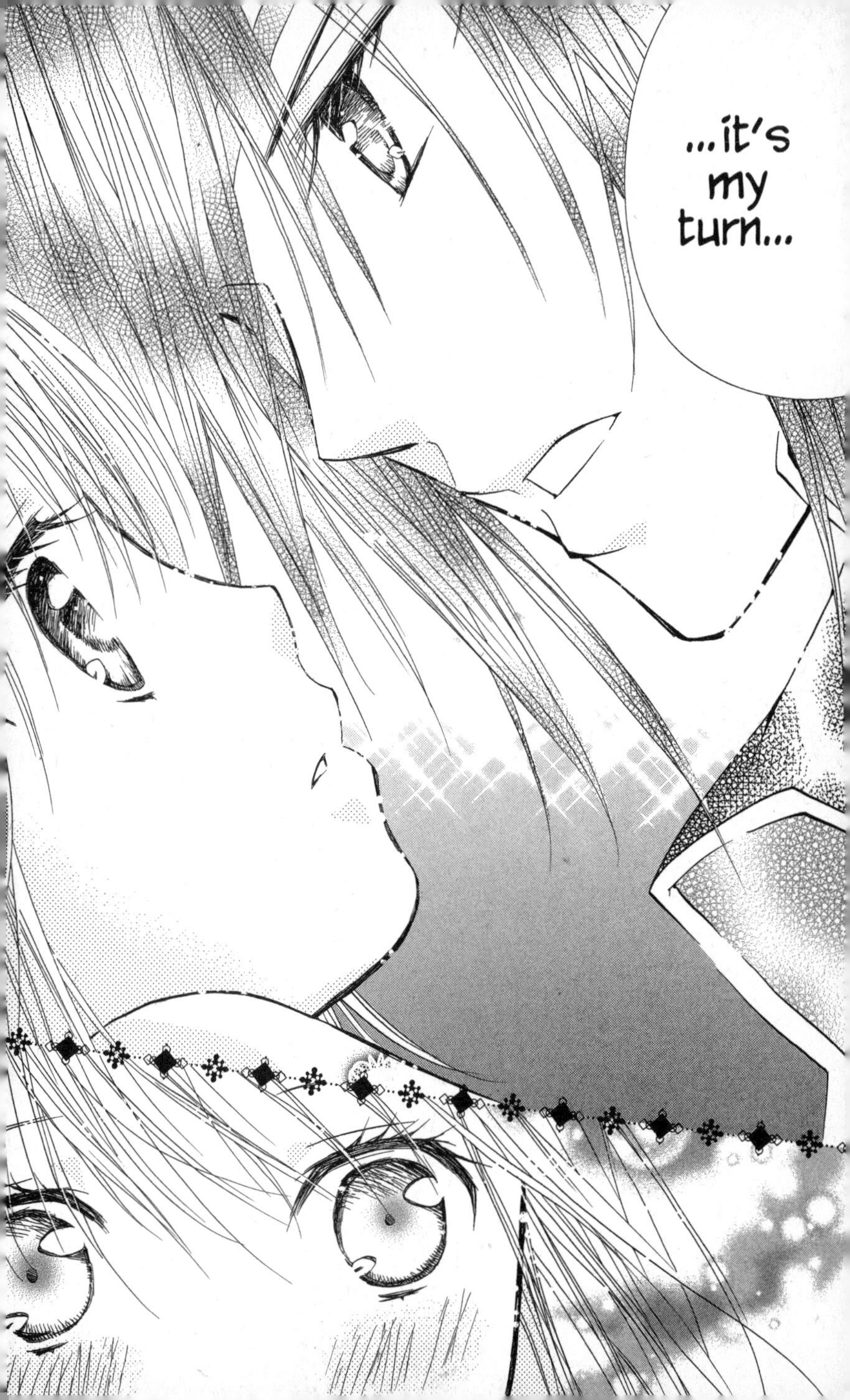
...it's my turn...

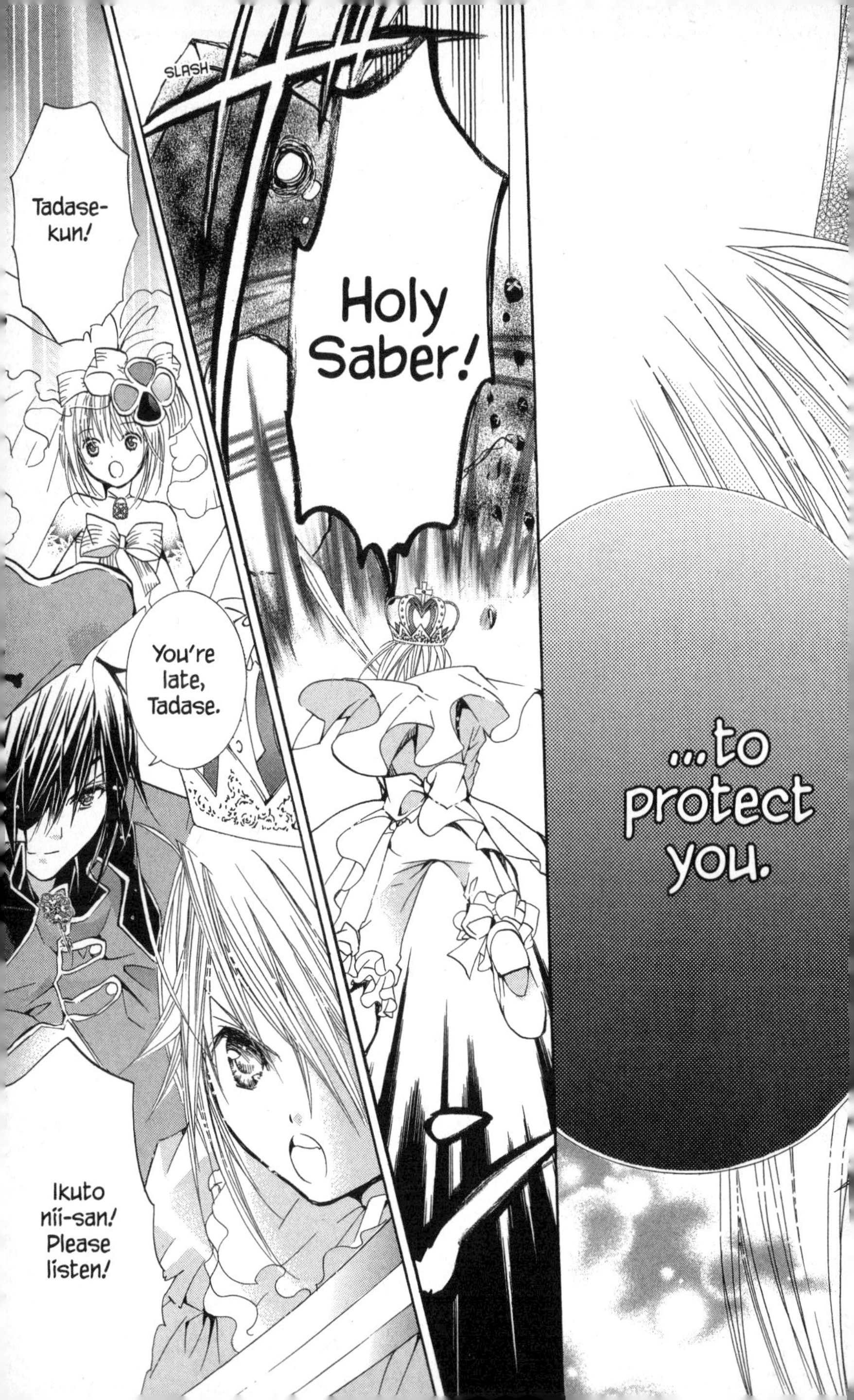
...to protect you.
SLASH
Holy Saber!
Tadase-kun!
You're late, Tadase.
Ikuto nii-san! Please listen!

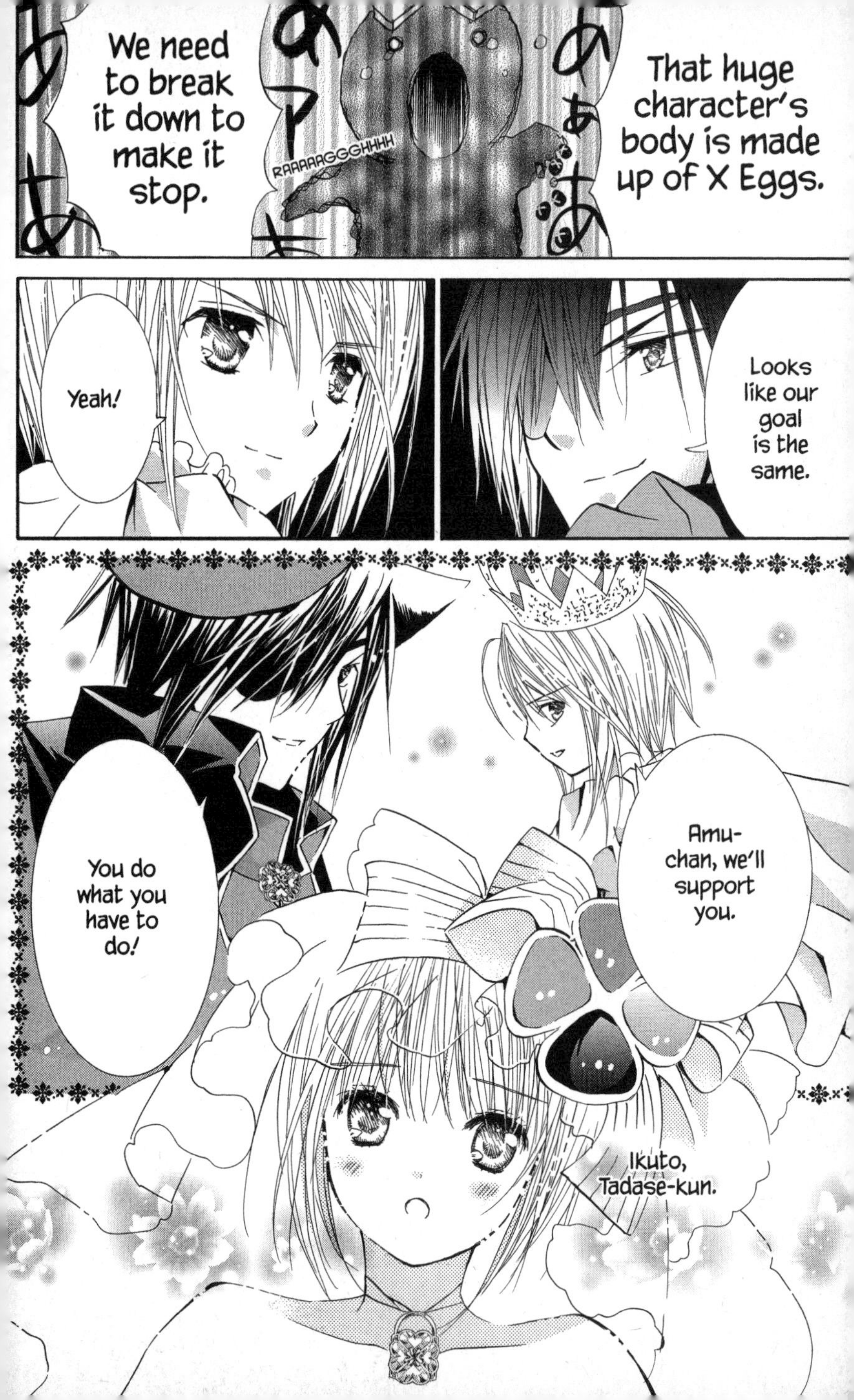
That huge character's body is made up of X Eggs.
RAAAAAGGGHHHH
We need to break it down to make it stop.
Looks like our goal is the same.
Yeah!
Amu-chan, we'll support you.
You do what you have to do!
Ikuto, Tadase-kun.

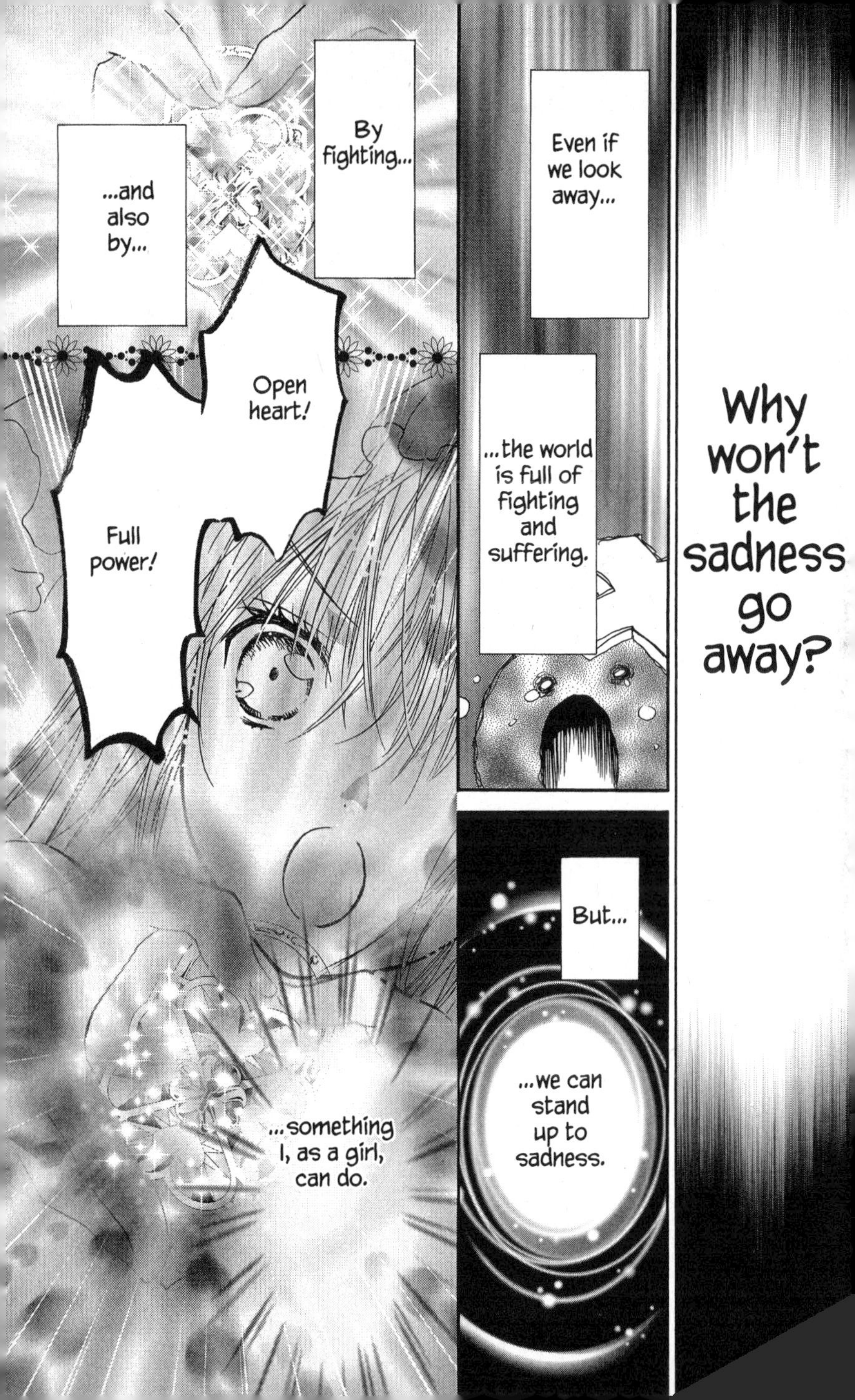
Why won't the sadness go away?
Even if we look away...
...the world is full of fighting and suffering.
But...
...we can stand up to sadness.
By fighting...
...and also by...
Open heart!
Full power!
...something I, as a girl, can do.

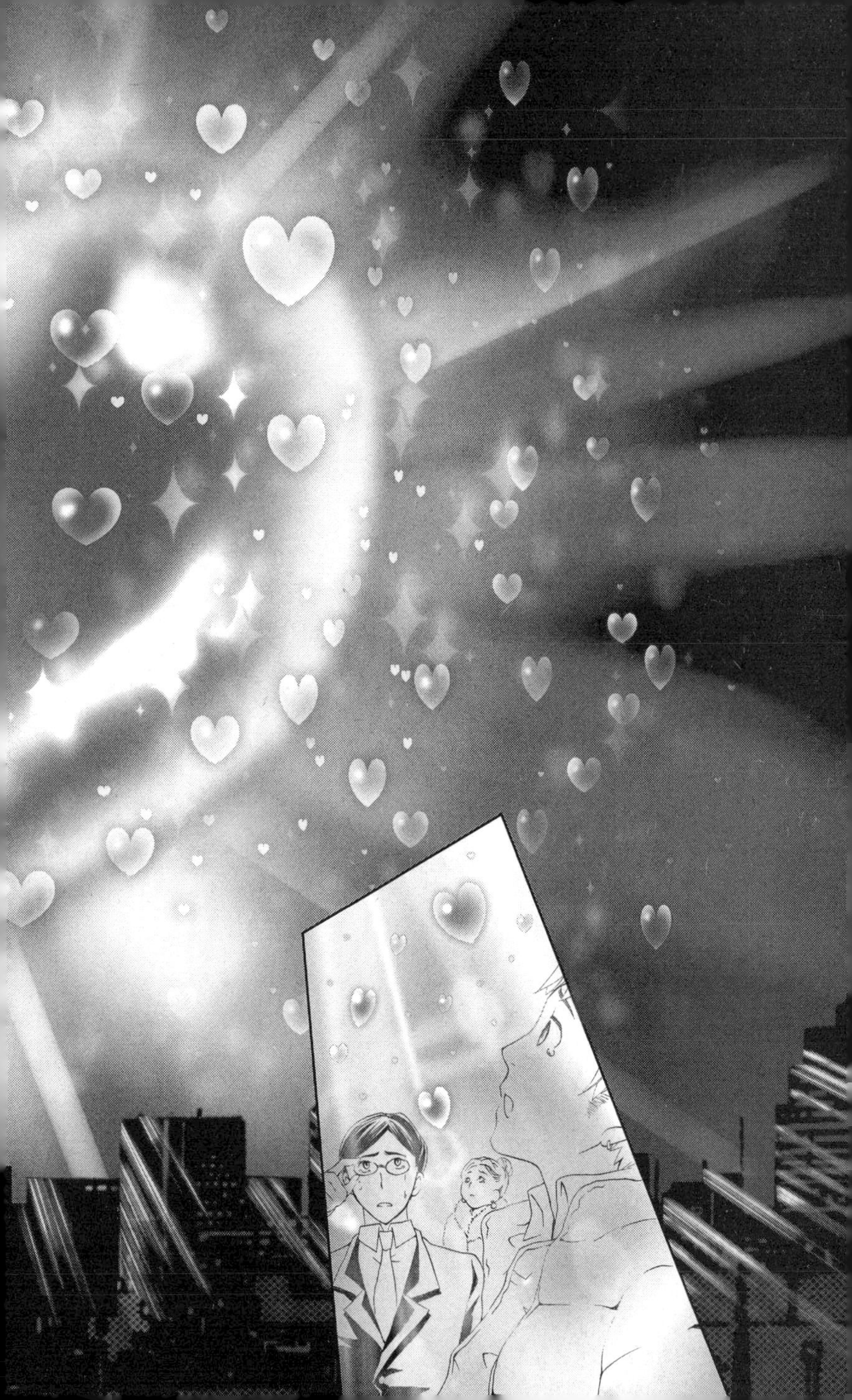

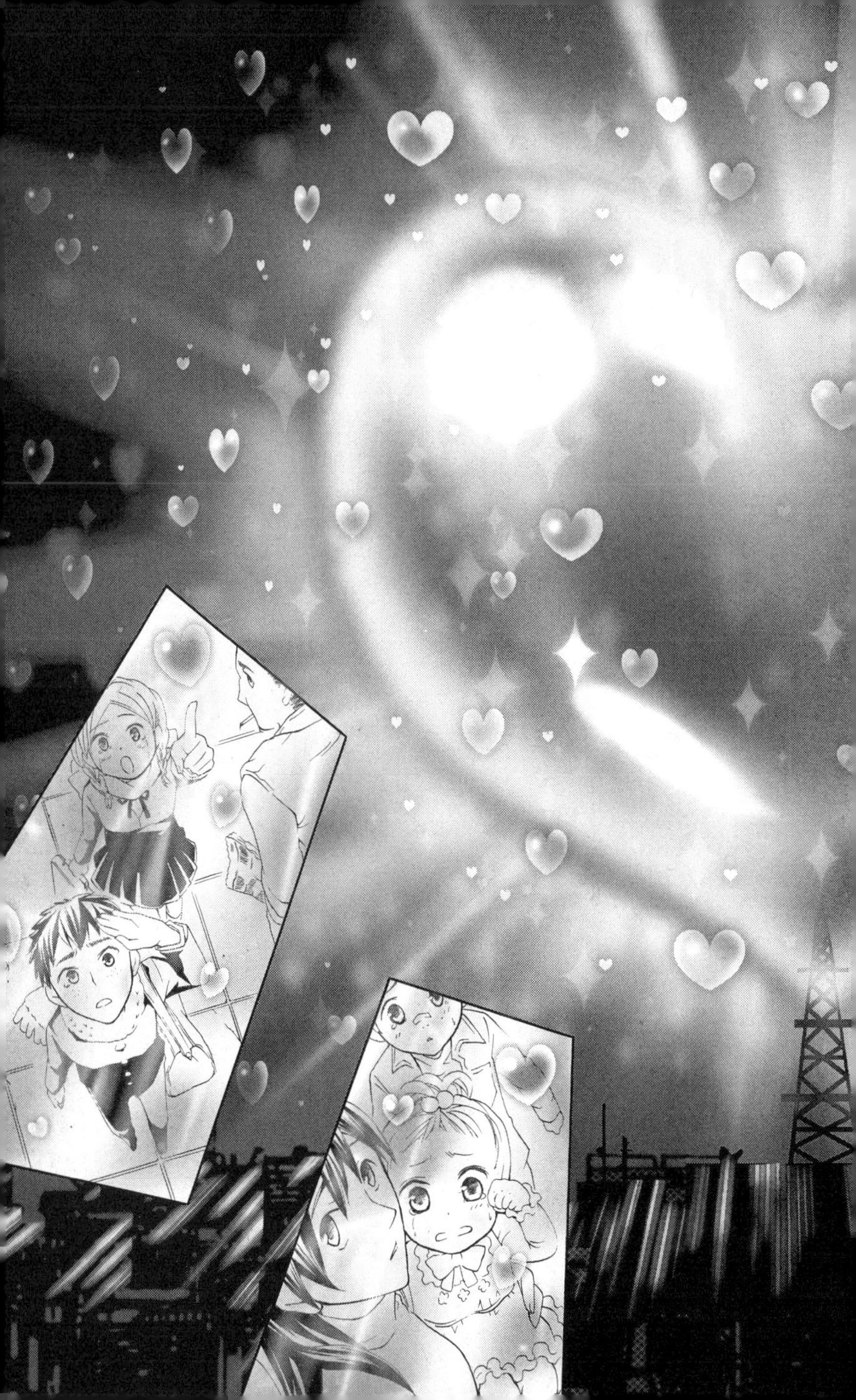

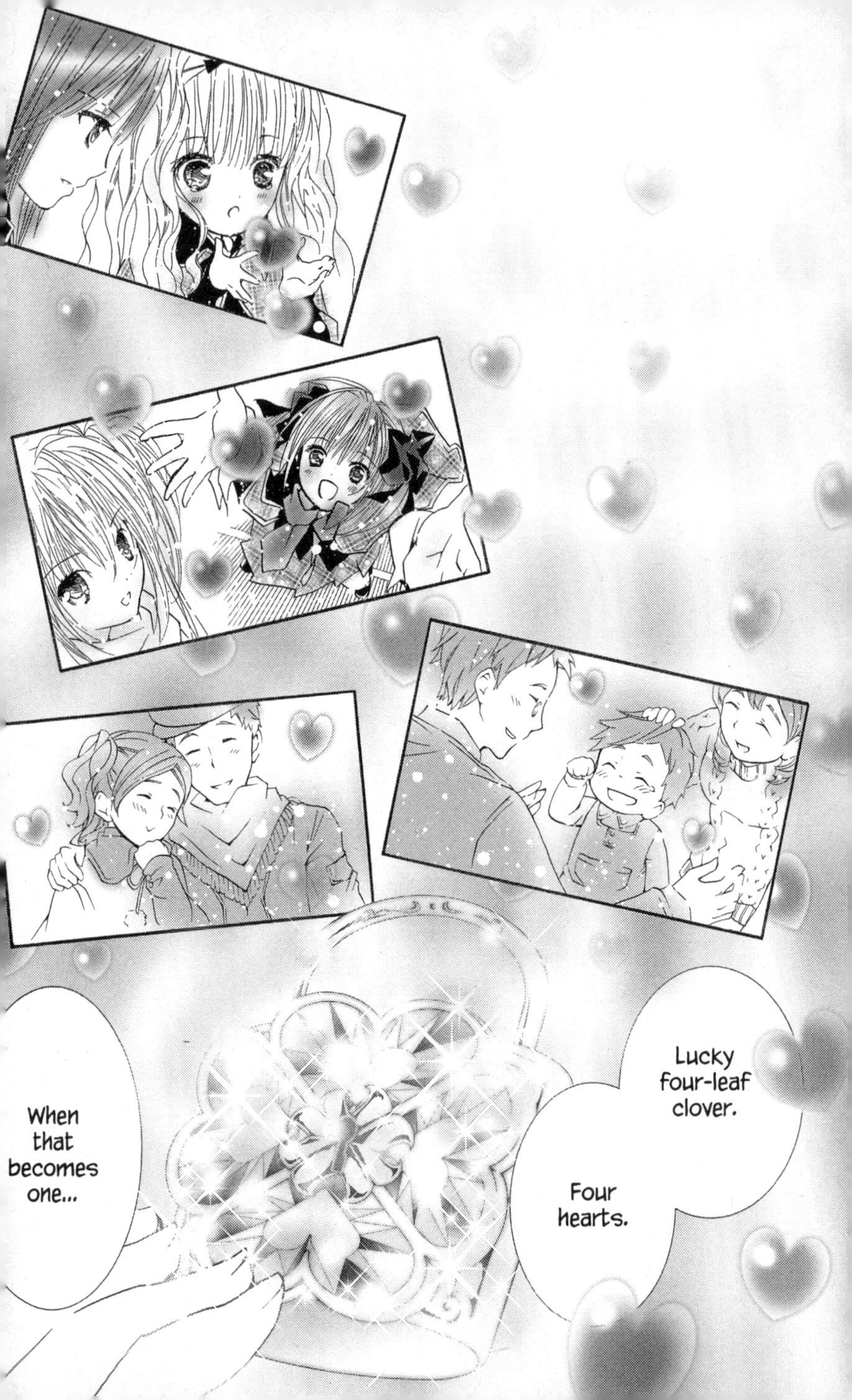
Lucky four-leaf clover.
Four hearts.
When that becomes one...

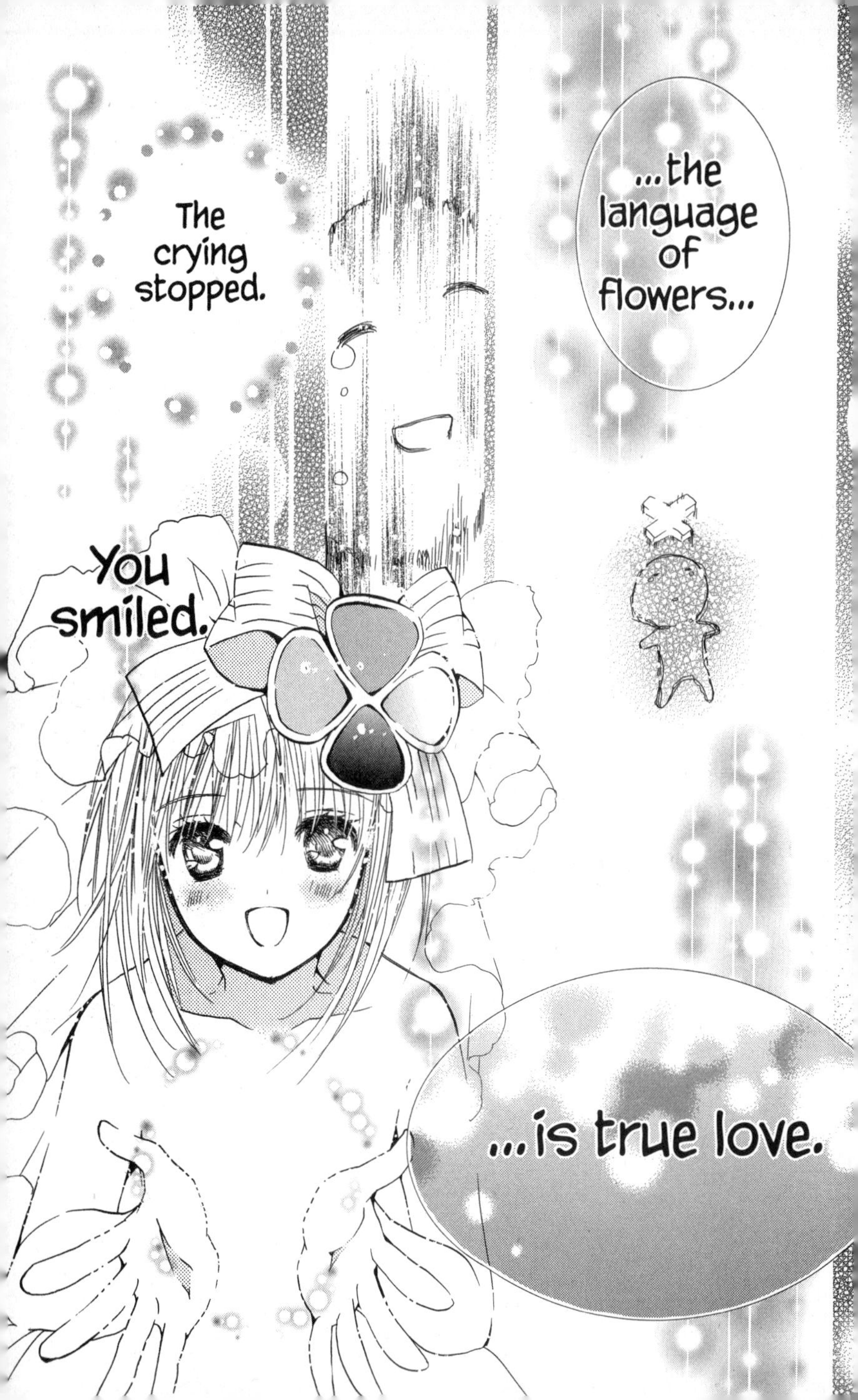

...the language of flowers...
The crying stopped.
You smiled.
...is true love.

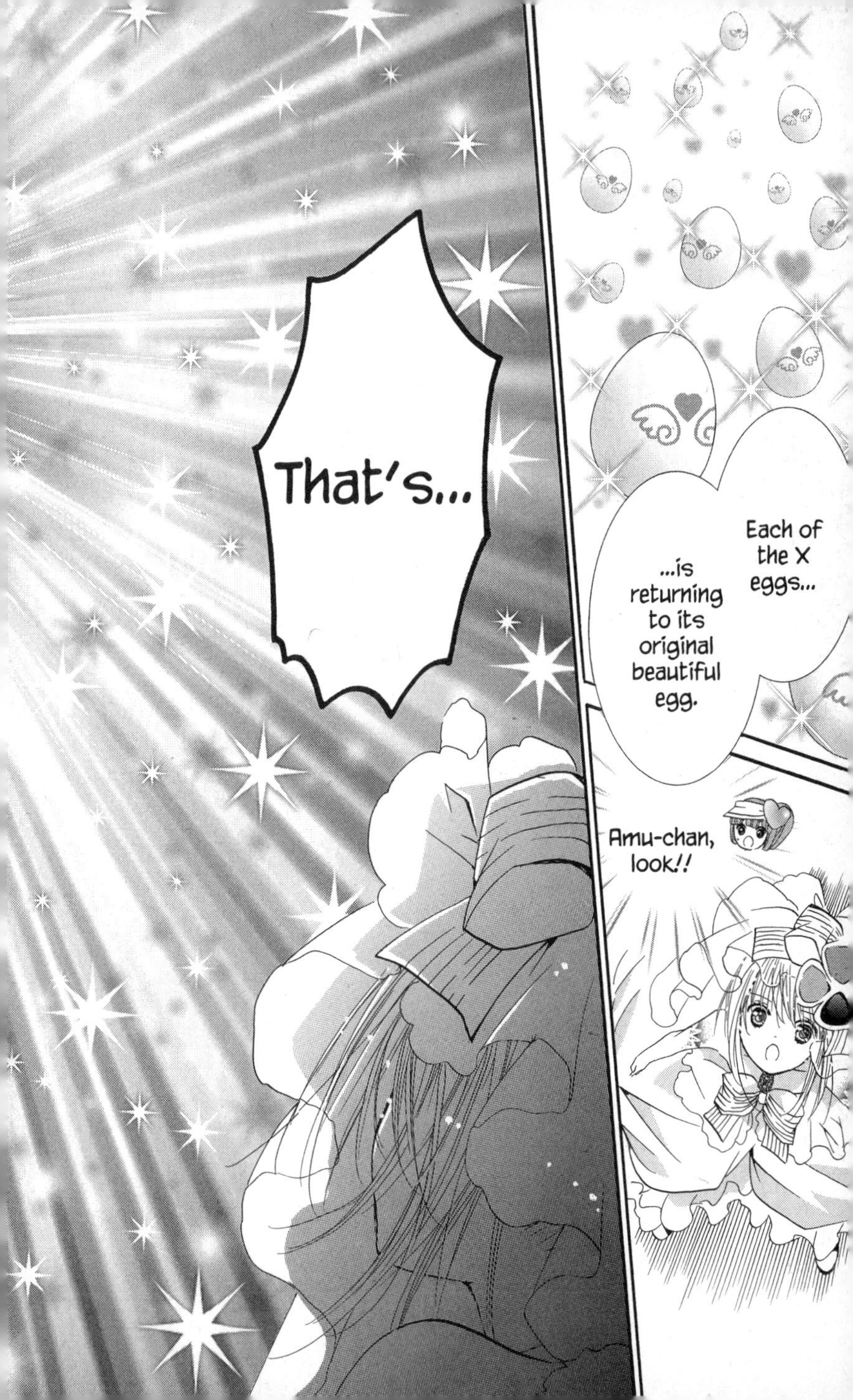
Each of the X eggs...
...is returning to its original beautiful egg.
Amu-chan, look!!
That's...

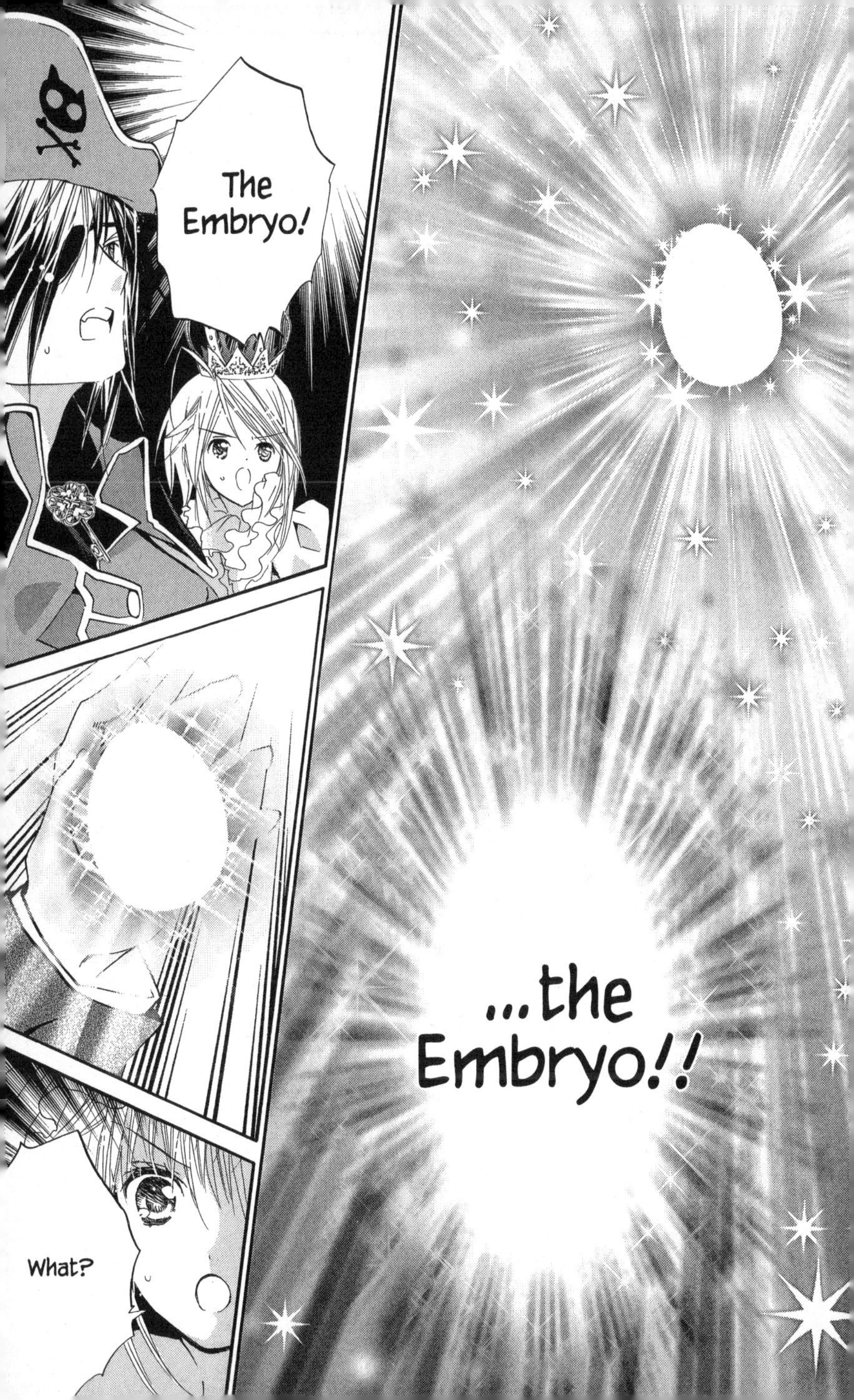
...the Embryo!!
The Embryo!
What?

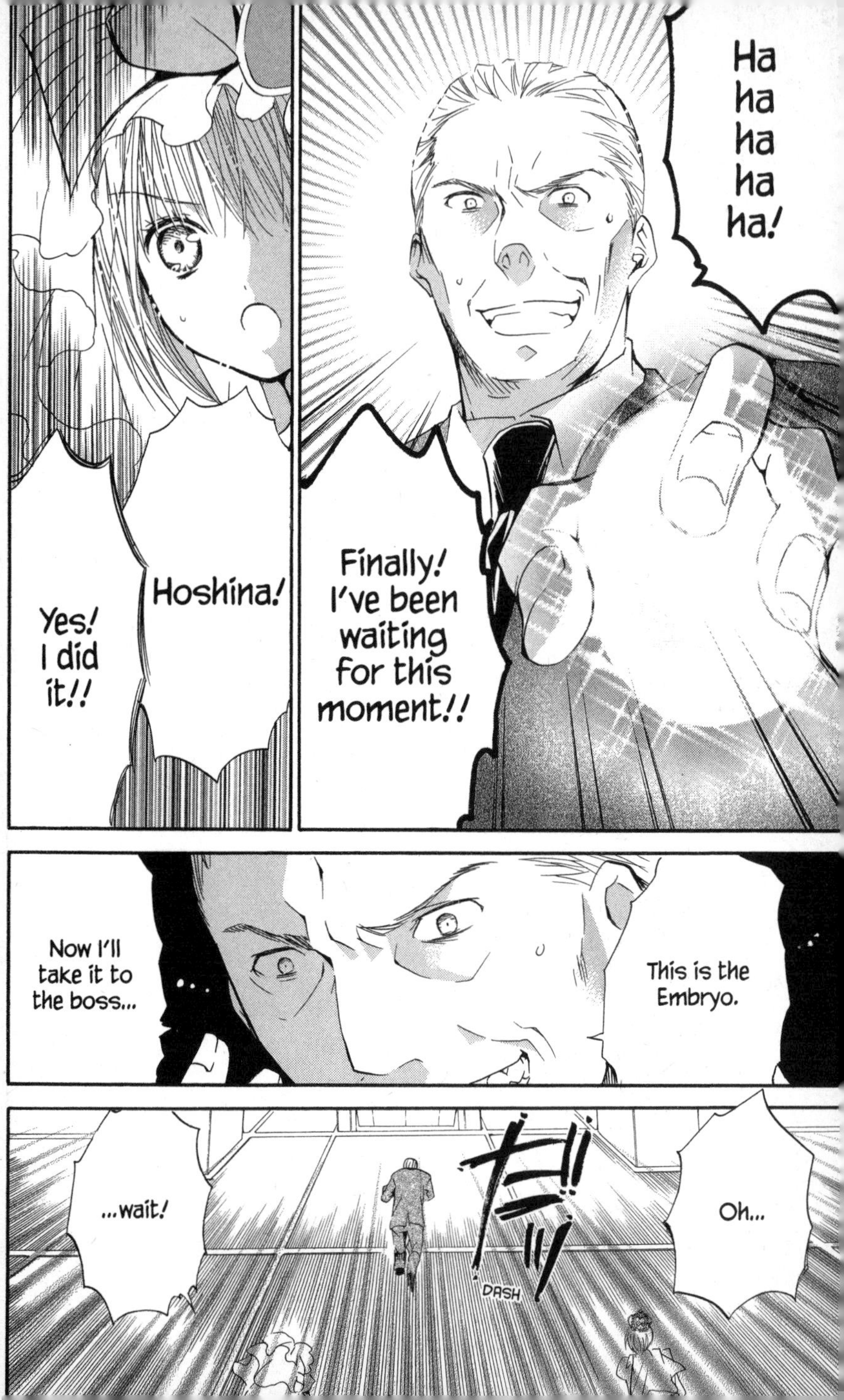
Ha ha ha ha ha!
Finally! I've been waiting for this moment!!
Hoshina!
Yes! I did it!!
This is the Embryo.
Now I'll take it to the boss...
Oh...
DASH
...wait!

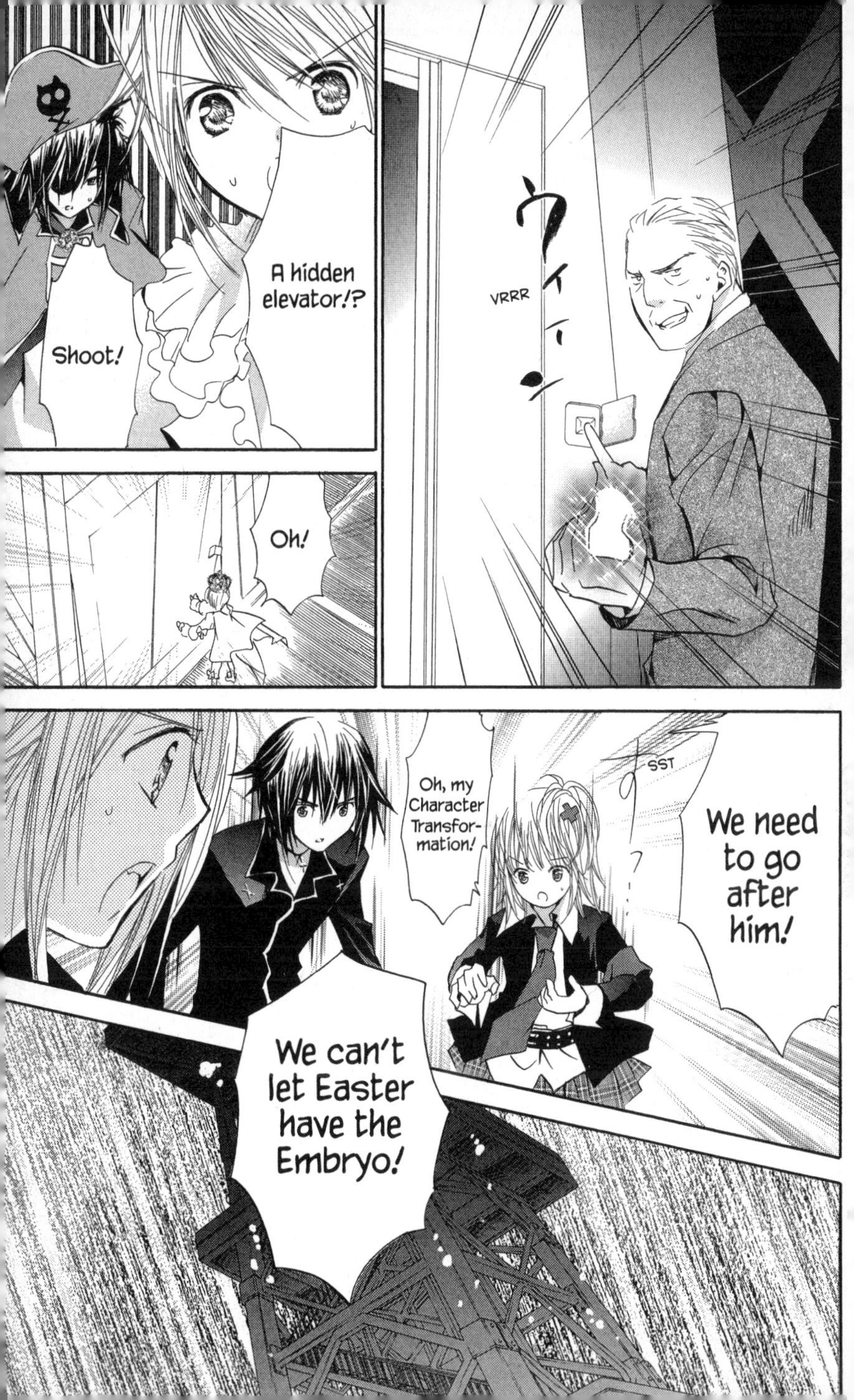
VRRR
A hidden elevator!?
Shoot!
Oh!
SST
We need to go after him!
Oh, my Character Transformation!
We can't let Easter have the Embryo!

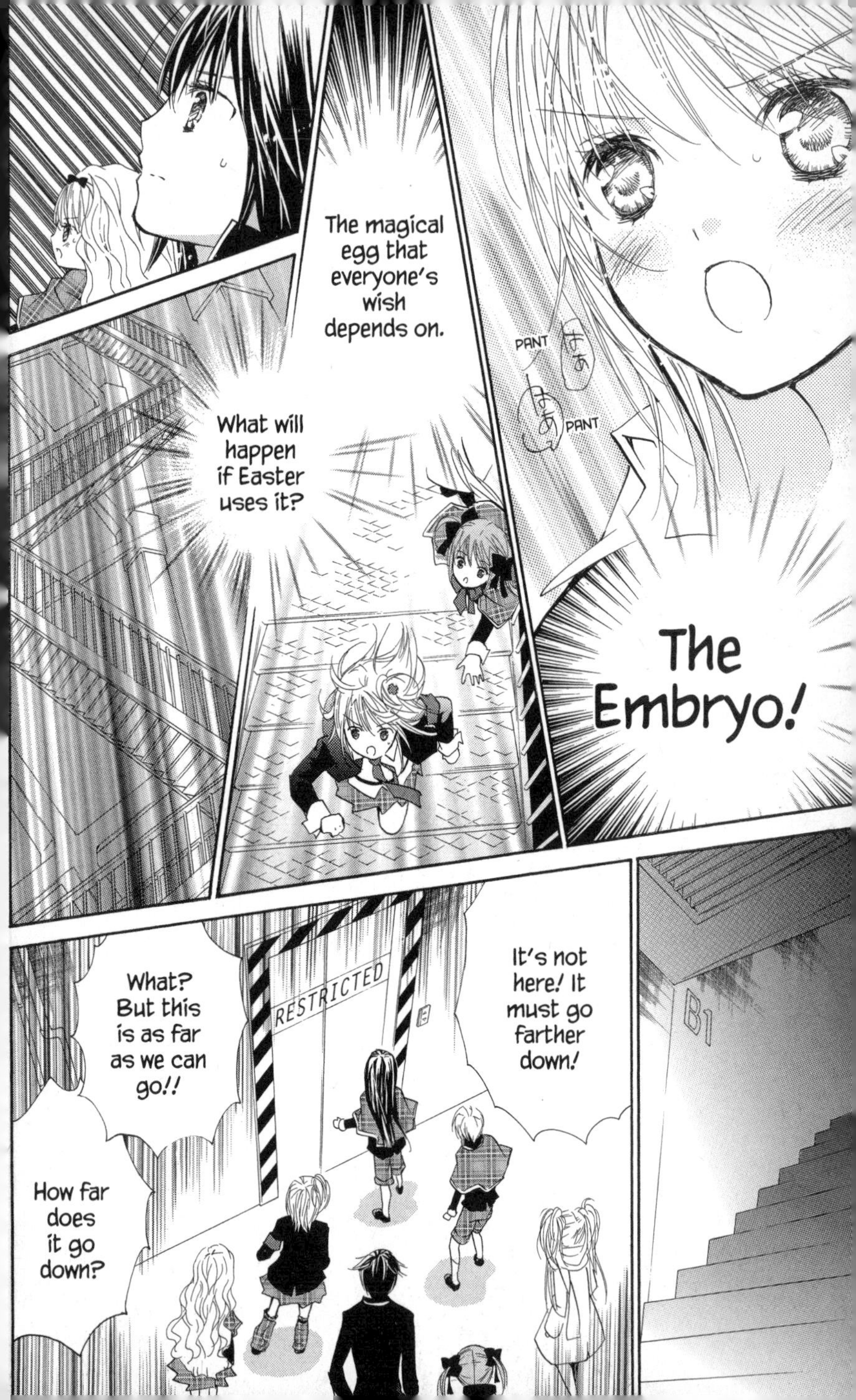
PANT
PANT
The Embryo!
The magical egg that everyone's wish depends on.
What will happen if Easter uses it?
B1
It's not here! It must go farther down!
RESTRICTED
What? But this is as far as we can go!!
How far does it go down?

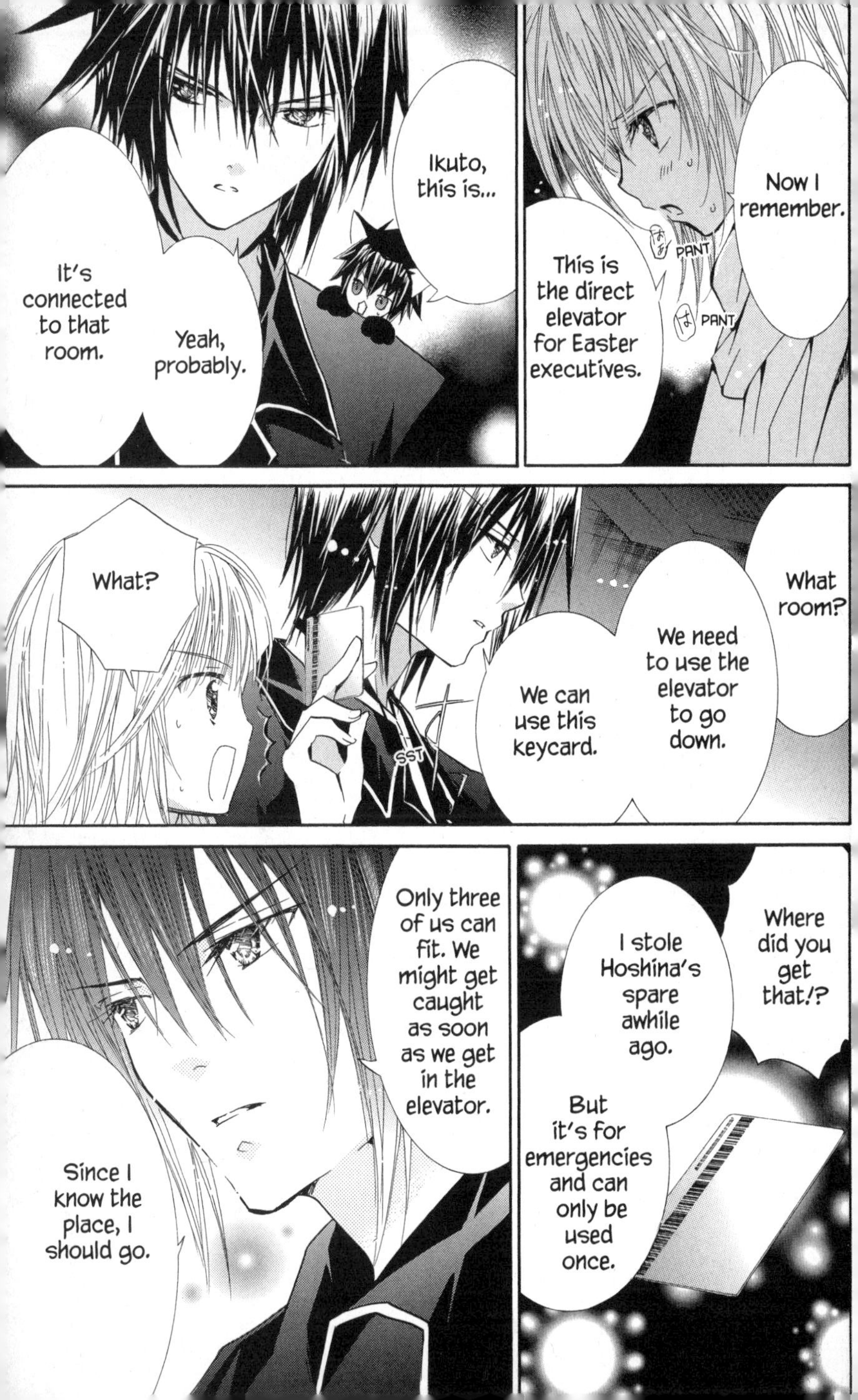
Now I remember.
This is the direct elevator for Easter executives.
はぁ PANT
は PANT
Ikuto, this is...
It's connected to that room.
Yeah, probably.
What room?
We need to use the elevator to go down.
We can use this keycard.
SST
What?
Where did you get that!?
I stole Hoshina's spare awhile ago.
But it's for emergencies and can only be used once.
Only three of us can fit. We might get caught as soon as we get in the elevator.
Since I know the place, I should go.

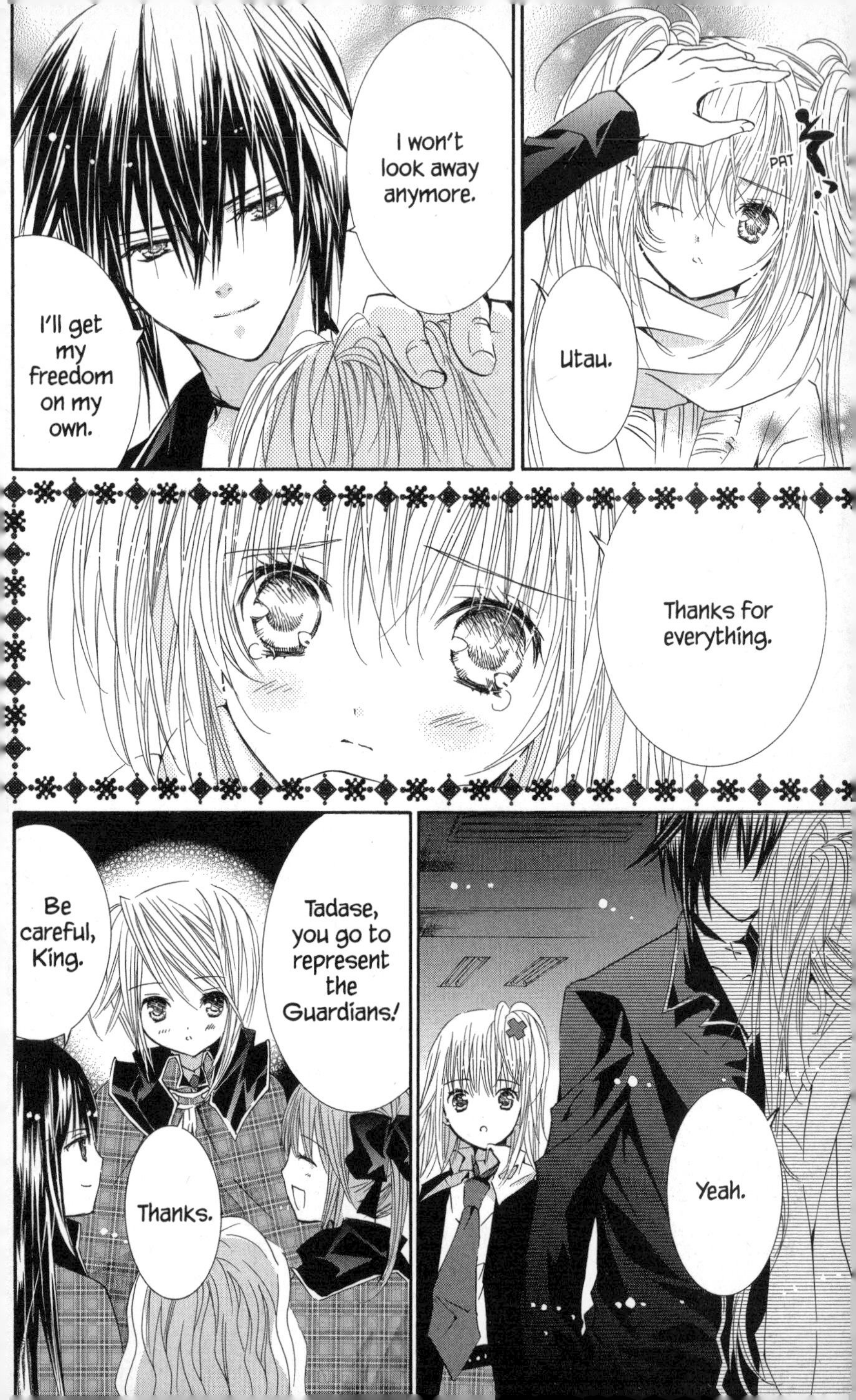
PAT
Utau.
I won't look away anymore.
I'll get my freedom on my own.
Thanks for everything.
Yeah.
Tadase, you go to represent the Guardians!
Be careful, King.
Thanks.

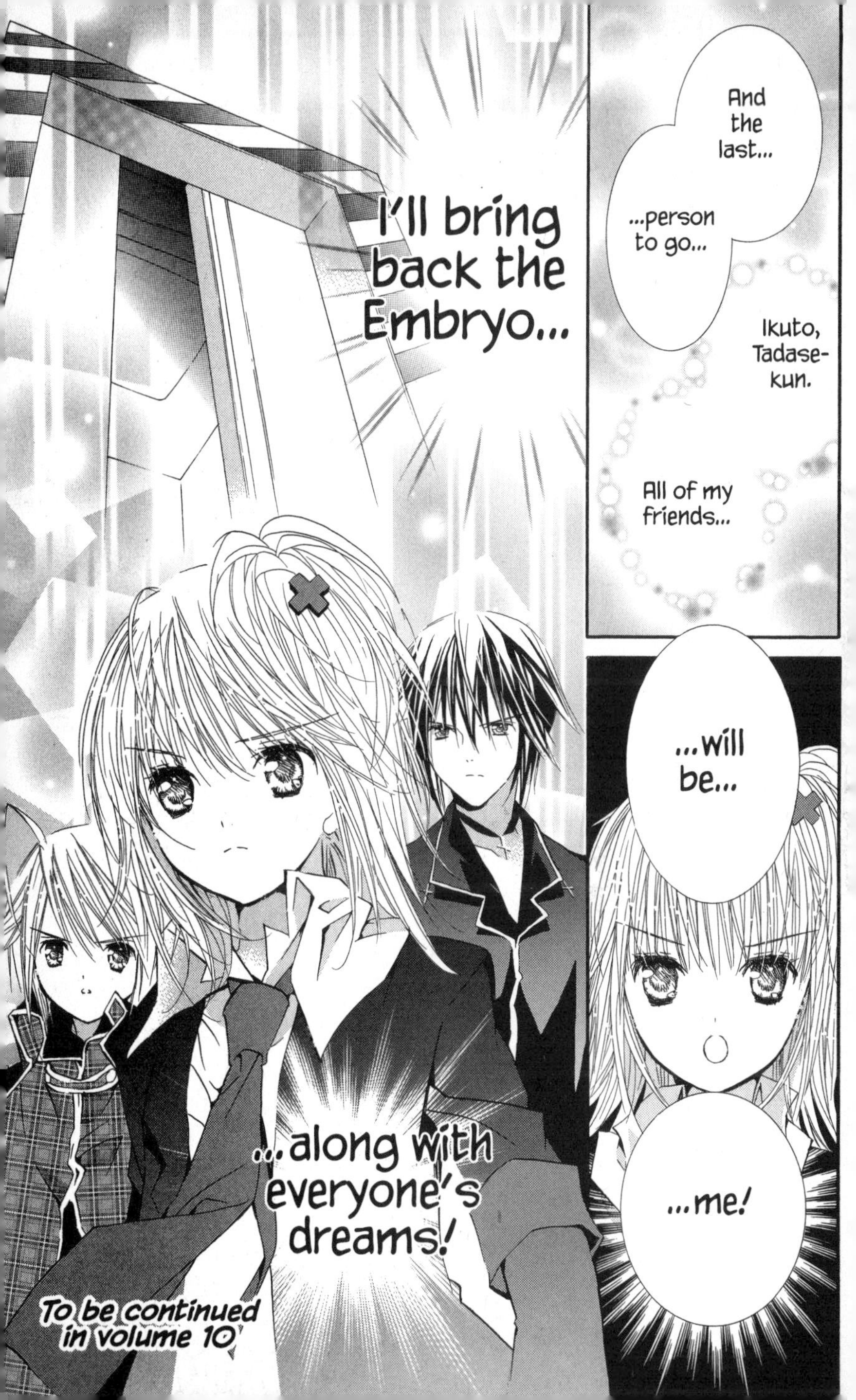
And the last...
...person to go...
Ikuto, Tadase-kun.
All of my friends...
...will be...
...me!
I'll bring back the Embryo...
...along with everyone's dreams!
To be continued in volume 10

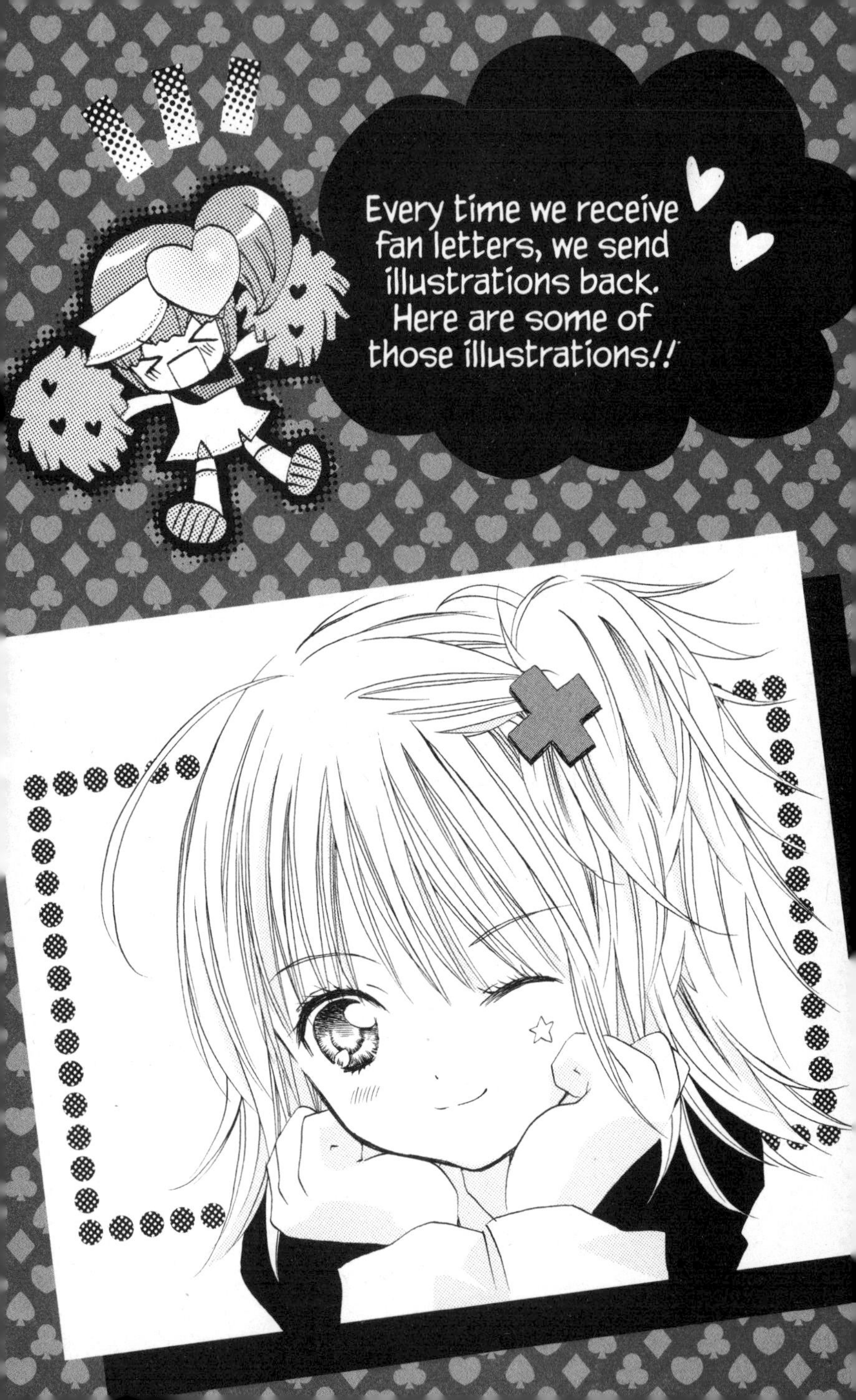
Every time we receive fan letters, we send illustrations back. Here are some of those illustrations!!

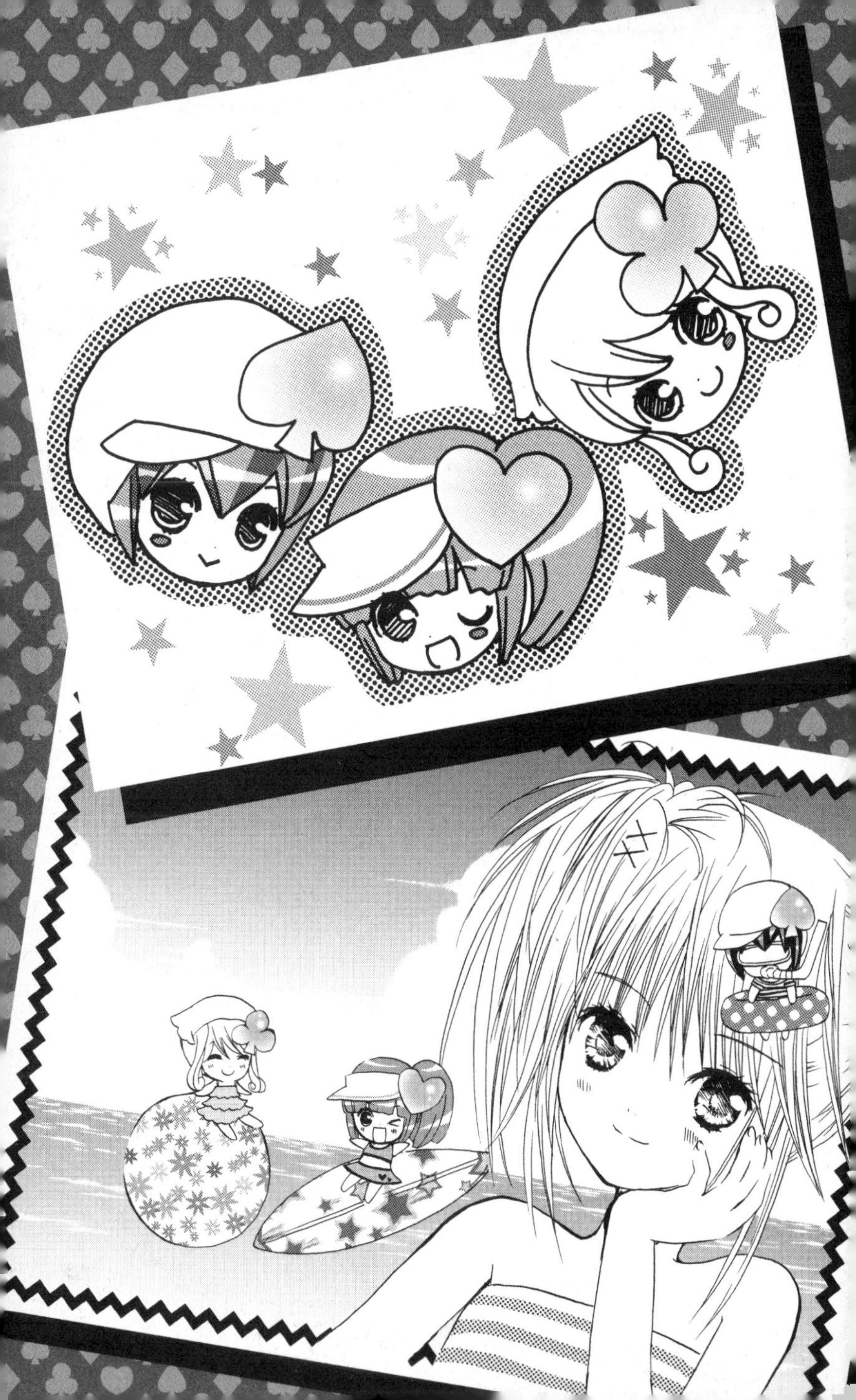

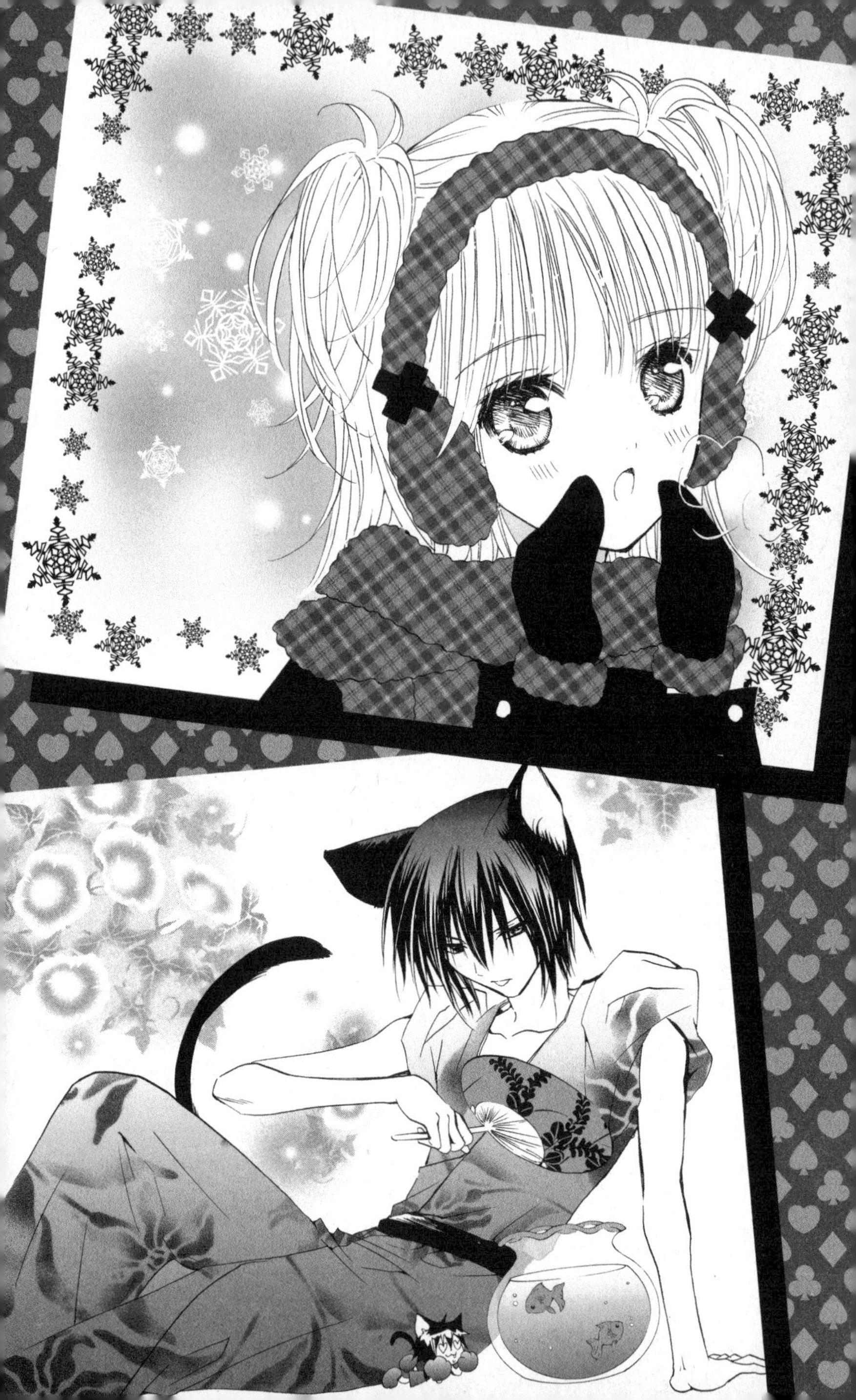

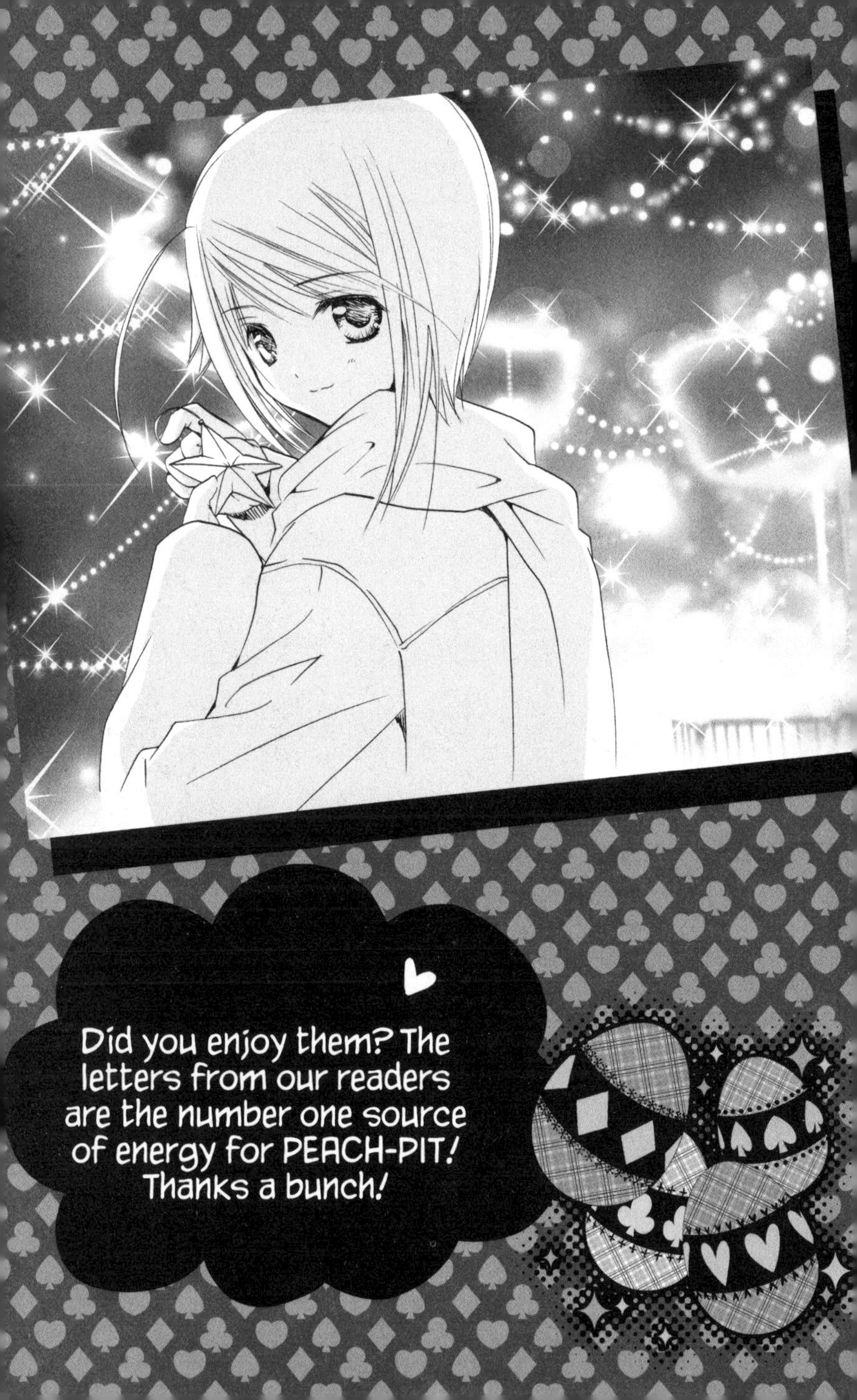
Did you enjoy them? The letters from our readers are the number one source of energy for PEACH-PIT! Thanks a bunch!

About the Creators

PEACH-PIT:

Banri Sendo was born on June 7. **Shibuko Ebara** was born on June 21. They are a pair of Gemini manga artists who work together. Sendo likes to eat sweets, and Ebara likes to eat spicy stuff.

"The number of Amu's fingers on the cover has been consistent with the volume number. Did you all notice that?" —PEACH-PIT

Translation Notes

Japanese is a tricky language for most Westerners, and translation is often more art than science. For your edification and reading pleasure, here are notes on some of the places where we could have gone in a different direction in our translation of the work, or where a Japanese cultural reference is used.

Rugby, page 14

Though rugby is not especially popular in America, it's become a fairly popular sport at Japanese universities. It was first introduced to Japan in 1899. In rugby, the aim of each team is to gain possession of the ball and take it into the goal area in the opposing team's territory. Players may score by carrying, passing, grounding, or kicking the ball.

You're weak because you play music when you're so young.
You need to play sports. I played rugby until college.

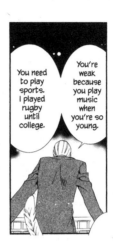

Hard noodles, page 64

For some types of noodles, particularly in the Hakata region, you can specify how hard you want your noodles. There is "extremely soft," "soft," "hard," and "extra hard." The softness is achieved by how long the noodles are boiled. Hakata is a ward of Fukuoka City in Fukuoka prefecture, which is in Kyushu. Kyushu is the third largest island and the southernmost of the four main islands of Japan.

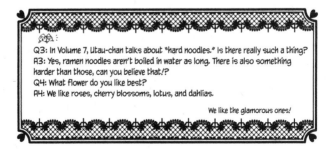

Q3: In Volume 7, Utau-chan talks about "hard noodles." Is there really such a thing?
A3: Yes, ramen noodles aren't boiled in water as long. There is also something harder than those, can you believe that!?
Q4: What flower do you like best?
A4: We like roses, cherry blossoms, lotus, and dahlias.

We like the glamorous ones!

Preview of *Shugo Chara!* volume 10

We're pleased to present you a preview from volume 10. Please check our website (www.kodanshacomics.com) for more information. For now you'll have to make do with Japanese!

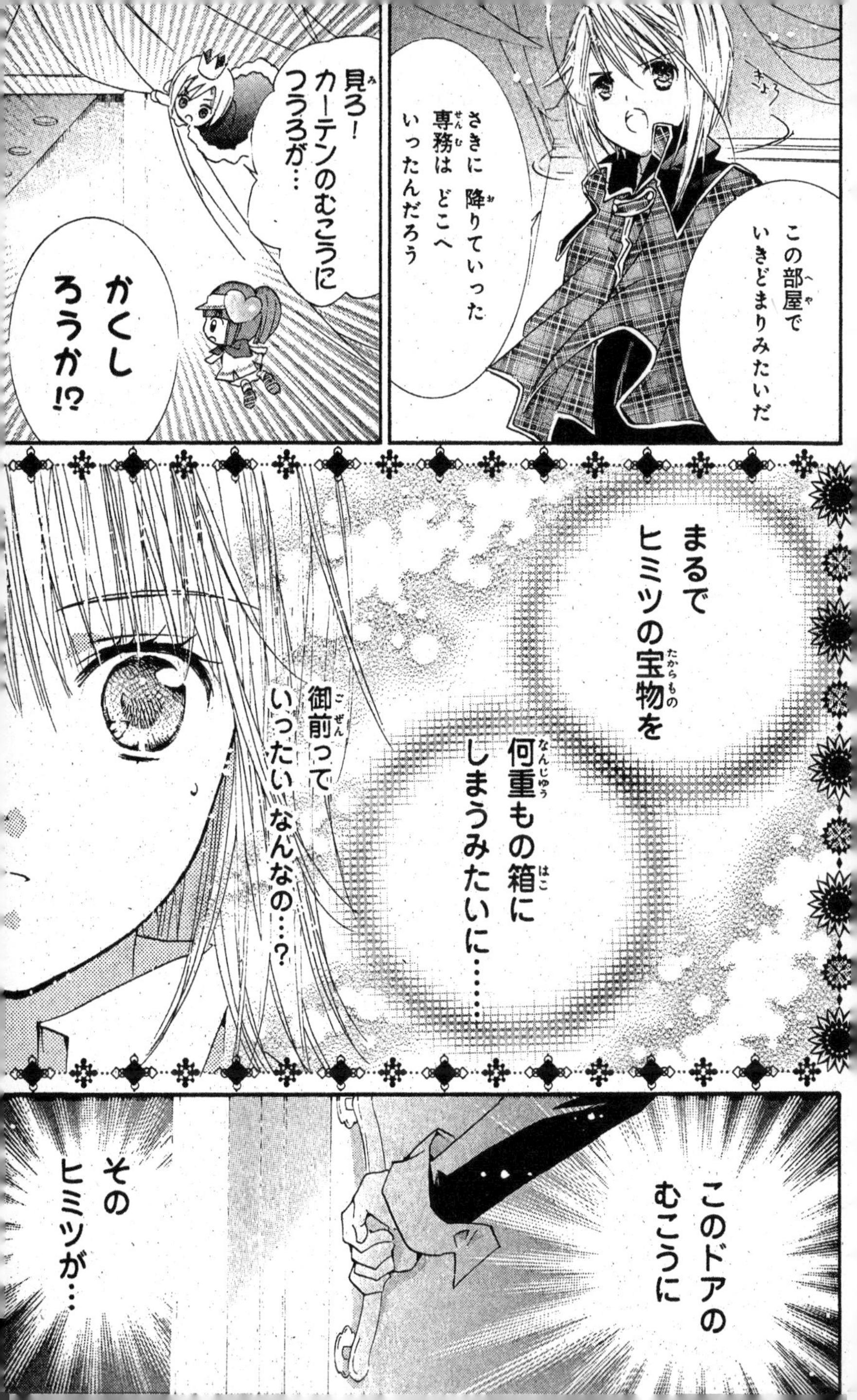
きょろ
この部屋でいきどまりみたいだ
さきに降りていった専務はどこへいったんだろう
見ろ！カーテンのむこうにつうろが…
かくしろうか!?
まるでヒミツの宝物を何重もの箱にしまうみたいに……
御前っていったいなんなの…？
このドアのむこうに
そのヒミツが…

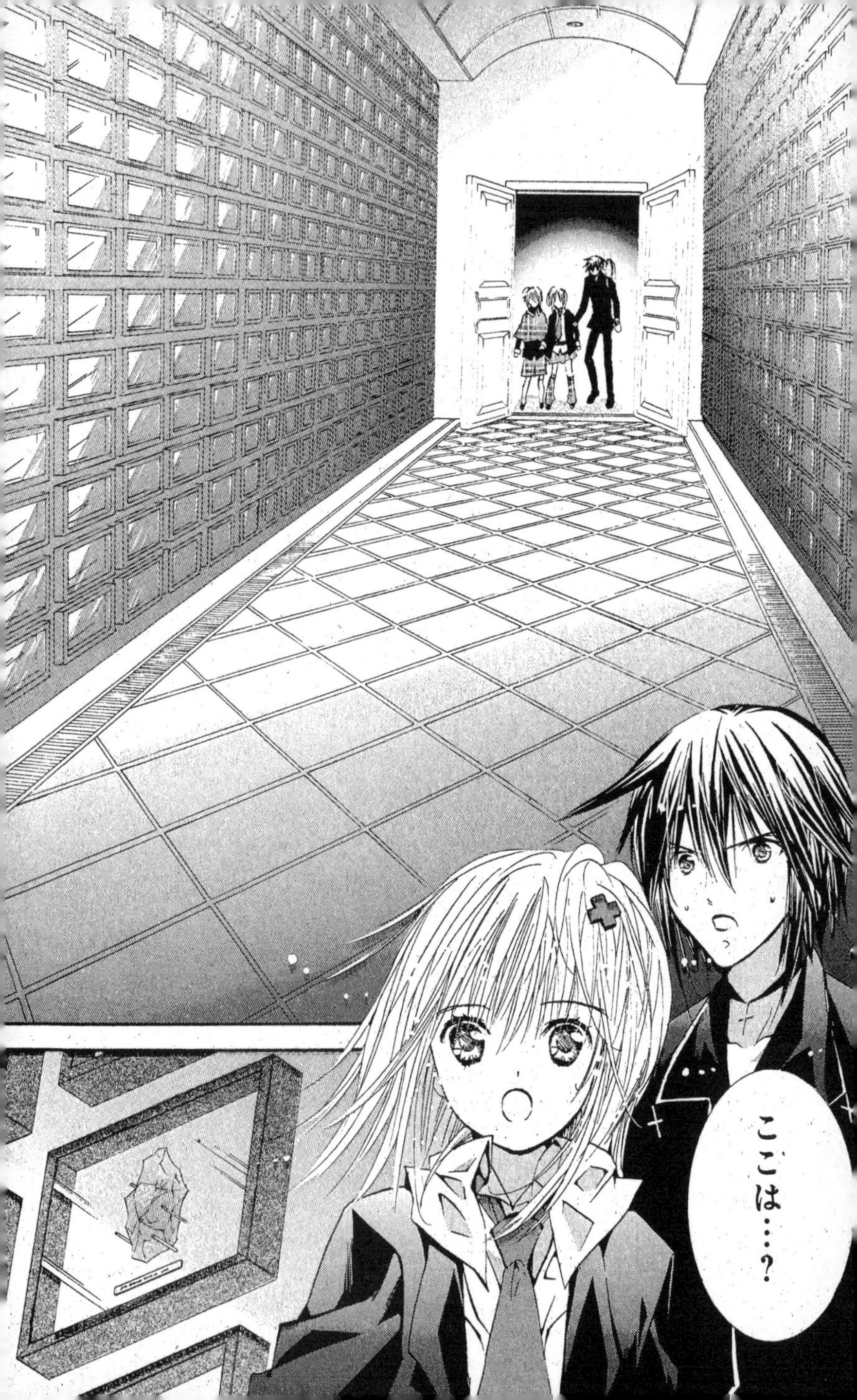
ここは…？

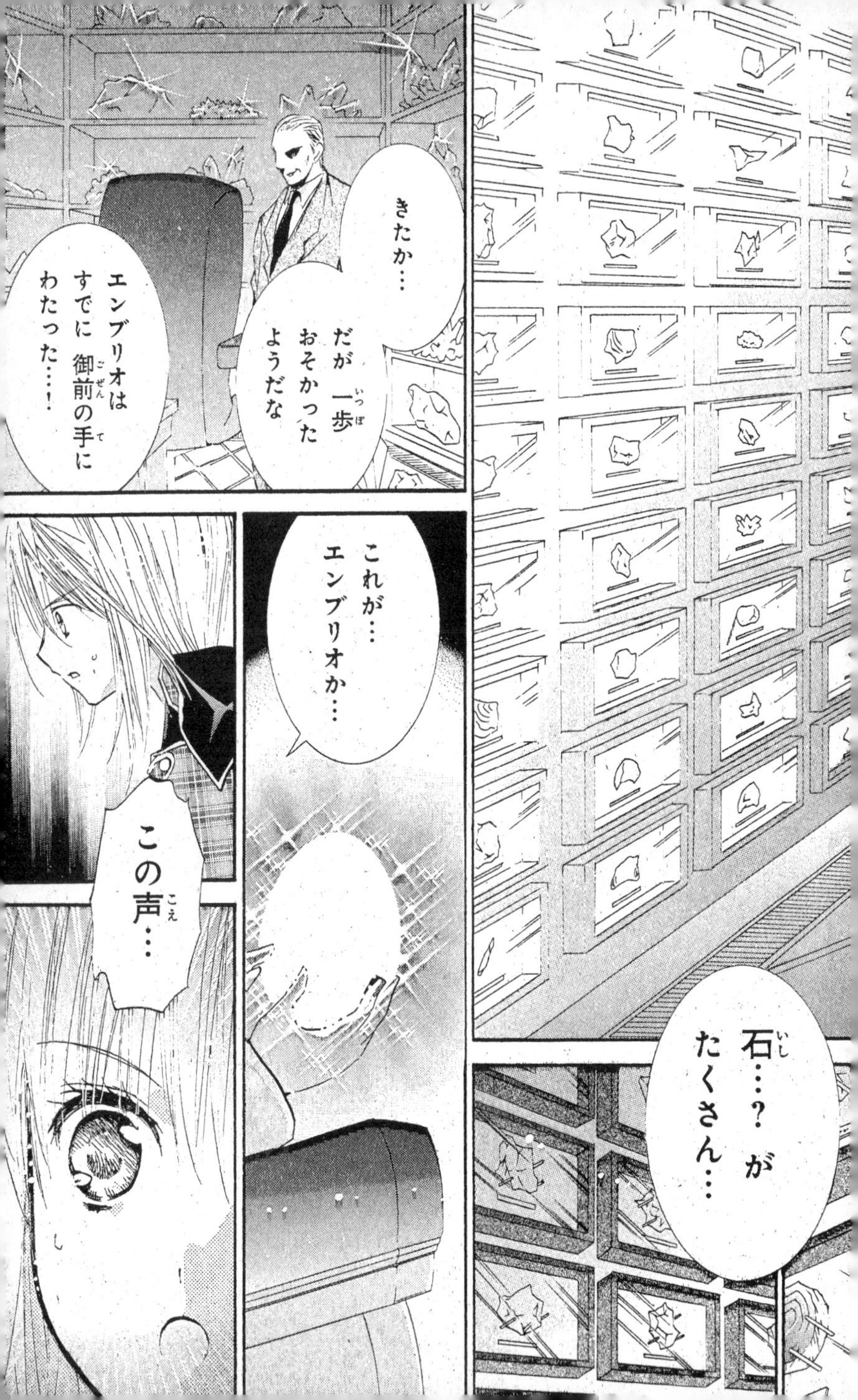
石…？が
たくさん…
きたか…
だが一歩
おそかった
ようだな
エンブリオは
すでに御前の手に
わたった…！
これが…
エンブリオか…
この声…

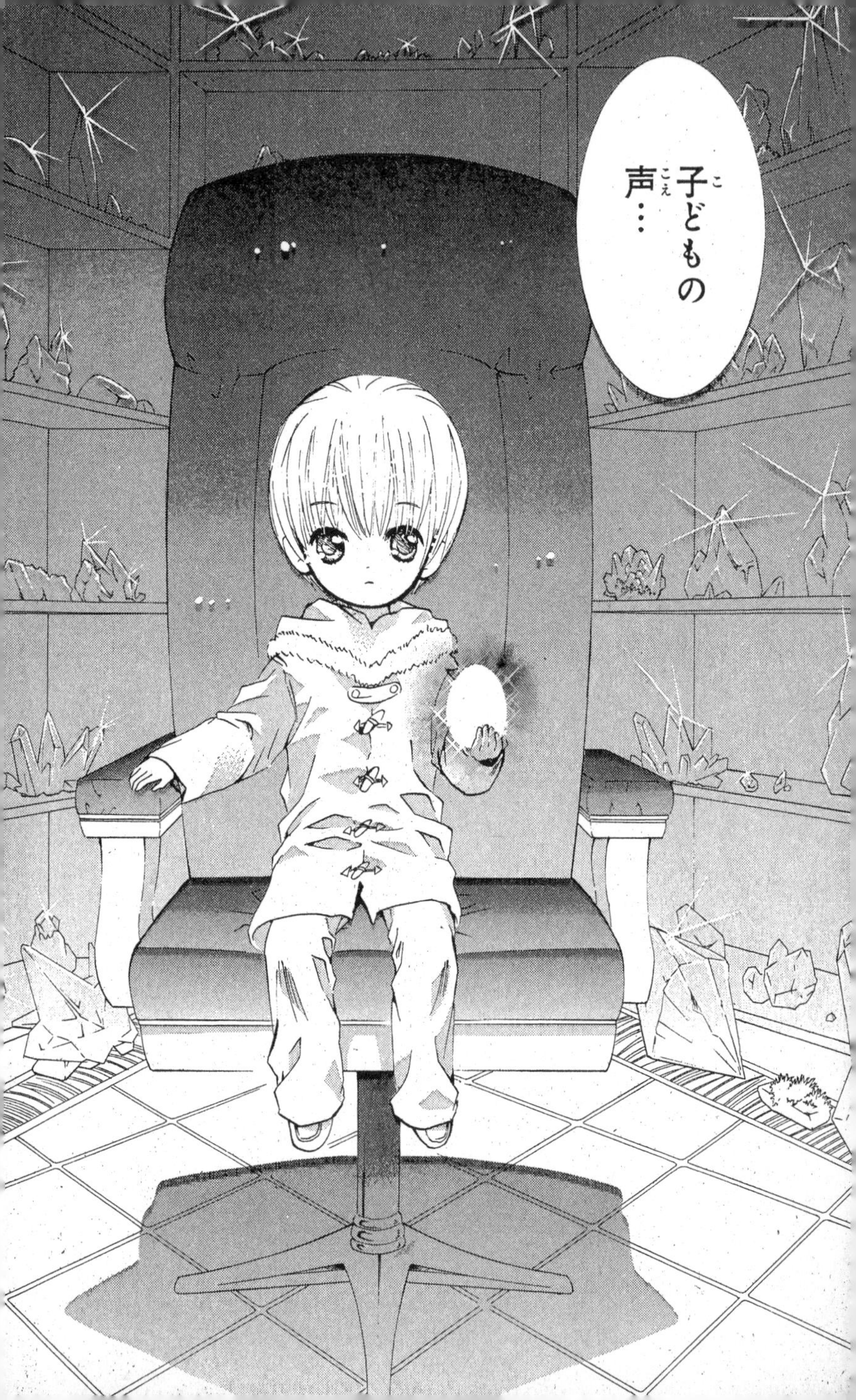
子どもの声……

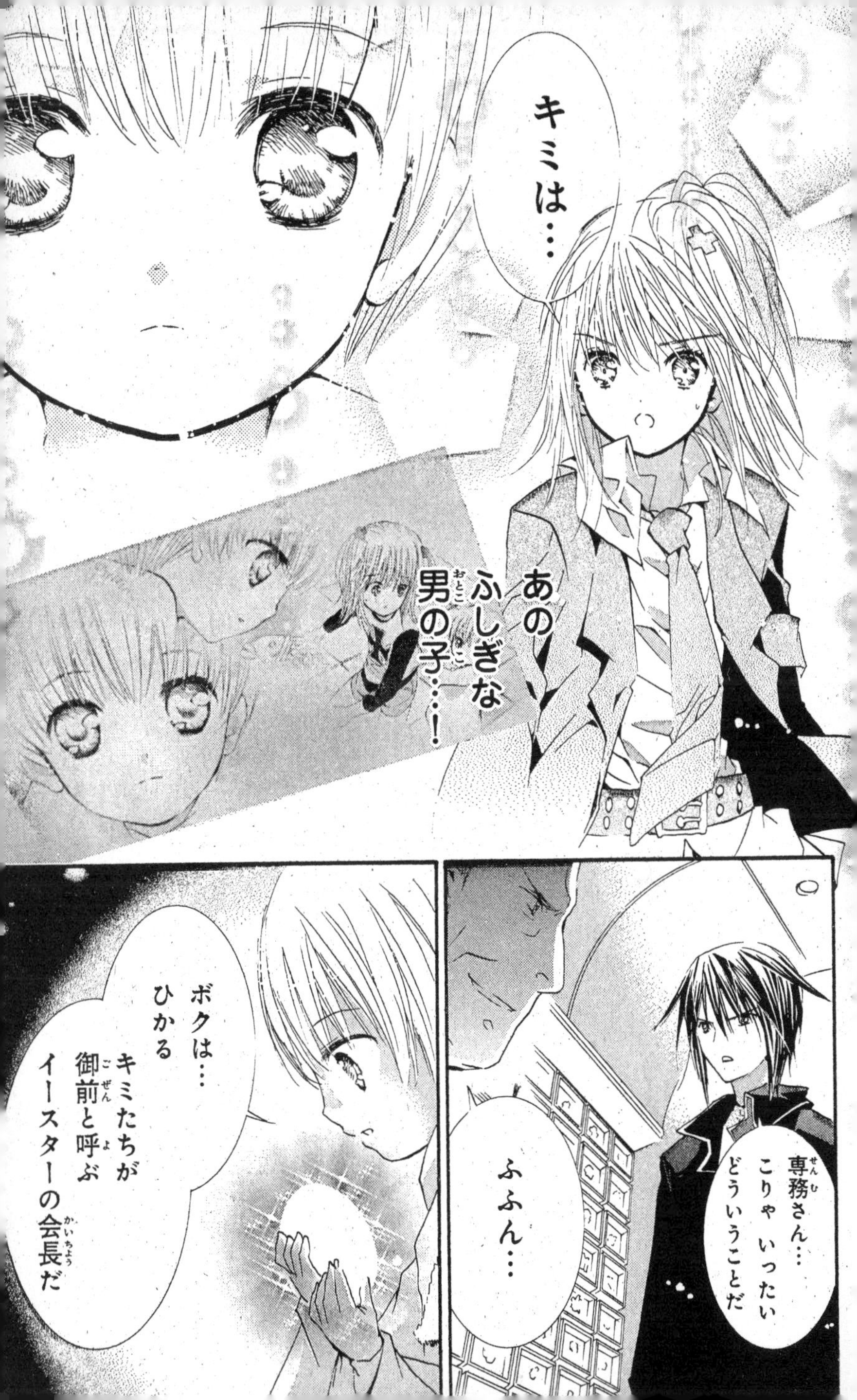
キミは…
あのふしぎな男の子…!
専務さん… こりゃ いったい どういうことだ
ふふん…
ボクは… ひかる
キミたちが御前と呼ぶ イースターの会長だ

TOMARE!

[STOP!]

You're going the wrong way!

Manga is a completely different type of reading experience.

To start at the *beginning,* go to the *end!*

That's right! Authentic manga is read the traditional Japanese way—from right to left. Exactly the *opposite* of how American books are read. It's easy to follow: Just go to the other end of the book, and read each page—and each panel—from right side to left side, starting at the top right. Now you're experiencing manga as it was meant to be!